James Henry Hackett

Notes, Criticism, and Correspondence upon Shakespeare's Plays and Actors

James Henry Hackett

Notes, Criticism, and Correspondence upon Shakespeare's Plays and Actors

ISBN/EAN: 9783337072858

Printed in Europe, USA, Canada, Australia, Japan

Cover: Foto ©ninafisch / pixelio.de

More available books at **www.hansebooks.com**

NOTES, CRITICISMS, AND CORRESPONDENCE

UPON

SHAKESPEARE'S PLAYS AND ACTORS.

NOTES, CRITICISMS, AND CORRESPONDENCE

UPON

SHAKESPEARE'S PLAYS AND ACTORS.

BY

JAMES HENRY HACKETT.

NEW YORK:
Carleton, Publisher, 413 Broadway.
(LATE RUDD & CARLETON.)
M DCCC LXIII.

R. CRAIGHEAD,
Printer, Stereotyper, and Electrotyper,
Carton Building,
81, 83, and 85 Centre Street.

New York, *March* 31st, 1863.

JAMES H. HACKETT, Esq.

My Dear Sir—

I have many thanks to render you for the high compliment you have paid me in inscribing to me your very interesting and valuable volume on Shakespeare and his characters and critics.

Your criticisms on the text and views of the characters of the great bard are of very great value and originality. On several of them I might be tempted to expand if I could write with more facility, but the return of an old sprain in the hand makes writing very laborious to myself as well as the handwriting obscure to others. The sprain is better to-day,—but as you see, not well. I can only make a single remark on Falstaff.

I have never read Maurice Morgann's Essay on the question of the Knight's courage or cowardice; but your remarks recall to me an observation of Col. Burr—a sagacious observer of men—that there were two quite distinct kinds of courage, the one purely physical, the other arising from moral or intellectual causes. Where the two are combined, the man is so far a hero. Where the purely physical or animal firmness or insensibility to danger is wanting, the deficiency may be supplied by moral or intellectual causes—sometimes of a high order, often not so, but still not physical. The sense of duty, patriotism, the feeling of personal honour, hate, revenge, party, fanaticism, may give courage.

Now, your and Shakespeare's Knight seems to me a cool man, but he has no moral courage high or low. Duty, patriotism, loyalty, are of course out of the question, and he scoffs at the sense of personal honour. Not troubled with any nervous trepidation, but utterly selfish, he skulks from danger nearly as coolly as a brave man would meet it.

In this view Morgann or your own thoughts may have anticipated me.

Again thanking you for the honour you have done me,

I am yours truly,

G. C. VERPLANCK.

This Volume

IS RESPECTFULLY DEDICATED

TO THE

HON. GULIAN C. VERPLANCK,

IN

GRATEFUL TESTIMONY

OF

THE MANY SERVICES HE HAS RENDERED TO THE PUBLIC;

AND

PARTICULARLY FOR HIS DEVOTION AS AN EDITOR

TO

The Shakesporean Drama,

AND HIS

ENLIGHTENED INTEREST IN EVERY HONEST EFFORT FOR ITS

PROMOTION IN LITERATURE, OR ON THE STAGE.

PREFACE.

THE sketches and essays which occupy the following pages, necessarily partaking more or less of a personal character—the author so often speaking of his own experience or observations—there would seem to be required no further preface at his hands. He cannot, however, neglect to avail himself of the time-honored privilege of saying a word to the reader, were it only to exchange the customary form of salutation when meeting. For he would have his book regarded not as an elaborate attempt at authorship— to which he makes no pretensions—but in the spirit of a familiar and friendly, yet earnest conversation, when one is listened to with partiality, as he discourses upon topics of admitted interest, or revises the traits of those whom the world has been accustomed to admire.

These papers have been written at intervals in the course of many and now by-gone years, as the respective occasions prompted.   In bringing them together at the present time, the writer would acknowledge his obligations to his accomplished friend, Mr. EDWARD S. GOULD, whose judgment he has consulted in the general arrangement of the volume, and to whose friendly assistance he has been indebted in seeing these pages through the press, during their writer's own unavoidable absence from the city.

JAMES H. HACKETT.

NEW YORK, *December*, 1862.

CONTENTS.

PART VI.

PART I.

HAMLET'S SOLILOQUY ON SUICIDE.

HAMLET'S SOLILOQUY ON SUICIDE.

THE classical Dr. Goldsmith commences his "Sixteenth Essay" thus:—Of all the implements of poetry, the metaphor is the most generally and successfully used, and indeed may be termed the Muse's caduceus, by the power of which she enchants all nature. . . . . . Over and above an excess of figures, a young author is apt to run into a confusion of mixed metaphors, which leave the sense disjointed, and distract the imagination. Shakespeare himself is often guilty of these irregularities. The soliloquy in *Hamlet*, which we have often heard extolled in terms of admiration, is, in our opinion, a heap of absurdities, whether we consider the situation, the sentiment, the argumentation, or the poetry. *Hamlet* is informed by the *Ghost* that his father was murdered, and therefore he is tempted to murder himself, even after he had promised to take vengeance on the usurper, and expressed the utmost eagerness to achieve this enterprise. It does not appear that he had the least reason to wish for death; but every motive which may be supposed to influence the mind of a young prince, concurred to render life desirable—revenge toward the usurper; love for the fair *Ophelia*, and the ambi tion of reigning. Besides, when he had an opportunity of dying without being accessory to his own death; when he had nothing to do but, in obedience to his uncle's command, to allow himself to be conveyed quietly to England, where he was sure of suffering death—instead of amusing himself with meditations on mortality, he very wisely consulted the means of self-preservation, turned the tables upon his attendants, and returned to Denmark. But granting him to have been reduced to the lowest state of despondence, surrounded with nothing but horror and despair, sick of this life, and eager to tempt futurity, we shall see how far he argues like a philosopher.

In order to support this general charge against an author so universally held in veneration, whose very errors have helped to sanctify his character among the multitude, we will descend to particulars, and analyze this famous soliloquy.

Hamlet, having assumed the disguise of madness, as a cloak under which he might the more effectually revenge his father's death upon the murderer and usurper, appears alone upon the stage in a pensive and melancholy attitude, and communes with himself in these words:

> "To be, or not to be ? That is the question.
> Whether 'tis nobler in the mind to suffer
> The slings and arrows of outrageous fortune,

Or to take arms against a sea of troubles,
And by opposing, end them?—To die—to sleep—
No more! and by a sleep, to say, we end
The heart-ache, and the thousand natural shocks
That flesh is heir to;—'tis a consummation
Devoutly to be wished.—To die—to sleep—
To sleep! perchance to dream; ay, there's the rub;
For in that sleep of death what dreams may come,
When we have shuffled off this mortal coil,
Must give us pause.—There's the respect
That makes calamity of so long life.
For who would bear the whips and scorns of time!
Th' oppressor's wrong, the proud* man's contumely,
The pangs of despised† love, the law's delay,
The insolence of office, and the spurns
That patient merit of th' unworthy takes,
When he himself might his *quietus* make
With a bare bodkin?   Who would fardels bear,
To groan and sweat under a weary life,
But that the dread of something after death
(That undiscovered country, from whose bourne
No traveller returns) puzzles the will—
And makes us rather bear those ills we have
Than fly to others that we know not of.
Thus conscience does make cowards of us all;
And thus the native hue of resolution
Is sicklied o'er with the pale cast of thought;
And enterprises of great pith and moment,
With this regard, their currents turn awry
And lose the name of action."

---

* The Folio reads—" the *poor* man's contumely;" the contumely
which the *poor* man is obliged to endure.—*Malone.*

† The Folio reads—" pangs of *disprized* love;" meaning a love
which is found to be *unvalued* or disregarded.—*J. H. Hackett.*

We have already observed that there is not any
apparent circumstance in the fate or situation of
Hamlet, that should prompt him to harbor one
thought of self-murder; and therefore these expressions of despair imply an impropriety in point of
character.   But supposing his condition was truly
desperate, and he saw no possibility of repose but
in the uncertain harbor of death, let us see in what
manner he argues on that subject.   The question is,
"To be, or not to be;" to die by my own hand, or
live and suffer the miseries of life.   He proceeds to
explain the alternative in these terms, "Whether
'tis nobler in the mind to suffer, or endure the frowns
of fortune, or to take arms, and, by opposing, end
them."   Here he deviates from his first proposition,
and death is no longer the question.   The only
doubt is, whether he will stoop to misfortune, or
exert his faculties in order to surmount it.   This,
surely, is the obvious meaning, and indeed the
only meaning that can be implied in these words,
"Whether 'tis nobler in the mind to suffer the slings
and arrows of outrageous fortune, or to take up arms
against a sea of troubles, and, by opposing, end
them."   He now drops this idea, and reverts to his
reasoning on death, in the course of which he owns
himself deterred from suicide by the thought of
what may follow death; "the dread of something
after death (that undiscovered country, from whose
bourne no traveller returns.")   This might be a good
argument in a heathen or pagan, and such indeed

Hamlet really was; but Shakespeare has already represented him as a good Catholic, who must have been acquainted with the truths of revealed religion, and says expressly in this very play—"Had not the Everlasting fixed his canon 'gainst self-murder?" Moreover, he has just been conversing with his father's spirit, piping hot from purgatory, which we presume is not within the *bourne* of this world. The dread of what may happen after death (says he)

> "Makes us rather bear those *ills* we have,
> Than fly to *others* that we know not of."

This declaration at least implies some knowledge of the other world, and expressly asserts, that there must be *ills* in that world, though what kind of *ills* they are we do not know. The argument, therefore, may be reduced to this lemma: "This world abounds with *ills* which I feel; the other world abounds with *ills* the nature of which I do not know; therefore, I will rather bear those *ills* I have, "than fly to *others* which I know not of;" a deduction amounting to a certainty, with respect to the only circumstance that could create a doubt, mainly, whether in death he should rest from his misery; and if he was certain there were evils in the next world, as well as in this, he had no room to reason at all about the matter. What alone could justify his thinking on this subject, would have been the hope of flying from the ills of this world, without encountering any *others* in the next.   Nor is *Hamlet* more accurate in the following reflection :

"Thus conscience does make cowards of us all."

A bad conscience will make us cowards, but a good conscience will make us brave.   It does not appear that anything lay heavy on his conscience : and from the premises we cannot help inferring that conscience, in this case, was entirely out of the question.   *Hamlet* was deterred from suicide by a full conviction that in flying from one sea of troubles which he did know, he should fall into *another* which he did not know.

His whole chain of reasoning, therefore, seems inconsistent and incongruous.   "I am doubtful whether I should live, or do violence upon my own life; for, I know not whether 'tis more honorable to bear misfortune patiently, than to exert myself in opposing misfortune, and by opposing, end it."   ·Let us throw it into the form of a syllogism; it will stand thus : "I am oppressed with ills; I know not whether 'tis more honorable to bear those ills patiently, or to end them by taking arms against them; *ergo*, I am doubtful whether I should slay myself, or live.   To die, is no more than to sleep; and to *say* that by a sleep we end the heart-ache," etc., "is a consummation devoutly to be wish'd."

Now, to *say it* was of no consequence, unless it had been true.   "I am afraid of the dreams that may happen in that sleep of death; and I choose rather to bear those ills I have in this life, than fly to *other ills* in that undiscovered country from whose bourne no traveller ever returns. I have ills that are almost insupportable in this life. I know not what is in the next, because it is an undiscovered country; *ergo*, I'd rather bear those ills I have than fly to others which I know not of." Here the conclusion is by no means warranted by the premises. "I am sore afflicted in this life; but I will rather bear the afflictions of this life, than plunge myself in the afflictions of another life; *ergo*, conscience makes cowards of us all." But this conclusion would justify the logician in saying, *negatur consequens;* for it is entirely detached both from the major and the minor proposition.

The soliloquy is not less exceptionable in the propriety of expression than in the chain of argumentation. "To die—to sleep—no more," contains an ambiguity, which all the art of punctuation cannot remove; for it may signify that "to die," is to sleep no more; or the expression "no more" may be considered as an abrupt apostrophe in thinking, as if he meant to say, "no more of that reflection."

"Ay, there's the rub"—is a vulgarism beneath the dignity of *Hamlet's* character, and the words that follow leave the sense imperfect:

> "For in that sleep of death what dreams may come,
>   When we have shuffled off this mortal coil,
>   Must give us pause."

Not the dreams that might come, but the fear of what dreams might come, occasioned the pause or hesitation. *Respect* in the same line may be allowed to pass for consideration; but

"Th' oppressor's wrong, the proud* man's contumely,"

according to the invariable acceptation of the words *wrong* and *contumely*, can signify nothing but the wrong sustained by the oppressor, and the contumely or abuse thrown upon the proud* man; though it is plain that Shakespeare used them in a different sense; neither is the word *spurn†* a substantive; yet as such he has inserted it in these lines:

"The insolence of office, and the spurns
That patient merit of th' unworthy takes."

If we consider the metaphors of the soliloquy, we shall find them jumbled together in a strange confusion.

If the metaphors were reduced to painting, we should find it a very difficult task, if not altogether impracticable, to represent with any propriety outrageous fortune, with her slings and arrows, between which, indeed, there is no sort of analogy in nature. Neither can any figure be more ridiculously absurd than that of a man taking arms against the sea, ex-

---

* The first folio reads "*poor* man's."

† Also, again "gives my soul the greatest spurn."

[Titus Andron., Act 3, Scene 1.

clusive of the incongruous medley of slings, arrows, and seas, jostled within the compass of one reflection. What follows is a strange rhapsody of broken images, of sleeping, dreaming, and shifting off a *coil*, which last conveys no idea that can be represented on canvas. A man may be exhibited shuffling off his garments or his chains; but how he should shuffle off a *coil*,* which is another term for noise and tumult, we cannot comprehend. Then we have "long-liv'd calamity," and "time armed with whips and scorns," and patient "merit spurned by unworthiness," and "misery with a bare bodkin going to make his own *quietus*," which at best is but a mean metaphor. These are followed by figures "sweating under fardels of burdens," "puzzled with doubts," "shaking with fears," and "flying from evils." Finally, we see "resolution sicklied o'er with pale thought," a conception like that of representing health by sickness; and a "current of pith turned away, so as to lose the name of action," which is both an error in fancy and a solecism in sense. In a word, this soliloquy may be compared to the *Ægri somnia* and the *Tabula cujus vanæ fingentur species.*†

---

* A *coil*, in Shakespeare, means a tumult, hubbub, etc.; shuffle off this mortal coil, *rid one's self of this mortal strife and confusion.*

† "*Ay, there's the rub*"—(Dr. Goldsmith remarks)—"is a vulgarism beneath the dignity of *Hamlet's* character." It might have been thus conventionally considered in Dr. Goldsmith's, but not in Shakespeare's day; and for the reason that besides, in numerous other instances of

Highly as I have been prepossessed in favor of Dr. Goldsmith's taste and purity of style in composition, I cannot unscrupulously swallow such a dose of sweeping condemnation, which seems to me hypercritical, despite his deprecation at the commencement of a shock to our sensibilities, founded upon a bias toward "an author so universally held in veneration, and whose very errors have helped to sanctify his character among the multitude." .

Let us first inquire whether some, at least, of his premises are not false—whether some of the *errors* imputed to Shakespeare are not the critic's own errors of perception. The reasoning, as well as some of the metaphors, have proved stumbling-blocks to other learned critics.

its use in rhythmical measure, the word *rub* is put into the mouths of, namely:

"To leave no *rubs* nor botches in the work."—*Macbeth.*

"Shall blow each dust, each straw, each little *rub*,
  Out of the path," etc.
> [*Cardinal Pandulph, (in King John.*)

" 'Twill make me think the world is full of *rubs*,
  And that my fortune runs against the bias."
> [*The Queen, (in Richard Second.*)

"Every rub is smoothed in our way."—*King Henry V.*

"What *rub*, or what impediment, there is."
> [*Duke of Burgundy.*

——"perceive
The least *rub* in your fortunes."
> [*Duke of Buckingham, (Henry VIII.*)

——"nor has Coriolanus
Deserved this so dishonored *rub*, laid falsely."
> [*Cominius, the Roman General.*

Dr. Johnson remarks:—" Of this celebrated soliloquy, which, bursting from a man distracted with a contrariety of desires, and overwhelmed with the magnitude of his own purposes, is connected rather in the speaker's mind than on his tongue, I shall endeavor to discover the train, and to show how one sentiment produces another.

" *Hamlet*, knowing himself injured in the most enormous and atrocious degree, and seeing no means of redress but such as must expose him to extremity of hazard, meditates on his situation in this manner: *Before I can form any rational scheme of action under this pressure of distress*, it is necessary to decide, whether, *after our present state*, we *are* to be, or not to be. That is the question which, as it shall be answered, will determine *whether 'tis nobler*, and more suitable to the dignity of reason, *to suffer the outrages of fortune* patiently, or take arms against *them*, and by opposing, end them, *though, perhaps*, with the loss of life. If to die, were *to sleep, no more, and by a sleep to end* the miseries of our nature, such a sleep were *devoutly to be wished;* but if *to sleep* in death be *to dream*, to retain our powers of sensibility, we must *pause* to consider, *in that sleep of death what dreams may come.* This consideration *makes calamity* so long endured ; *for who would bear* the vexations of life, which might be ended *by a bare bodkin*, but that he is afraid of something in unknown futurity? This fear it is that gives efficacy to conscience, which, by turning the mind upon *this regard*, chills the ardor of *resolution*, checks the vigor of *enterprise*, and makes the *current* of desire stagnant in inactivity.

"We may suppose that he would have applied these general observations to his own case, but that he discovered *Ophelia*."—*Johnson*.

Mr. Malone, in his edition of Shakespeare, quotes the foregoing, and then adds:—"Dr. Johnson's explication of the first five lines of this passage is surely wrong. *Hamlet* is not deliberating whether after our present state we are to exist or not, but whether he should continue to live, or put an end to his life—as is pointed out by the second and the three following lines, which are manifestly a paraphrase on the first:—'Whether 'tis nobler in the mind to suffer,' etc., 'or to take arms.' The question concerning our existence in a future state is not considered till the tenth line:—'To sleep! perchance to *dream*,' etc. The train of *Hamlet's* reasoning from the middle of the fifth line, 'If to die, were to sleep,' etc., Dr. Johnson has marked out with his usual accuracy. In our poet's 'Rape of Lucrece' we find the same question stated, which is proposed in the beginning of the present soliloquy:

> ———'With herself she is in mutiny,
> To live or die, which of the twain were better.'"—*Malone*.

A precedent for the figure—"*arrows* of outrageous *fortune*"—Mr. Steevens finds in one of Cicero's Epistles: Fam. v. 16.

Mr. Theobald remarks :—"*A sea of troubles*, among the Greeks, grew into a proverbial usage. So that the expression figuratively means the troubles of human life, which flow in upon us, and encompass us round like a sea."

Dr. Johnson observes :—"Mr. Pope proposed *seige*. I know not why there should be so much solicitude about this metaphor. Shakespeare breaks his metaphors often, and in this desultory speech there was less need of preserving them."

Mr. Steevens says :—"A similar phrase occurs in Ryharde Morysine's translation of 'Ludovicus Vives's Introduction to Wysedome,' 1544 : 'how great a sea of evills every day over-runneth,' etc."

And Mr. Malone concludes his notes with—"One cannot but wonder that the smallest doubt should be entertained concerning an expression which is so much in Shakespeare's manner ; yet to preserve the integrity of the metaphor, Dr. Warburton reads *assail* of troubles. Shakespeare might have found the very phrase that he has employed, in the tragedy of Queen Cordila, 'Mirrour of Magistrates,' 1575, which he undoubtedly had read :

'For lacke of frendes to tell my *seas* of giltlesse *smart*.'"

"*Shuffled off this mortal coil—i.e.*, turmoil, bustle."—*Warburton*.

"A most intelligent Shakespearian critic, Thomas Caldecott, remarks upon the word *coil :*—'*Coil* is here used in each of its senses—that of turmoil or

bustle, and that which entwines or wraps round.'
'This muddy *vesture* of decay.' Those folds of mortality that *encircle* and entangle us. Snakes generally lie in folds like the coils of ropes; and it is
conceivable that an allusion is here had to the
struggle which that animal is obliged to make in
casting his slough, or extricating himself from the
skin that forms the exterior of this coil, and which
he throws off annually.'"—*J. II. II.*

" *There's the respect*—*i.e.*, the consideration. See
Troilus and Cressida, Act 2, sc. 2."—*Malone.*

" *The whips and scorns of Time.*—The evils here
complained of are not the product of time or dura-
tion simply, but of a corrupt age or manners. We
may be sure, then, that Shakespeare wrote:

> ——' the whips and scorns of th' time.'

And the description of the evils of a corrupt age,
which followed, confirms this emendation."— *Warburton.*

" It may be remarked, that *Hamlet*, in his enumeration of miseries, forgets, whether properly or not,
that he is a prince, and mentions many evils to
which inferior stations only are exposed."—*Johnson.*

I think we might venture to read:—" The whips
and scorns o' the *times*"—*i.e.*, times satirical as the
age of Shakespeare, which probably furnished him
with the idea, etc., etc.

Whips and scorns are surely as inseparable companions as public punishment and infamy.

Quips, the word which Dr. Johnson would introduce, is derived, by all etymologists, from whips.

Hamlet is introduced as reasoning on a question of general concernment. He therefore takes in all such evils as could befall mankind in general, without considering himself at present as a prince, or wishing to avail himself of the few exceptions which one in high place might have claimed.

In part of "King James I.'s Entertainment, passing to his Coronation," by Ben Jonson and Decker, is the following line, and note on that line :—

> "And first account of years, of months, *of time.*
> By *time* we understand *the present.*"

"This explanation affords the sense for which I have contended, and without change."—*Steevens.*

Time, for *the times,* is used by Jonson in "Every Man Out of His Humour :"

> "Oh, how I hate the monstrousness of *time.*"

So, in Basse's "Sword and Buckler," 1602 :

> "If I should touch particularly all
> Wherein the moodie spleene of captious *Time*
> Doth tax our functions——"

So, also, to give a prose instance, in "Cardanus Comfort," translated by Thomas Bedingfield, 1576, we have a description of the miseries of life, strongly resembling that in the text :—" Hunger, thurste, sleape not so plentiful or quiet as deade men have, heate in sommer, colde in winter, *disorder of tyme*, terroure of warres, controlement of parentes, cares of wedlock, studye for children, slouthe of servants, *contention of sutes*, and that (whiche is moste of all) the *condicion of tyme* wherein *honestye is disdaynd*, and folye and crafte is honoured as wisdome."— *Boswell.*

The word *whips* is used by Marston in his " Satires," 1599, in the sense required here :

" Ingenious Melancholy,—
Inthrone thee in my blood ; let me intreat,
Stay his quick jocund skips, and force him run
A sad-pac'd course, untill my *whips* be done."—*Malone.*

" *The* PROUD *man's contumely.*—Thus the quarto. The folio reads ' the *poor* man's contumely ;' the contumely which the poor man is obliged to endure :

" *Nil habet infelix paupertas durius in se,*
Quam quod ridiculos homines facit."—*Malone.*

" *Of* DESPIS'D *love.*—The folio reads, of *dispriz'd* love.   So too, ' Great deal disprizing the knight opposed.'   (Troilus and Cressida, Act 4.)"—*Steevens.*

Dispriz'd, the word found in the first folio (1623), has seemed to me the most suitable adjective in such connection ; for the reason that as Love begets Love, and Hate *his* kind, so *Love* that finds itself *despised*, instead of returned, by its object, soon leaves the heart, and its place is not unapt to be filled by rank *hatred ;* but, the pangs of *disprized* love are those of one whose spirit sinks and writhes under the pride-stung consciousness that the being towards whom their own heart yearns *disprizes* their irresistible affection.　It is *this* species of love which *disprized* (unvalued, or unrequited, or entertained with indifference) cannot be diverted or superseded, or, as if *despised*, find a relief in *hatred*—but brooding over its own subtile mortification, produces that poignant melancholy, which, rankling within a proud soul, may stimulate to suicide.　(See my quotation from this in my Correspondence with Hon. John Quincy Adams, 1839.)

> " Might his *quietus* make

With a bare BODKIN."—The first expression probably alluded to the writ of discharge, which was formerly granted to those barons and knights who personally attended the king on any foreign expedition.　This discharge was called a *quietus*.

It is at this time the term for the acquittance which every sheriff receives on settling his accounts at the Exchequer.

The word is used for the discharge of an account, by Webster, in his " Duchess of Malfy," 1623 :

> " And 'cause you shall not come to me in debt,
> (Being now my steward) here upon your lips
> I sign your *quietus est.*"

Again :

> " You had the trick in audit time to be sick,
> Till I had sign'd your *quietus.*"

A *bodkin* was the ancient term for a *small dagger.* So, in the second part of the " Mirrour for Knight-hood," quarto, 1598 :—" Not having any more weapons but a poor poynado, which usually he did bear about him, and taking it in his hand, delivered these speeches unto it.   Thou, silly *bodkin*, shalt finish the piece of work," etc.

In the margin of " Stowe's Chronicle," edit. 1614, it is said, that Cæsar was slain with *bodkins ;* and in " The Muses' Looking-Glass," by Randolph, 1638 :

> " *Apho.*—A rapier's but a *bodkin.*
> *Deil.*—And a *bodkin*
> Is a most dang'rous weapon ; since I read
> Of Julius Cæsar's death, I durst not venture
> Into a taylor's shop, for fear of *bodkins.*"

Again, in " The Custom of the Country," by Beaumont and Fletcher :

> ——" out with your *bodkin,*
> Your pocket-dagger, your stiletto."

Again, in " Sapho and Phao," 1591 : " There will be a desperate fray between two, made at all weapons, from the brown bill to the *bodkin.*"   Again, in Chaucer, as he is quoted at the end of a pamphlet, called " The Serpent of Division," etc., whereunto is annexed the " Tragedy of Gorboduc," etc., 1591 :

> "With bodkins was Cæsar Julius
>   Murdered at Rome of Brutus Crassus."—*Steevens.*

By "a *bare* bodkin," does not perhaps mean, "by so *little* an instrument as a dagger," but "by an *unsheathed* dagger."

"In the account which Mr. Steevens has given of the original meaning of the term *quietus*, after the words, ' who personally attended the king on any foreign expedition,' should have been added, ' and were therefore exempted from the claims of scutage, or a tax on every knight's fee.' "—*Malone.*

" *To* GRUNT *and sweat.*—Thus the old copies. It is, undoubtedly, the true reading, but can scarcely be borne by modern ears."—*Johnson.*

Stanyhurst, in his translation of Virgil, 1582, for *supremum congemuit*, gives us, "for sighing it *grunts.*" Again, in Trubervile's translation of Ovid's Epistle from Canace to Macareus:

> "What might I wiser do? greefe forst me *grunt.*'

Again, in the same translator's Hypermnestra to Lynceus:

> ——" round about I heard
>   Of dying men the *grunts.*"

The change made by the editors [to *groan*] is, however, supported by the following line in " Julius Cæsar," Act. 4, sc. 1 :

> " He shall but bear them as the ass bears gold ;
>   To groan and sweat under the business,
>   Either led or driven, as we point the way."

I apprehend that it is the duty of an editor to exhibit what his author wrote, and not to substitute what may appear to the present age preferable; and Dr. Johnson was of the same opinion. See his note on the word *hugger-mugger*, Act 4, sc. 5. I have, therefore, though with some reluctance, adhered to the old copies, however unpleasing this word may be to the ear. On the stage, without doubt, an actor is at liberty to substitute a less offensive word. To the ears of our ancestors it probably conveyed no unpleasing sound; for we find it used by Chaucer and others:

> "But never *gront* he at no stroke, but on," etc., etc.
>
> *The Monke's Tale.*

Again, in "Wily Beguiled," written before 1596:

> "She's never well, but *grunting* in a corner."—*Malone.*

> "The undiscover'd country, from whose bourn

No TRAVELLER *returns.*"—This has been cavilled at by Lord Orrery and others, but without reason. The idea of a traveller in Shakespeare's time was, of a person who gave an account of his adventures. Every voyage was a discovery. John Taylor has "A Discovery by Sea from London to Salisbury."— *Farmer.*

Again, Marston's "Insatiate Countess," 1603:

> ——"Wrestled with death,
> From whose stern cave none tracks a backward path."
> "*Qui nunc it per iter tenebricosum,*
> *Illuc unde negant redire quemquam.*"—*Catullus.*

Again, in Sandford's translation of " Cornelius Agrippa," etc., 1569 (once a book of uncommon popularity): " The *countrie* of the dead is irremeable, that they *cannot retourne*.'   Again, in " Cymbeline," says the *Gaoler* to *Posthumus* : " How you shall speed in your journey's end [after execution], I think you'll *never return to tell one.*"—*Steevens.*

This passage has been objected to by others on a ground which, at first view of it, seems more plausible.   *Hamlet* himself, it is objected, has had ocular demonstration that travellers do sometimes return from this strange country.   I formerly thought this an inconsistency.   But this objection is also founded on a mistake.   Our poet, without doubt, in the passage before us, intended to say, that from the *unknown* regions of the dead no traveller returns with all his *corporeal powers*, such as he who goes on a voyage of *discovery* brings back when he returns to the port from which he sailed.   The traveller whom *Hamlet* had seen, though he appeared in the same habit which he had worn in his lifetime, was nothing but a shadow ; " invulnerable as the air," and consequently *incorporeal.* If, says the objector, the traveller has reached this coast, it is not an undiscovered country.   But by *undiscovered*, Shakespeare meant, not undiscovered by departed spirits, but undiscovered, or unknown to " such fellows as we who crawl between earth and heaven ;" *superis incognita tellus.*   In this sense every country, of which the traveller does not return *alive* to give an *account*, may be said to be *undiscovered*. The *Ghost* has given us no account of the region from whence he came, being, as he himself informed us, " forbid to tell the secrets of his prison-house."

Marlowe, before our poet, had compared death to a journey to an undiscovered country :

> ————"weep not for Mortimer,
> That scorns the world, and, as a *traveller*,
> Goes to *discover countries* yet unknown.
> —*King Edward II.* 1598, (*written before* 1593)' "—*Malone.*

Perhaps this is another instance of Shakespeare's acquaintance with the Bible: " Afore I goe thither, from *whence I shall not turne againe*, even to the land of darknesse and shadowe of deathe ; yea, into that darke, cloudie lande and deadlye shadowe wherein is no order, but terrible feare as in the darknesse."   (Job, ch. x.)

" 'The way that I must goe is at hande, but *whence* I shall *not turne againe*.'   (Job, ch. xvi.)   I quote Cranmer's Bible."—*Douce.*

Thus conscience does make cowards of us all.

> " I'll not meddle with it; *it makes a man a coward.*"
>   [*Rich. III.* : *Act* 1, *sc.* 4.
> " O coward conscience, how dost thou afflict me."
>   [*Ibid* : *Act* 5, *sc.* 3."—*Blakeway.*

" Great PITH."—Thus the folio.   The quartos read, " of great *pitch.*"—*Steevens.*

" *Pitch* seems to be the better reading.   The allusion is to the *pitching* or throwing the *bar;* a manly exercise, usual in country villages."—*Ritson.*

Not to speak it profanely, Mr. Ritson's idea is *far fetched.* *Pith* (as per *folio*) was the word, and used in a similar sense, as in—

> ——" that's my *pith* of business."—*Meas for Meas.*
> ——" marked not what's the *pith* of all."
> [*Taming of the Shrew.*
> ——" the *pith* and marrow of our attribute."—*Hamlet.*
> ——" let it feed even on the *pith* of life."—*Ibid.*
> ——" arms of mine had seven years *pith.*"—*Othello.*

TURN AWAY.—Thus the quartos. The folio, " turn *away.*" The same printer's error occurs in the old copy of " Antony and Cleopatra," where we find, " your crown's *away,*" instead of " your crown's *awry.*"—*Steevens.*

Thus have I quoted the most erudite and eminent of Shakespeare's commentators upon such words and metaphors as are comprised in *Hamlet's soliloquy on suicide,* and the meaning or propriety of which has suggested their doubts or questions. But, as in the early part of this nineteenth century, there was discovered, in the library of the Duke of Devonshire, a single edition of " Hamlet," 1603, (the only known copy of the play as originally written by Shakespeare, and the same which he afterward altered and enlarged to that which appears in the folio of 1623,) containing many of Shakespeare's original crude or undigested thoughts, which he afterward worked over or elaborated, and among others, his previous sketch or draft of this famous soliloquy, a reference to it may assist to elucidate some point that has been involved in doubt, and also gratify the curiosity of any one inclined to discover where Shakespeare thought fit to turn critic and improve upon his own earlier compositions.

It should be premised, however, perhaps, to a modern reader, that, besides standing as a numeral for *one*, the ninth letter of the alphabet, *I*, which in later times became confined to signify the *pronoun of the first person*, was in Shakespeare's day written also to express *ay* or *yes*.   Wherever Shakespeare wrote *aye*, the word means *ever* or *always*.

> *Ham.*—"To be, or not to be, I there's the point,
> To die, to sleepe, is that all?   I all:
> No, to sleepe, to dreame, I mary there it goes,
> For in that dreame of death, when wee awake,
> And borne before an everlasting Judge,
> From whence no passenger ever returned,
> The undiscovered country, at whose sight,
> The happy smile, and the accursed damn'd.
> But for this, the joyful hope of this,
> Whoe'd beare the scornes and flattery of the world,
> Scorned by the right rich, the rich curssed of the poore.
> The widow being oppressed, the orphan wrong'd,
> The taste of hunger, or a tirant's raigne,
> And thousand more calamities besides,
> To grunt and sweat under this weary life,
> When that he may his full quietus make,
> With a bare bodkin, who would this indure,
> But for a hope of something after death?

> Which pusles the braine, and doth confound the sence,
> Which makes vs rather beare those evilles we have,
> Than flie to others that we know not of.
> I that, O this conscience makes cowards of vs all,
> Lady in thy orizons, be all my sinnes remembered."

The soliloquy here consists of twenty-two lines only; in the folio of 1623 it fills thirty-three lines. Shakespeare found occasion in that to introduce new or different subject-matter for reflection. He also strengthened many of his original expressions, and, indeed, seems to have almost entirely reformed, by diffusion and compression alternately, the links in the chain of the self-argument.

In the edition of 1603, preserving the first half of the opening line—" To be, or not to be "—the author struck out " ay, there's the point," and substituted " that is the question."   Then he introduces:

> " Whether 'tis nobler in the mind, to suffer
>   The slings and arrows of outrageous fortune,
>   Or to take arms against a sea of troubles,
>   And by opposing, end them ?"

At this point he falls back upon his second original line :

> " To die, to sleep, is that all? ay, all :"

and resolves it *for the continuity:*

> ——" To die ?—to sleep !—
> No more."

There Shakespeare stopped to reconnoitre *Hamlet's*

postulate and the natural consequences, and pursuing his self-inquiry, added:

> ——" and, by a sleep, to say, we end
> The heart-ache, and the thousand natural shocks
> That flesh is heir to,—'tis a consummation
> Devoutly to be wish'd."

Here he again returns, and resumes his self-debate
from the third line of the original soliloquy:

> " No, to sleepe, to dreame, ay mary there it goes,"

first reiterating,

> " To die—to sleep—"

and then suggesting the likelihood of a *dream :*

> " To sleep ! perchance to dream; ay, there's the rub,"

he specifies the respective considerations which
should restrain his impulses or compel him to hesitate. He changes the expression from *dream* to
" sleep of death ;" and substitutes for

> ——" when we awake
> And borne before an everlasting Judge,"

> ——" what dreams may come,
> When we have shuffled off this mortal coil."

Possibly Shakespeare may have considered that
his own ideas were not quite clear in their inception,
and had been rather conglomerated in their original
expression ; as he continued to separate and to arrange

them in a more logical and intelligible order : for example, in place of his first hypothesis of being "in a *dream* of death, and awakened and borne before an everlasting Judge, from whence no *passenger* ever returned," and also, of the opening to " sight an undiscovered country " which should have the effect to make "the happy smile, and the accursed (feel) damn'd," we find the author has changed the idea to one suggestive of "*sleep* of death," (which knows no waking,) together with that dread—"*what*" (possibly horrid) "dreams" in the *eternal* sleep a suicide might discover as *his* fate, who, aware that the Everlasting had "fixed his canon 'gainst self-slaughter," had thus defiantly attempted to rid himself of life's turmoils, and had hastily " SHUFFLED OFF this *mortal* coil," and those ill fortunes which Destiny had seen fit to *deal* out, as his lot in *this* world.

Referring to the immediate antecedent—

> " The undiscovered country, at whose sight
> The happy smile," etc.,

the line—

> " But for this, the joyful hope of this "

is omitted, and, instead of retaining entire,

> " But for the *hope* of something after death,"

the author thought fit to alter " *hope* " to " *dread*."

> " But that the DREAD of something after death
>   (That undiscovered country, from whose bourn
>   No *traveller* returns) puzzles the will "—

(not " puzzles the *braine*," as previously written,) and, after apostrophizing " conscience " in a line, *adds*, finally :

> " And thus the native hue of resolution
>   Is sicklied o'er with the pale cast of thought;
>   And enterprises of great pith and moment,
>   With this regard, their currents turn awry,
>   And lose the name of action."

The idea connected with the words " *shuffled off* " may be discovered in its concordance in another play :

> ——" Often good turns
> Are *shuffled off* with such uncurrent pay ;
> But, were my worth, as is my conscience, firm,
> You should find better *dealing*."
>
>   [*Twelfth Night*, Act 3, sc. 3.

In conclusion, with reference to the matter contained in this soliloquy as it appeared in the earlier edition, (1603,) it is highly interesting to imagine what *thoughts* might have originated in the brain of such a mighty genius, and what his motives were for each change of word, or sentence, or order in expression ; but, with what a nice regard to a combination of poetry with philosophy and human nature, Shakespeare has condensed the spirit of his first ideas and less digested reflections in the *latest* edition of this soliloquy, only such as may have the taste, time and patience to investigate for themselves can thoroughly appreciate.

In March, 1828, happening, when engaged in discursive reading, to pick up a volume of "The British Classics," containing Goldsmith's Essays, I quoted the preceding matter, and wrote the previous comments and the following remarks upon that portion of Goldsmith's XVIth Essay which relates to "Hamlet's Soliloquy on Suicide:"—

In reference to the first charge preferred against Shakespeare, that he has given *Hamlet* not "the least reason to wish for death," it should be recollected, that *Hamlet's* mind was, upon our first introduction to him, strongly operated upon by the recent and sudden death of a parent whom he had dearly loved, and whose memory he reverenced—that, whilst in the full and unabated indulgence of his grief, his mother, forgetful of his father's recent decease, and in defiance of common decency, had been actually won, within a month after that fatal event, to the incestuous bed of his paternal uncle.

Perhaps a touch of disappointed ambition, but more apparently the continual recurrence of these facts to his sensitive mind, at times disgusted him with life; and, to add to his mortification, his succession had been hindered, and the throne usurped, by one whose very dethronement, since his marriage with his mother, would tend more deeply to disgrace the royal family of Denmark, which, as appears by the catastrophe, consisted of these three only.

In the midst of these afflictions, he is informed that the ghost of his father has been seen "two nights together" upon the platform before the castle, where,

> "With martial stalk, hath he gone by our watch;"

has sought and had an interview *apart* with the apparition, learned that *murder* has been joined to the crime of incest in obtaining the crown, his own by right; but, though *Hamlet* is expected to revenge upon his beastly uncle his father's "foul, strange and unnatural" murder, his pursuit of it is embarrassed by the *Ghost's* injunction:

> "Taint not thy mind, nor let thy soul contrive
> Against thy mother aught; leave her to heaven,
> And to those thorns that in her bosom lodge
> To prick and sting her."

As soon as *Hamlet* recovers from the appalling effect of that horrid revelation, sufficient of itself to overwhelm and prostrate his faculties, without the superadded and preternatural agency of his father's disembodied spirit to render it still more terrific and impressive, he resolves that the preliminary step of his policy shall be the semblance of madness; because, such a reputed state of mind will at once exempt him from being an object of further machinations from his murderous uncle, whose security in the throne would be greatly enhanced by *Hamlet's* incapability; and, also, whilst evident insanity would protect his life and neutralize any apprehension in his uncle's mind of *Hamlet's* attempt to vindicate his own rights, would afford *Hamlet* more opportunity to reconnoitre his uncle's unguarded licentiousness.

In order that the story of the *Ghost* may not get currency, and thereby discover any clue to his stratagem and assumed madness, *Hamlet* has prayed of the only three others who have seen the apparition—

> " If you have hitherto concealed this sight,
>   Let it be tenable* in your silence still "—

and, of the two officers of the watch, particularly, and under their oath, not to divulge anything concerning him, should he " think meet to put an antick disposition on."

One of the most signal traits of *Hamlet's* idiosyncrasy is his fickleness of purpose or irresolution. Of that morbid fertility is his imagination, that often before he is able to realize to himself an idea it has started, another dispels or displaces it, and his utterance, incapable of keeping pace with their flow, and blending their expression, becomes confused and unintelligible without scrutiny.

---

* The folio of 1623 reads, " let it be *treble* in your silence still," and, although Steevens thinks "tenable" in the quarto "right," I doubt it; as the meaning of *treble* (or triple) may be, " the sight *remain* known to you *three* only," namely, *Horatio, Marcellus* and *Bernardo.*

Dr. Johnson says:—"Of the feigned madness of *Hamlet* there appears no adequate cause, for he does nothing he might not have done with the reputation of sanity." Granted, that he accomplishes little or nothing in any of his plans or objects; but he repeatedly purposed to do a great deal; and it is the differing shades of his discrepancy between the understandings and moral habits and actions of mankind which constitute our peculiarities of character. *Hamlet* was of an impulsive temperament, and very dissimilar to such as are naturally phlegmatic, and who resolve, after mature and deliberate reflection, and steadily execute their purposes. *Hamlet's* nature is like the flint-struck steel, which " shows a hasty spark, and straight is cold again." All his resolutions must be formed out of some excitement of the blood. When the *Ghost* first intimates, and calls upon him to revenge, his *murder*, he impatiently interjects :

> " Haste me to know it; that I, with wings as swift
> As meditation, or the thoughts of love,
> May sweep to my revenge "—

and could he *immediately* have encountered his murderer, whilst his blood was inflamed, would unhesitatingly have fulfilled his vow of vengeance then, as he did, upon an after-occasion, in " his brainish apprehension," kill *Polonius.* The moment his blood cools, he relapses into the philosopher. Hardly does one incentive to action present itself to his mind, before it is blasted in the bud, or neutralized by some paralyzing obstacle. His inconsistency of conduct has in some instances been undeservedly complained of through ignorance of *Hamlet's* motives. Once, particularly, he summons all his resolution, and fully bent on sacrifice, seeks his uncle, whom he then chances to find at prayer:—his heart, which revolted even at retributive slaughter in cold blood, failed him, and suggested to his judgment a parley before procedure, and the sophism that it would be "hire and salary—not revenge,"

> "To take him in the purging of his soul,
>   When he is fit and seasoned for his passage,"

who had killed his brother

> "With all his crimes broad blown, as flush as May;"

and, under the alleged pretext that slaying his uncle *then* "would be scann'd" and be regarded as an encouraging example to a murderer, *Hamlet* determines with himself that it is inexpedient at that juncture to kill *King Claudius*, and prefers to await some opportunity when his uncle may be

> ——"about some act
> That has no relish of salvation in't:
> Then trip him, that his heels may kick at heaven:
> And that his soul may be as damn'd, and black,
> As hell, whereto it goes."

This obvious subterfuge for his own irresolution has been *barbarously* misconstrued by some ignorant or superficial critics, who impute to *Hamlet* the possession of a demoniacal spirit of revenge, unsatisfied with the killing of the body only, and desirous of extending its gluttonous malignancy to the *soul* after its separation: whereas, the real motive which underlies the sophistry ought to be transparent to any one reading carefully *Hamlet's* conduct and character, either before or after. Take, for one of the many examples, his own acknowledgment of his instability of purpose and self-reproof:

> "How all occasions do inform against me,
> And spur my dull revenge;" etc.

Dr. Johnson continues:—"*Hamlet* plays the madman most when he treats *Ophelia* with so much rudeness, which seems to be useless and wanton cruelty." With regard to its *uselessness*, I would suggest a reference to the fact, that *Hamlet*, having, immediately after the *Ghost's* revelation, thought fit to put an antic disposition on, sought a subject and a medium for circulating through the Court a report of his *insanity;* some strange freak of conduct was necessary as a preliminary, and what sort of mental derangement so likely to be esteemed harmless to all, and afford perfect security to the suspicious mind of the guilty usurper, as the madness proceeding from unrequited love? The notoriety of his tender passion for *Ophelia*, and the fact that she had recently, by the command of her father, returned his letters and rejected his visits, afforded a promising opportunity to establish such a starting-point without exciting anyone's suspicion.

However strongly the current of *Hamlet's* passion for *Ophelia* had been set previously, it had been checked by his then mourning his father's recent and sudden death, and, now particularly that he had vowed to *remember* his perturbed spirit, and

> " Thy commandment *all alone* shall live
>   Within the book and volume of my brain,"

his thoughts had been diverted from a course of *love* and bound in another channel, *filial duty.*

If an origination of the report of *Hamlet's* madness, and its apparent cause from the least suspicious source (and *Hamlet's* object was to secure such report's ready access to the King and Queen), could he have selected a more fit, inoffensive, and sure course, than through *Ophelia*, who would naturally, and dutifully, and *forthwith* communicate *Hamlet's* behavior to her father, whose propensity would lead to its immediate promulgation to the King and the Court? I think the means *Hamlet* adopted were exceedingly well calculated to produce the impression he wished to make, and that up to this stage of his proceeding, there is no evidence of his *madness* being other than *assumed.* His "rudeness," then, was not—if it could be so considered at all—"*useless* and *wanton* cruelty." But was *Hamlet* either *rude* or *cruel* to *Ophelia?* To judge from her description of *Hamlet's* behavior, when she had "been *affrighted*, as she was sewing in her closet," *Ophelia* did not regard it as either rude or cruel, but "*piteous*," in its effect upon her; and, in reference to his conversation with her, when her father and the King had conspired to send for *Hamlet*, when he might, as 'twere by accident, meet *Ophelia*, whilst they, so bestowed as to be unseen by him, could thus covertly see and hear what should pass between them, and to which *espionage* she has lent herself by *walking* in *Hamlet's* way and seeming to *read a book*, as instructed, it should be premised that the text furnishes a reasonable inference that *Hamlet* has acquired, either by a personal glimpse of his spies, or other incident of the scene, some idea of *Ophelia's* duplicity and unfair, not to say unfaithful or ungenerous, position with respect to him, when he commences to interrogate, and she to equivocate—he to animadvert and she at last to answer his direct question, "Where's your father?" with "At home!" which *Hamlet* may have known to be as *palpable*, as she did it was an absolute, *falsehood*. *Hamlet's* language, however, though earnest and pungent, was neither rude, nor wanton, nor cruel; nor were his sentiments, as it seems, in any way offensive. The effect was to impress her, by the sudden change, from his habitually mild and gentle language and manners to strong and ungallant invective, with a belief that he was hopelessly mad.

Kean (Edmund), as *Hamlet*, after concluding his words to *Ophelia*—"To a nunnery, go!" and departing abruptly out of sight of his audience, used to come on the stage again and approach slowly the amazed *Ophelia* still remaining in the centre; take her hand gently, and, after gazing steadily and earnestly in her face for a few seconds, and with a marked expression of tenderness in his own countenance, appeared to be choked in his efforts to say something, smothered her hand with passionate kisses, and rushed wildly and finally from her presence. The conception was clearly indicated and neatly executed in each point, whether justified by the circumstances of the interview or not. A more effective bit of serious pantomime by way of episode that master of his art never exhibited upon any stage. It was *a whole history in little!*

Reverting to the situation of *Hamlet* immediately preceding the soliloquy on suicide. He had no sooner put on the guise of insanity than he discovered that the king had sent for and made spies of his two friends, *Rosencrantz* and *Guildenstern*, whom he had found bent upon plucking out the very heart of his own mysterious behavior, and resolved to scrutinize his every movement. It is now that the consciousness of the wrongs he has suffered— the perplexity he finds in steering the course he has adopted—the delicacy of his situation with respect to his mother—the uncertainty of the stratagem for making his uncle's "occulted guilt" "*itself unkennel*" by the effect of the play—then the melancholy and bitter satisfaction its success at best must afford him, together with its reflections upon his own infirmity of purpose when compared with the ability of the player to assume upon an imaginary occasion—these all conspire to predispose his mind to philosophize concerning the value or worthlessness of human existence, and particularly under his own embarrassing circumstances. It is in such a frame of thought, that *Hamlet* enters just before the mock-play and commences the soliloquy—"To be, or not to be," etc.

The assertion that "*Hamlet* deviates, after the first line, from the proposition—to die by his own hand, or to live and suffer the miseries of life"—when he follows up with, "Whether 'tis nobler in the mind to suffer," etc.—is a different construction of the metaphor it contains from that which I understand the passage to convey. Instead of supposing him to be debating with himself, "whether he will stoop to misfortune, or exert his faculties in order to surmount it," thereby (as the critic observes) "giving over his reasoning on death, which, he alleges, is no longer the question," though he admits that "*Hamlet* instantly reverts to it," I will endeavor to show it to be thus far one unbroken continuation of the same chain of ideas. The fact is, *Hamlet* never alludes to the alternative of ending his difficulties by raising an army or claiming his rights by force of arms; the arm to which he contemplates the effect of a recourse is no other than the unsheathed *dagger*—(particularized afterward in the course of his reasoning as "*a bare bodkin*")—and *by opposing* (it to his *heart*—the fountain of existence, and comparing it, in its then *agitated* condition, to "*a sea of troubles*") *end them.* *That* is the kind of *arm*, and *such* the *sea*, the poet intended to prefigure in *Hamlet's* hypothesis. The analogy between the *sea*, with the ebbing and flowing of its tides, as they are propelled and returned back and forth through various branching rivers, channels, and tributary creeks, and other passages, and the *heart*, by whose impulses the *blood* is constantly forced and courses through the veins and arteries of the body until it returns to its source and is again emitted, must be obvious to every one upon reflection ; thus, instead of "a ridiculously absurd figure," is the idea beautifully poetic. Among Shakespeare's numerous figures in reference to the *heart*, he thus associates with the *sea*

——"a heart,

As full of troubles as a *sea*—of sands."

[*Two Gent. of Verona.*

Othello, too, in allusion to his *heart*, calls it—

"The fountain from the which my current runs
        Or else dries up."

Hamlet, in his self-debate on suicide, by "sea of troubles," *had only and* special *reference to his* heart *and its* physical functions—*namely*—

> *" The tide of* blood *in me*
> *Hath proudly* flowed *in vanity till now,*
> *Now doth it* turn and ebb back to the sea.*"
>
> *[Second Part of King Henry IV.*

That the word "sea," *in* this *context, is used as figurative or suggestive of the* heart, *is* undeniable; *because the* "blood" can "*turn and ebb back*" *to no* other "*sea.*"

DR. GOLDSMITH's classical taste discerns and complains that " Shakespeare himself is often guilty of an excess of figures and of running into mixed metaphors, which leave the sense disjointed and distract the imagination."   As " from the fulness of the heart the mouth speaketh," so it may be natural to a richly endowed poetical genius to be apt to indulge in a profusion even unto a redundancy, occasionally, and the breaking unavoidably, sometimes, or a mixing of metaphors.   It is an evidence of a meagre mind when its figures are too continuously pursued and attenuated.

As to there being " nothing analogous in nature to Fortune with her *slings* and *arrows*," I do not perceive any special " disjointure of the *sense*," if there be any particular transgression of *poetical license.*

Among " the thousand natural shocks that flesh is heir to," what is there so very absurd or poetically unnatural in representing " outrageous Fortune"— that blind, and fickle, and inexorable goddess—with a *sling*, hurling stones and stunning the sense of some unlucky victim? or in her shooting an *arrow*

and lacerating the kind heart of another undeservedly, and in her wantonness?   Have not *slings*
and *arrows* been primitive instruments of human
torture, and may they not be used with equal propriety as *symbols* of *suffering*, as the poisoned bowl
and the ruthless dagger are as *figurative* of *death?*

With respect to the flat contradiction charged in
making *Hamlet* speak of "'the undiscovered country from whose bourn no traveller returns,' when
the ghost of his father, piping hot from purgatory
(a place not within the bourn [or limit] of this
world), had just been conversing with him," it has
been freely and ingeniously canvassed by discerning
commentators, whom I have quoted copiously in a
former paper.   I may add, in the way of remark,
that *Hamlet* is constantly wavering in his mind, and
betwixt the supernatural revelation from the ghost,
and the irreconcilability of the *source* of the information with his philosophy, he seems at times to
doubt even the evidence of his senses, and to
imagine that his faculty of eyes and ears has been
fooled by his other senses, and to impute the deception to the effect of an overheated imagination :—

> "The spirit that I have *seen*
> May be a devil, and the devil hath power
> To assume a pleasing shape ; yea, and, perhaps,
> Out of my *weakness* and my *melancholy*,
> (As he is very potent with such spirits),
> Abuses me to damn me : I'll have grounds
> More *relative* than this : the play's the thing
> Wherein I'll catch the conscience of the king."

The confirmation his mind receives from the incident at the play, and the emotion that so conclusively, to him, betrayed his uncle's guilt, seems to be again superseded when the *Ghost* appears and talks to him, yet is invisible and inaudible to his mother at the same time. The *Ghost*, too, in the closet, thus seen only by himself, appears clad in his father's *habit as he lived*, whilst that which visited the glimpses of the moon upon the platform, in figure like his father, appeared in *armor*, was seen at the same time by *Hamlet's* three companions, and might have been heard, too, had the *Ghost* not beckoned him to a more removed ground; as though the apparition some impartment did desire to *Hamlet* alone.

Shakespeare may have, however, designed by this difference to indicate the turning-point of *Hamlet's* brain, where his madness is no longer assumed, but has become real and constitutional, and ready to burst into paroxysms upon any occasional excitement, and again to subside and leave to reason an interval of temporary sway. Such a self-conviction may, in some measure, account for his neglect thereafter to pursue actively his revenge, and for the fact of his seldom alluding to it in subsequent conversation. The shock inflicted upon his nervous system when mistaking and killing *Polonius*, seems to have produced a climax touching the subject whereon his melancholy had been sitting on brood, and absolutely deranged his intellect.

When Shakespeare needed a ghost to come from
the grave in order to tell *Hamlet* what his prophetic
soul had previously suggested to his imagination, he
was, I presume, not supposed to be restricted from
investing each, according to circumstances, with any
quality requisite for the occasion. Finally, when
poets have need of the influence of departed spirits
upon the affairs of this world, and find it expedient
to their purposes to recall their apparitions to
scenes familiar in their lives, what may be their
righteous limits, license, faculties of communicating
what they know or desire, of perceiving what occurs
upon this earth, or of rendering themselves only
visible to certain persons, and at particular hours of
the night most favorable to the imagination of such
as they would be noticed by, I have never studied;
but have ever yielded the utmost latitude to the
erratic fancy of an author—never attempting to
reconcile to my *natural philosophy* a consistency
with *preternatural* agencies and influences; because
such things have strong imagination, and a poet's
eye, in a fine phrensy rolling, requires space and
scope for any utility.

The mystery complained of, contained in the
lines—

> " But that the dread of something after death
> * * * * * * * *
> * * * * * * * *
> And makes us rather bear those ills we have,
> Than fly to others that we know not of.
> Thus conscience does make cowards of us all;"

may be removed at once by admitting *Hamlet's* creed to be, that " there *are* ' ills ' in the next world, and I would fly to them, *but* that I fear such as might be measured out to me as a *suicide*, and the severity of which ' I know not of,' may be greater than the miseries I bear here; and therefore I am deterred from rushing into those of the world to come, in order to escape these which I endure in *this* life."

" Thus conscience does make cowards of us all."

" The logician might be justified in saying of such a conclusion, *negatur consequens*," if the signification of the word " *conscience*," was confined to this critic's understanding of its sense, and had not a legitimate latitude of which he does not appear aware. The meaning of " conscience " in this context is, *an internal sense of right or wrong*, and which modern lexicographers distinguish by the word (not expressed in Shakespeare's vocabulary, though frequently implied) *consciousness*, (the *knowledge* of what passes in the mind) whilst they have defined *conscience* to signify—" The faculty within us which *decides* upon the lawfulness or unlawfulness of our actions."

In Shakespeare's comprehensive use of the word, a conscience may be good or bad, according to its owner's *knowledge* of what passes in his mind, and not necessarily implying that he is *conscientious* or *scrupulous in obeying its dictates*. Conscience, as a synonyme of *consciousness*, is also used by Bacon, Hooker, Pope and other writers. I take *Hamlet's* meaning to be, as we would with our modern distinction of terms express it, " It is the *consciousness* that we would merit the ills or condign punishment that may be reserved by the Everlasting for such as may commit forbidden acts, which " makes cowards of us all."

Then, after recapitulating the points of his previous objections, Goldsmith asserts that

"'Ay, there's the rub'

is a vulgarism beneath the dignity of *Hamlet's* character." If the vulgarism consists in the use of the word " rub," (a hindrance or obstacle,) it is put by Shakespeare repeatedly into the mouths of several of his kings and queens and other dignified personages; had its particular quantity for the metre of his versification been the cause of its use in this context, we should not find the word *rub* so often elsewhere; besides, from its frequent use by Dryden, Davenant, Swift and others, its conventional degradation in the vocabulary becomes very doubtful; but how " it leaves the sense imperfect," according to the critic's own showing, I am unable to comprehend.

The sense and propriety of " the oppressor's wrong, the proud man's contumely," as governed in the possessive case by the preceding verb " bear," to me are obvious. The objection to the use of the word "*spurn*" as a substantive is also hypercritical, if Milton be allowed as authority. "What defence can properly be used in so desperate an encounter as this, but either the slap or the *spurn*."—*Colasterion*.

Finally, it seems to me that "the strange rhapsody of broken images," of which the critic complains, is perfectly characteristic of *Hamlet's* idiosyncrasy in his peculiar predicament; indeed, such unprecedented and unrivalled individuality has Shakespeare shown in drawing and sustaining each of his characters throughout, and so peculiarly adapted to the respective situations is their language, that any attempt to transpose it, or to change the medium of its use, or to disconnect sentences and examine certain ideas separately or from an abstract point of consideration, must be foreign to the spirit and purpose of the bard of Avon.

Dr. Goldsmith's essay, at least so far as concerns the *sense* of the soliloquy on suicide, I consider weak and abortive. It is a proof that a critic may have a refined taste, be learned and classical, and yet not qualified to fathom the more profound meanings of such an author as Shakespeare.

It is a singular fact that, of all the critics I have read, *Schlegel* and *Goethe*, with whom Shakespeare's was not their vernacular, should seem, by their general remark, to have the more clearly penetrated his designs.

Goethe, particularly, has given a key to the character of *Hamlet*. He says :—

"It is clear to me that Shakespeare's intention was to exhibit the effects of a great action, imposed as a duty upon a mind too feeble for its accomplishment. In this sense I find the character consistent throughout. Here is an oak-tree planted in a china vase, proper only to receive the most delicate flowers. The roots strike out and the vessel flies to pieces. A pure, noble, highly moral disposition, but without that energy of soul which constitutes the hero, sinks under a load which it can neither bear, nor resolve to abandon altogether. *All* his obligations are sacred to him. Observe how he turns, shifts, hesitates, advances, and recedes! Now he is continually reminded and reminding himself of his great commission, which he, nevertheless, in the end, seems almost entirely to lose sight of, and this without even recovering his former tranquillity."— *Wilhelm Meister's Apprenticeship.*

PART II.

HAMLET.

FROM MY JOURNAL OF CORRESPONDENCE, RESPECTING

HAMLET.

In January, 1839, I spent a few weeks socially at *Washington*, D.C.—a city which I have very seldom visited professionally—and met the Hon. and Ex-President *John Quincy Adams* occasionally.

In a conversation with him respecting the drama in general, and Shakespeare's especially—of which he was notoriously a constant reader—I observed to him that from boyhood I had read *Hamlet* with great attention, and had interleaved my copy of the play, and interspersed copiously annexations, which had been regarded by several of our literary friends as involving some new and singular ideas of the character. I reminded Mr. Adams of the delight he had once afforded me as well as a number of his friends, by his *remarks* upon that same character, after dinner at the table of Mr. Hone (Ex-Mayor Philip), of New York, and I proposed to send him my MS. notes for *perusal*, which he politely intimated he would "gladly give them."

When Mr. Adams returned my *noted*-copy of *Hamlet*, it was accompanied by a very charming and instructive letter, dated, "Washington, 19 Feb., 1839," commencing:—"I return herewith your tragedy of *Hamlet*, with many thanks for the perusal of your manuscript notes, which indicate how thoroughly you have delved into the bottomless mine of Shakespeare's genius. I well remember the conversation, more than seven years by-gone, at Mr. Philip Hone's hospitable table, where at the casual introduction of *Hamlet* the Dane, my enthusiastic admiration of the inspired (Muse-inspired) Bard of Avon, commenced in childhood, before the down had darkened my lip, and continued through five of the seven ages of the drama of life, gaining upon the judgment as it loses to the imagination, seduced me to expatiate at a most intellectual and lovely convivial board, upon my views of the character of *Hamlet*, until I came away ashamed of having engrossed an undue proportion of the conversation to myself. I look upon the tragedy of *Hamlet* as the master-piece of Shakespeare—I had almost said the master-piece of the human mind. But I have never committed to writing the analysis of the considerations upon which this deliberate judgment has been formed. At the table of Mr. Hone I could give nothing but *outlines* and *etchings*. I can give no more now—snatching, as I do from the morning lamp to commune with a lover and worthy representative of Shakespeare upon the glories of the immortal bard."

In reference to Mr. Adams' "*morning lamp*" of *February*), it should be observed that, at his date, it was his custom to rise at four o'clock, in order to dispatch all his private affairs, that they might not interfere with his *duties* of the day in the House of Representatives, where he sat as a member from Massachusetts. As Mr. Adams complimentarily calls me "a lover and worthy representative of Shakespeare," I ought, in justice to his judgment, to observe also, that he had reference *particularly* to my *Falstaff* of *King Henry IV.* and in *The Merry Wives of Windsor;* because, before loaning him my notes upon *Hamlet* for his perusal, I had mentioned that, " I had never *acted*, nor had *thought* of acting that character; and for the reason that, I should probably, owing to the *comic* department of the Drama which I professed, be either neglected or laughed at by the *public*, for any attempt to *embody* my own conception in my own person; and had, therefore, not only *noted* my own peculiar understanding of various *texts*, but had elaborately *described how* I thought my particular views might be *illustrated* and made *perceptible upon the stage* by a *good* actor of *Hamlet*."

Mr. Adams' letter continues—"What is tragedy?" —of which he wrote a classical analysis as a preface, and then a concise one which he calls—" a hasty outline of his own view of the character of *Hamlet;*" and concludes his four autographic pages of letter-sheet, closely written, with—

" I regret that time will not allow me to fill the canvas with lights and shades borrowed from the incidents and dialogues of the play. But after bestowing so much of my own tediousness upon you, I can only repeat my thanks for the perusal of your own very ingenious comments upon this incomparable tragedy, and add the assurance of my best wishes for your health and happiness, and of my cordial sympathies with your devotion to the memory of the immortal bard."

(Signed) JOHN QUINCY ADAMS.

See this epistle in full, on a subsequent page.

Though I considered Mr. Adams' personal compliments to emanate more from his benevolence and acquaintanceship with me than from his unbiassed judgment of my pretensions, yet, if an earnest desire from my youth to become familiar with Shakespeare's dramas—beginning at twelve years of age with *Macbeth,* which inspired me to peruse the others, when I had yet never seen *one acted*—if to explore the vast intellectual magazine which the Bard of Avon has bequeathed to posterity—to try to penetrate his moral and dramatic designs—discover and elucidate even a few of the many poetic gems which he has set, and diffused amid his copious, and admirable, and unequalled diction—and to have become by such study enamored, and ambitious of performing some of his many matchless characters upon the stage (for which all were expressly designed), and overcoming my constitutional and habitual love of ease and my aversion to close study or any prolonged physical labor—to have attained to be or have been accounted by the *public generally* "a good actor" of at least *one* of his greatest characters—if, I repeat, this allowance to me of such particular *elements* may constitute and reflect any merit or *claim* in my favor for even a *passing notice* in this wonder-working age, I can't conscientiously deny that I am not insensible to, but *grateful* for its public acknowledgment, expressed or implied.

When the first letter from Mr. Adams (out of which I have quoted) reached my hand at New York, I was just embarking for England, whither I carried it before I had time to reply.   It was esteemed so very interesting by several literary friends of mine in London, and became so eagerly and frequently sought, for the purpose of being copied, that at last, to rescue it from further mutilation, I caused it to be *lithographed in fac-simile*, together with my *reply*, and a few hundred of such copies presented to certain friends and literary institutions there ; also, I sent some of the copies of that correspondence to several friends in New York, and prior to my return from England (March, 1840), it had been obtained by the *New York Mirror* (a weekly), and published, without regard to the *notice* thereupon—"*lithographed for private distribution only.*" The consequence was, Mr. Adams' letter and my reply were copied extensively by newspapers throughout the United States. After my return, and upon visiting Washington, when I met Mr. Adams, I mentioned that I had been very much vexed for his sake when I heard of the liberty which had been taken in publishing our letters in my absence, and without my knowledge or his consent, and that I had written Mr. Clay soliciting that gentleman's explanation of the facts in advance of my coming. Mr. Adams laughed, and observed—"I told Mr. Clay, when, at your instance, he referred to the circumstance and entered your disclaimer, that it not only did not offend—it did not surprise me—I *expected* it would be published one day or other. Indeed, I never *write* upon any subject, the *publication* of which at some time or other is unexpected or might prove disagreeable."

En passant, Mr. Adams writes—"I look upon the tragedy of *Hamlet* as the master-piece of the drama —the master-piece of Shakespeare—I had almost said the master-piece of the human mind." That distinguished litterateur, the present *Earl of Carlisle*, whom, as "*Lord Morpeth*," I was accustomed to meet occasionally when he visited the United States about 1842–43, and to whom in England, in 1844, I carried a special letter of introduction from our eminent statesman, the Hon. Henry Clay, and was there entertained by him, and subsequently have enjoyed his *correspondence*, in one of his letters, referring to that point, observes—"I see none of your criticisms are addressed to the play of *Macbeth*: in my mind the very highest, in order, of all the few which seem to me indisputably higher than all the rest—*Macbeth, Hamlet, Othello, Lear*. When I say this, however, I never could quarrel with a person who puts *Hamlet* even above *Macbeth*."—*See letter, on a subsequent page*.

Horatio Smith—the *brother* of my witty and familiar London acquaintance at the Garrick Club, James, and the *younger* of those two—(called "the handsomest men in England," and who became renowned for their surprising imitations of the different styles of their various contemporary poets, in the little volume entitled "*Rejected Addresses*," which required some *twenty* editions to satisfy the demand of the reading world), in a letter to me, dated at Brighton, where he resided, upon the subject of *Hamlet*, coincides with Mr. Adams in the rank he allowed *that* in the *order* of Shakespeare's plays; and, with characteristic discernment, refers to *Goethe's* practically-beautiful comparison of *Hamlet's* character. ("An oak tree planted in a china vase, proper only to receive the most delicate flowers. The roots strike out, and the vessel flies to pieces."—*See Wilhelm Meister's Apprenticeship, B. iv. Ch.* 13.)

By the way, I wonder if Mr. Adams ever heard

our gentle and amiable friend, and universally admired writer and revered countryman, Mr. *Washington Irving*, mention what in his latest letter to me, he remarked, referring to his many singular and particular reminiscences of the *stage*, within the current century—"I have seen the *Ballet* of *Hamlet* gravely *danced* at Vienna." Had *Mr. Adams* happened to see such a desecration, when "a looker on in Vienna," it would have recalled—if it did not *realize* to him—the reflections of *Hamlet* in the grave-yard. "To what base uses we may return, Horatio. Why may not imagination trace the noble dust of Alexander till he find it stopping a bung-hole?"—because then and there was one of the most exquisite poetic gems, ever germinated by dramatic genius in the brain of the Intellectual Minerva and devoted to the special service of Melpomene, debased, perverted, and sacrificed to *subserve* the mazy and meretricious "*poetry of motion;*" a province peculiar to the fantastic Terpsichore.

I should perhaps in this connexion note that the particular letter of Mr. Irving, from which the foregoing sentence is extracted, is dated "New York, April 17, 1848;"—for the reason that, this eminent author had done me the favor to open a correspondence with me, "Jan. 3, 1837," in special reference to his "*Knickerbocker's History of New York*," when I, in a private and friendly way, had sought his opinion of its susceptibility of *dramatic* effect. In 1847 I had mentioned to Mr. Irving socially and incidentally, that I had been in the practice of carefully noting and recording in a manuscript volume kept for that special purpose, the performance and apparent conception of every actor of distinction whom I had seen in the character of *Hamlet*, both in our country and in England, from 1816 to 1845; which our venerable friend Mr. Adams had borrowed for perusal, and, when returning it, had written me *another* and particularly interesting and instructive letter; first thanking me for what he had the indulgence to call "*the privilege* of perusing" such notes, and then, "asking my acceptance of a few scattered leaves, containing his own remarks upon *Othello*, *Romeo* and *Juliet*, and *Lear*, which had been originally written to a friend who thought them worthy of *publication* with his consent, &c.," and at same time communicating to me in that letter, his own first impressions of the *London*, and the effect of an incident he witnessed on the Paris stage, in the time of Louis XVIth.

Mr. Irving, too, complimented me by soliciting my "*Notes upon the Actors of Hamlet*" for perusal. I sent him the volume during the autumn of 1847, and he did not return it until the following spring, (April 17,) when he promised in his letter—

"I have detained your manuscript notes an unconscionable time, but I could not help it. I wished to read them attentively, for they are remarkably suggestive, and not to be read in a hurry," &c., &c.—*See letter, on a subsequent page.*

Upon examining thereafter my returned manuscript, I discovered that, as another eminent literary friend, Mr. James Fenimore Cooper, had done, Mr. Irving, when struck by my graphic record of the personal peculiarities of some well-remembered Actor, had stopped occasionally, and upon the margin, favored me, by adding his own autographic annotations, in "lead-pencillings by the way."

About the middle of October, 1841, the late Edmund Simpson, then Manager of the Park theatre, New York, referring to the prevailing interest taken by the play-going community in my novel conceits, as manifested respecting the character of *Hamlet* in my then recently transpired correspondence with the Hon. John Quincy Adams, and which being transcribed and published throughout the land, was attracting great attention from critical admirers of Shakespeare, suggested, urged, and finally persuaded me to *impersonate* my own conception and as soon as *six days thereafter*, when my benefit was appointed, assuring me that "my performance under the circumstances could not fail to attract greatly." The celebrated singer Mrs. Wood (ci-devant Miss Paton, the renowned prima donna of Covent Garden and Drury Lane, London) then an immense favorite at New York, as an inducement and encouragement to me, generously *volunteered* to act *Ophelia*, a part she had repeatedly played when Edmund Kean acted *Hamlet* at Drury Lane.

So far as Shakespeare's text went, I felt sure I

could become perfect in it; but, when I reflected that having never before thought of *acting Hamlet*, there was no time to acquire by practice, which alone makes perfect on the stage, the requisite ease of a gentleman, the dignity of a prince, appropriate action and flexibility of voice, in order to give proper variety to the vehement passions, weight to the declamatory and poignancy to the spirited and satirical portions; I became frightfully nervous at the responsibility I had undertaken, and was vexed with my own want of forethought and circumspection.

For

"Fools rush in where angels fear to tread."

It is true that I had within a month or two previously been performing *King Lear* (some dozen times in Philadelphia and New York) and had acquired a certain confidence in the power and compass of my *voice*, and in the accompaniment of natural and expressive action and attitude in the *passionate* scenes; but then the physical training for *Lear* included little or nothing towards the adaption of my person for representing *Hamlet:*—

"Our strange garments cleave not to their mould,
    But with the aid of *use*,"

Consequently I passed six days of continuous nervous excitement, which made my system restless at night and my faculties sleepless the greater portion of each, and until that of my performance, when in the presence of my audience, I endured *too* a constant and violent palpitation of the heart. Nevertheless I said I would go on for *Hamlet*—

"What! a soldier, and afeard?"

and I felt ashamed afterward to say, "I am afraid!" John Kemble, the greatest *Hamlet* of his day, is reported to have declared that he studied *Hamlet* seven years before he acted it; and, though he had then played it more than thirty years, *every time he repeated it, something new in it struck him.* I remembered that I felt alarmed for my own temerity, but was resolved to do my best at such short notice of requirement, and deprecate public *exactness.* I headed the play-bill of the day with a short *apology* for my attempt to impersonate *Hamlet*, because, though my sock was not, my buskin was *new*, and my habitual *study* of characters had been very systematic and conscientious. At that time, I was unsophisticated enough to presume that every one who might go to see me *act Hamlet* would be a competent *critic*, and, that such at least as had curiosity excited by reading my *letter* to Mr. Adams, would expect of me some good *acting*, as well as novelty, nicety, and undeniable correctness of perception of the poet, philosopher, and dramatist, to whose tragedies I generally had riveted my most serious attention, and whose *Hamlet* especially, though I had analysed it, I now approached a *representation* of with a profound awe and reverence, and particularly with apprehension before that many-headed monster, *the public*, whom I *then* dreaded. To do justice on the stage to my own conception in my closet, it was indispensably necessary that I should revise it minutely, dissect the component parts of the character, and where the text seemed unintelligible or ambiguous, and might have been corrupted by an editor or printer of the folio of 1623, to collate the various editions since, and, if a sentence *then* did not clearly indicate to me a *consistent* signification, to find a recourse in the poet Roscommon's suggestion—

> " When things appear unnatural and hard,
>   Consult your author with *himself* compar'd."

To avail myself of which, it was necessary to take each *important word* in the sentence, search every line in each of Shakespeare's plays where *such* word was incorporated, for the reason that the *same* author would seldom be found to use the same *word* in very *different* senses, and try to detect a concordance of sentiment in some one of that *word's* various connexions, settle fully with myself every verbal meaning and special point, as well as contexts having a general bearing upon the character; all which seemed to me necessary, prior to re-uniting the dissected articles or resolved particles into a compendious, and harmonious, and completely-compounded *conception*, for the *actor* to *begin* his own peculiar art with reference thereto :* *then*, in regular course of study, has arrived the time for an *artist* to apply his *rhetorical* powers to the elucidation of his conception, and ascertain, to his own satisfaction at least, by untiring practice in his *chamber*, how far *nature* has qualified him or denied him the requisites for a *perfect* personation of his own ideal, in order to make the most of any natural fitness, and by art to overcome any physical drawbacks. Such I considered for *Hamlet* requisite in *advance* of any stage-*rehearsal ;* and then, very essential to the effects before an *audience*, that such *rehearsals* should be carefully conducted, and frequent enough to assure the actor of his own ease, and that the others who should support him, might thoroughly understand his intentions or objects, and not, through ignorance, defeat them at night. It is a mistake to imagine that even a *soliloquy* can be perfectly studied and delivered without practice on the STAGE; *where only*, could *I* ever acquire the necessary abstraction and the faculty of identifying myself with my character assumed, as also the proper regulation of my voice, and of the action suitable to a passion according to situation. These reflections, after my hasty consent to undertake a performance of *Hamlet* with only six days of preparation, a *novice* too in the tragic department of the

* Refer here to my noted opinion of the habitual *difference* in this respect (study) between *Kean* and *Macready*, 1844.

art, and the responsibility, I began to realize were the *cause* of that *apology* upon the play-bill, of which the following is an extract:—

PARK THEATRE.

Mr. Hackett's Benefit,

on which occasion the Distinguished Favorite

Mrs. Wood

has, in the kindest manner, tendered her aid, as

OPHELIA.

With the Original Music.

Mr. Barry

has kindly volunteered his services, and will also

appear.

———

Mr. Hackett respectfully informs his friends and the public that, encouraged by the gratifying approbation bestowed upon each of his personations of *King Lear*, he will attempt, for the first time, to embody his own conception of Shakespeare's *Hamlet, Prince of Denmark*, well assured that in his native city he can depend upon every reasonable allowance for such deficiency of mechanical manner as can be supplied only by longer and more frequent practice in the loftier departments of the Drama, than he has yet had opportunity to acquire.

Wednesday Evening, *Oct.* 21, 1840.
HAMLET.

HAMLET (for the first time on any stage), ...	*Mr. Hackett.*
GHOST OF HAMLET'S FATHER, .	*Mr. Barry.*
OPHELIA (for the first time in this country), ...	*Mrs. Wood.*
CLAUDIUS, King of Denmark, .	*Mr. Gann.*
HORATIO, ...	*Mr. Field.*
LAERTES, ...	*Mr. Wheatly.*
POLONIUS, ...	*Mr. Chippendale.*
OSRICK, ...	*Mr. Fisher.*
GERTRUDE, Queen of Denmark, .	*Mrs. Barry.*

To which will be added the Ludicrous Scene of
A MILITIA TRAINING.

HATEFUL W. PARKINS (an Independent Disorderly), ...	*Mr. Nickinson.*
THE YANKEE MAJOR, ...	*Mr. Hackett.*

The Militia, by an *awkward squad.*

The Entertainment to Conclude with the First Act of
THE KENTUCKIAN.

COL. NIMROD WILDFIRE, ...	*Mr. Hackett.*

The theatre was full, and I was warmly greeted
on appearance—all my soliloquies were surprisingly

well received, and more or less interrupted by applause in their course of delivery—my scenes generally were marked either by mute applause or eloquent approbation, whilst my impassioned utterance of Hamlet's *self*-condemnation after witnessing what the *player* could do " in a dream of passion," was applauded to the echo, which, after I had left the stage, called me back to acknowledge the compliment of my audience; also, the earnestness which I manifested in the course of Hamlet's contrivance to detect the " occulted guilt," and the happy attitude which I happened to strike, as the usurper, at its climax, rushed away conscience-stricken, were honored by such loud vociferation and thunders of applause as required a long suspension of the progressive scene. Such portions of the play and certain points in the closet-scene (after which I was *again* called before the curtain), proved the most effective of any which I attempted to mark.

In my youth I had read the work called *Wilhelmeister's Apprenticeship*, and been struck with and remembered *Goethe's* idea of causing, in representation, Hamlet's description and comparison of his father's and his uncle's respective persons to be painted as full length portraits, and suspended in the Queen's closet, and, with the aid of Mr. Thomas Barry (a most capital stage-director as well as good and sound actor), I determined to *try* such an effect on the occasion. Mr. Barry, who acted the *Ghost,* consented to change the costume (*armour*) worn when it was seen upon the *platform*, and which, as it would seem, was designed to suggest surprise and increase Hamlet's wonder—(" My father's spirit— *in arms!* all is not well!")—and to adopt one similar to *that* worn by "My father in his *habit as he lived*," and *painted* for the portrait. The canvas was so constructed—by Mr. Barry's direction—and split, but backed with a spring made from whale-bone, which rendered its practicability unperceived by the audience, that it enabled him at the proper juncture, as the *ghost* behind, to step apparently *out* of it upon the stage; the rent through which the figure had passed was closed up again, and the canvas, with a light behind it, then looked *blank* and illuminated; but, the instant after the departure of the spirit from sight of the audience, the light was removed, and the *painting* appeared as before. The whole effect proved wonderful and surprising, and was vehemently applauded. The audience, at the close of the tragedy, as a matter of course, called me once more before the curtain, and I thanked them cordially for their manifestations of satisfaction; though, in my heart, I attributed their apparent enthusiasm more to their own perception of what I was earnestly *trying* to do than to my own accomplishments upon the stage; for I was anything but *self*-satisfied with my performance. I knew—what they did not, or were too kind to *seem* to perceive—my *deficiency* in that case and smooth-

ness which is only acquirable by much practice.
Next day, however, I was warmly congratulated by
numerous personal friends, and received, through
the Box-office of the Park Theatre, some verses in
a female hand, signed " *Minerva*," so complimentary that I suspected them as designed for a practical *quiz*. Such causes might, and perhaps *ought*,
to have stimulated me to exert myself and make a
complete study of the art necessary to act, to my
own satisfaction, my *conception* of *Hamlet*, as I *had*
been, eight years previous, to undertake that of the
Falstaff of *King Henry IV.*, after I had so far succeeded as to be tolerated by an audience in my first
and very crude attempt to personate that character;
but I lacked an equally strong motive for *Hamlet*
that I had had to elaborate my performance of
Falstaff. My first representation of the *Falstaff* of
Henry IV. attracted only a moderate audience—not
equal to the Manager's expenses—whilst my local
characters, for which I was then and *only* famed,
produced more than double to the theatre's treasury.
The Press—such as noticed my *debût* at all—con-
demned not only my acting, but my *conception*
and even my *readings* of the text, and denied me
both the mind to grasp, and the physical elements
(for training) to represent the character of *Falstaff*
respectably. Of my natural qualifications or impediments for a " respectable" *performance* I could
not judge, but, considering that I had on my first
night succeeded in keeping my audience in good

humor throughout, I was determined to persevere, and endeavor to make my toleration a sort of entering-wedge with public opinion, for riving and prostrating what I looked upon as a traditionary and time-honored but *erroneous conventionalism*, and for introducing and establishing instead, if not a better, at least an *original* conception of that masterly compound of wit and philosophy with vice and sensuality. Therefore, when the Manager inquired of me (his Star) what I would "act the next night" (I was playing alternately with another Star), I replied—"I'll *repeat Falstaff !*" "Any of your *other* characters would *draw better !*" observed he, and left me evidently vexed. The second night the *receipts* improved upon the first a little, but still were under the *expenses*, though the audience seemed more attentive and liberal of applause at certain points. The next day, however, when the Manager feared I might persist in again repeating *Falstaff*, he prevailed upon a certain newspaper editor with whom he was intimate and I esteemed "a friend" of mine, to be at the Box Office when I should come there (as usual about 10 o'clock A.M.), and to suggest the *inexpediency* of my persistence in any further repetition at present of *Falstaff*. The gentleman (and he was a benevolent one, and often good-humoredly afterwards alluded to the conversation) intimated that "though the public acknowledged me to possess wonderful powers of *imitation*, precedent had proved that no great imitator had

ever become even a *good original* actor." I asked
him if he was familiar with David Garrick's *beginning*, as well as his establishment of himself as a
great actor? and if he was aware that he started by
playing characters "*after the manner of a Mr.
Smith*"—then a great favorite in London—and that
he did not discontinue his *imitation* until he had
secured the notice of the town, and extracted their
acknowledgment of his (Garrick's) *original* abilities.
"Well!" added my expostulator, "*our* public have
been accustomed, since you adopted the stage a few
years ago, to see you only in *imitations* of Kean,*
and Macready, and Barnes, and Hilson, and perform a Yankee (*Solomon Swop*), and a Dutchman
(*Rip Van Winkle*), or a Kentuckian (*Nimrod
Wildfire*), and a Frenchman (*Monsieur Morbleu*),
which are (what are technically called) '*character-
parts*;' but you cannot persuade them *now*—if ever
—that you are able to play FALSTAFF." Such dis-
paragement of my ability aroused my indignation,
and I observed with some warmth—"Look you!
Mr. ——, the Manager has *instigated* you to put me
out of conceit of myself in this part, in order that I
may fall back—as he prefers—upon my local and
hackneyed characters to-morrow night, and which
he thinks would be more *attractive*. *I will play
nothing but Falstaff* again *to-morrow* night! With
reference to your prediction, that I may '*never* be

* In 1826, in my novitiate, I acted *Richard III. in imitation of
Kean* repeatedly at New York, and in London in 1827, with applause.

able,' I say, and mark you my words, *when* I have had a reasonable time by stage-practice—say three years—to ripen my acting and become mellowed in the part like a second-nature, if *then* I can't convince the public *generally* that I *can* act it—not only to their *satisfaction* but *more so* than will any rival—I'll forswear my adopted profession, and never appear again upon the stage." The third performance, however, proved an agreeable surprise to the Manager, Mr. Simpson, who played the *Prince of Wales.* When he and myself in our respective characters met at "Gadshill," and unavoidably noticed the *crowd* in the pit and boxes, I muttered to him in an undertone, "Which of us was right about to-night's bill?" He very pleasantly whispered back—"You! you understand the monster better than I *this* time!" Often as I repeated the part after that, during a series of years, I seldom if ever acted it to less than expenses *anywhere.*

But times and circumstances (which alter cases) were different when I first appeared as *Hamlet.* In 1832 I was comparatively young as an actor, and *ambitious,* and my energies were aroused to combat prejudice and opposition, and to acquire fame and a moderate independence ; besides supporting my family and educating three sons, who, after my bankruptcy as a merchant of New York, had no resources or expectations other than what might be obtained through my own exertions. In 1840, I had acquired an extensive credit for *Protean* ability and a surfeit of theatric *honors*, which no longer fired my ambition. The country had not yet recovered from the effects of the monetary revulsion of 1837, and theatricals generally were at a very low ebb, and *tragedy especially neglected.* I had begun to consider the expediency of then *withdrawing* myself from—as I had in 1826 of adopting—the stage, and of returning and resuming some branch of *mercantile* business after that season ; and also, only how to make the acting of my most popular of established parts most available to my purse. I reflected upon the years of practice I had devoted to *Falstaff*, before I could make it tolerable in my own or quite acceptable in *general* opinion, and I apprehended a greater and a longer task to obtain the like for *Hamlet*, together with a difficulty of inspiring in advance various and unfamiliar audiences (throughout the lands where I might wander as a star) with confidence in a candidate for their *tragic* instruction and delight, who had never before been heard of by them but as an " irregular comedian," and in order to command an attendance of numbers equal to those attracted by my *local* parts. The occasion of my *debût* in *Hamlet* being for my " benefit and last night of engagement" for some time in New York (owing to an interval of some months to be occupied with *other* stars engaged at the Park), precluded me from *immediately* following up my comparative success, by frequent repetitions of *Hamlet* upon the stage where I had obtained it,

and of striking the public-iron whilst hot, and clench-
ing as well as diffusing and circulating throughout
the community any strong impression I had made
in that part.

Not many weeks prior to my first appearance in
Hamlet at New York, I had been persuaded to perform *King Lear* at Philadelphia, by Mr. Manager
Burton (1840), with new scenic appointments which
he got up with care and liberality. It *filled* his
theatre for a *week*, and gave me a strong foothold
for *tragic* promise in *that* city; whereupon the New
York Park theatre had imitated Burton's example,
and incurred considerable expense forthwith to *get
up Lear* for me. I played it three nights with great
applause from the audience and unprecedented
commendation from the press; but it *did not attract
expenses either night*, and I then refused *ever to play
it at the Park again*, and have *kept my word;* but
the town did *not* go into mourning. That was one
reason I had urged against the policy of trying to
act Hamlet, but which Manager Simpson overcame,
by his assurance of a peculiar prestige, viz. : " the
popularity of my *conception* as evolved in my
widely-circulated correspondence with Mr. Adams,
and also by reason of the play's more general
favoritism, and consequently *greater attraction* of
the masses towards the character of *Hamlet* than
that of *Lear*," a fact which he intimated could be
proved by reference to the latter's smaller treasury-
receipts of the theatre, and the comparatively few

repetitions *King Lear* would bear, even when represented by such famous actors as George Frederick Cooke and Edmund Kean.

Nevertheless, I allowed my own first and favorable impression and upon a single audience as *Hamlet*, to fade out of its memory by neglect and delay; whereas, by immediate and frequent repetition I should have endeavored to "bite it in," as engravers do *their* work, with *aquafortis*, and have tried to thoroughly establish it: hence, my glory in it was transient, and with the occasion the achievement soon passed away from my own mind. My habitual love of ease, aversion to extraordinary physical or mental exertion, together with a consciousness and dread of painful effects upon my sensitive nervous system, and, from its ready excitability, how much and how often it would surely be wrought upon by my efforts to push on to fame as an *actor* of *Hamlet*,

> "Some craven scruple
> Of thinking too precisely on the event,
> A thought, which, quartered hath but one part wisdom,
> And ever three parts *coward*,"

combined to discourage my ambition in such pursuit. I resolved rather to continue to act easily and quietly and with moderate profit, my former though limited number of *popular* parts, than to embark in a struggle at that time against popular prejudice or stage-precedent of an acknowledged comedian trying to make his *Hamlet* attractive and add that to his repertoire.

Not long after I had thus neglected to take at "young flood" the indicated tide of extended popular favor, for,—

> "There is a tide in the affairs of men,
>   Which, taken at the flood, leads on to fortune;
>   Omitted, all the voyage of their life
>   Is bound in shallows and in miseries,"

my old friend William E. Burton, the manager at Philadelphia, sought and chid me for "keeping the noiseless tenor of my way," and especially for my impolitic and censurable inertness in my profession when Fortune had opened to me an opportunity. Mr. Burton proposed, and I accepted an engagement to act at his *New National Theatre, Philadelphia*, in the March following, assuring me that he could do with *that* public what was necessary to draw its attention to my pretensions which he pronounced "extraordinary and constituted unmistakably good material." When I visited Philadelphia, accordingly, I found indeed that Mr. Burton had not forgotten his managerial designs thus intimated, and that Philadelphia was pretty generally placarded, and all his playbills headed with a puff-announcement as follows :—

New National Theatre.

W. E. BURTON, ... *Sole Proprietor.*
P. RICHINGS, ... *Stage Manager.*

☞THE MANAGER takes pride in respectfully soliciting the attention of the American Public generally, to the following rare impersonations of a variety of Shakespeare's heroes, and of dissimilar American Originals (all of which are to be performed at this theatre *This Week*) by one of their own distinguished Native actors, viz.:

MR. HACKETT

who has always been a particular favorite in Philadelphia, and is now UNIVERSALLY acknowledged to combine a higher degree of EXCELLENCE with VERSATILITY than has been recorded in the annals of the Stage of any individual since the days of Garrick.

Mr. Hackett will appear

Tuesday—as *Falstaff*, in the *Merry Wives of Windsor*.

Monday—as *King Lear*, and also in *The Kentuckian*.

Thursday—as *Falstaff*, in *King Henry IV. Part 1st*.

Friday—as *Hamlet*, and also as the Yankee, *Solomon Swop*.

Saturday—as *Rip Van Winkle*, and *Horse Shoe Robinson*.

Monday—as *Falstaff*, in *The Second Part of King Henry IV*.

Though I was well received in each of these characters by the notoriously cold and reserved audiences of Philadelphia, Mr. Burton did not succeed in making my performance of *Hamlet* and of *King Lear* nearly as attractive as most of my *comic* characters proved, and without vexation or regret I struck them both from my repertoire, and soon thereafter studied and produced *Sir Pertinax Mac-Sycophant* in Macklin's Man of the World, and also *O'Callaghan*, in Bernard's farce of *His Last Legs;* in both which parts I have been a favorite with every public in either hemisphere.

PART III

NOTES UPON KING LEAR.

GENIUS AND TASTE.

" *Genius* all sunbeams where he throws a smile,
Imprégnates Nature faster than the Nile;
Wild and impetuous, high as Heaven aspires,
All science animates, all virtue fires,
Creates ideal worlds and there convenes
Aërial forms and visionary scenes.
But *Taste*, corrects by one therial touch,
What seems too little and what seems too much;
Marks the fine point, where each consenting part
Slides into beauty with the ease of art;
This bids to rise, and *That* with grace to fall,
And rounds, unites, refines, and heightens all."

CAWTHORN.

NOTES UPON KING LEAR.

"Take pains the genuine meaning to explore;
  There sweat, there strain; tug the laborious oar;
  Search every comment that your care can find;
  Some here, some there, may hit the poet's mind:
  When things appear unnatural and hard,
  Consult your author with himself compar'd."

Roscommon.

KING LEAR is not a popular play with the million; because the *young*, who constitute the great majority of play-goers, are too inexperienced to comprehend the dotage of the aged and tender father, and to sympathize with his consequent afflictions;—regarding *Lear*, as they generally do, merely as an old despot, and his sorrows and sufferings as measurably deserved by his own folly and tyranny; nor can youth have acquired knowledge enough of mankind to detect and appreciate Shakespeare's exquisite art and profound philosophy in the drawing of *Lear's* madness, its origin, progress, and climax; nor his frightfully faithful portraiture towards the fatal denouement of nature's last and abortive struggle

with extreme old age and bodily infirmity to restore
Lear's mental balance, and to re-establish his *reason :*
therefore, this play is better adapted to the understanding of the sage and philosopher, and the mad
scenes, especially, to the appreciation of experienced
and scientific physicians, who have been accustomed
professionally to witness and contemplate the subtle
workings of the maniac's mind.

"The proper study of mankind is man."—*Pope.*

Coleridge, in his *Table Talk*, says :—"*Lear* is the
most tremendous effort of Shakespeare as a poet,
Hamlet as a philosopher and meditator, and *Othello*
is the union of the two. There is something gigan-
tic and unformed in the former two; but in the
latter (*Othello*), everything assumes its due place
and proportion, and the whole mature powers of his
mind are displayed in admirable equilibrium."

My opinion is, that the difference noticed does
not arise so much from an inequality in Shakespeare's genius for drawing perfectly these three
distinctive characters, but in the critic's taste for the
different *subjects* they respectively comprehend, and
their several moral *spheres* of action.

A critic, in the *Edinburgh Review* for July,
1840, (Article, "*Recent Shakesperian Literature*,")
asserts :—

"The whole circle of Literature, ancient and
modern, possesses nothing comparable to that world

of thoughts, feelings, and images which is displayed in the five great tragedies of Shakespeare." * * * * *

Comparing them with each other the same writer remarks :—

" *Lear* is at once more original in invention, more active in imagination, more softly pathetic in feeling; *Romeo and Juliet* has more pure feeling; *Macbeth* a closer amalgamation of tragic action with thoughts purely ethical ; and *Hamlet* traverses a world of thought in which all other existing dramas linger at the frontier: but *Othello*, above every other drama, unites vehemence and nature in tragic emotion, with truth and vigor in the delineation of character. This play, above all others, harmonizes those two elements, and makes each the counterpart, the supplement, the condition of the existence of the other."

The poet, Percy Bysshe Shelley, regarded *Lear* as a drama " universal, ideal, sublime; and the most perfect specimen of dramatic art in existence."

Philadelphia, December 1, 1840.   I saw Mr. Forrest as *Lear* last night, at the Chestnut Street Theatre.   He and myself often and materially differ in our conceptions as well as in our tastes in personifying them upon the stage.   He exhibits too much nerve and too little flexibility of voice and countenance generally ; his physical impetuosity in the curse, beginning " Hear, Nature ! Hear ! " and in *Lear's* rage, wheresoever it occurs, seems to me overstrained and unnatural, whilst his pathos is whining and wants intensity, and seems to spring more from a cool head than a warm heart. He evidently aims to make sternness and the mortified pride of the pagan despot *Lear's* strongest characteristics; whilst I think they should show only as sudden and transient flashes of a consuming heart, but most clearly alternate and *secondary* to the philanthropy which pervades the nature of the sensitive old father. *Lear's* occasional bursts of anger certainly require of an actor earnest and forcible expression, in order to realize fully to an audience *Lear's* outraged sensibility; but anger which can find words should, at the same time, acquire a comparative temperance, to give it smoothness; and though a passion torn to tatters may obtain more noisy applause from the barren spectators, it is the innate benevolence of the man, as is seen in his calm and reasoning intervals, which affords opportunity in acting for those tender strokes of art which wake the souls of the reflecting and judicious, and stamp the deepest and most enduring impression upon their hearts.

Mr. Forrest seems to "come tardy off" in all Lear's gushes of tenderness, as though his own nature was too rough or unrefined to receive the impress, and too sterile to cherish such delicate impulses; the apostrophes, too, he uttered in the speculative tone of a stoic and without a touch of that plaintiveness which should characterize the sententiousness of a soul overcharged with its own accumulated wrongs. The gentler emotions of an afflicted bosom beget deeper sympathy in the beholder than the most startling paroxysms of rage; for, *anger*, duly considered, is one of the lowest order of the passions, and just in proportion that any man allows it to rise and obtain the mastery does it dispel his reason and reduce his nature to that mere instinct which is common to the fiercest of the *brute* creation; it is a relic of barbarism which social refinement has abolished by crowning mildness and equanimity with its good graces, and by stigmatizing a loss of temper as rudeness and ill-breeding.

Mr. Forrest recites the text as though it were all prose, and not occasionally written in poetic measure; whereas, blank verse can, and always should be distinguishable from prose by proper modulations of the voice which a listener with a nice ear and a cultivated taste could not mistake, nor if confounded detect in their respective recitals: else Milton, as well as Shakespeare, has toiled to little purpose in the best proportioned numbers.

Mr. Forrest's countenance, as made up for *Lear*, is inflexible, stern, and forbidding: he has, too, a favorite grim scowl: his eyebrows are made so shaggy and willowy, they hide the eyes too much: and his beard, though long and picturesque, covers some useful and important muscles of the face, making it rigid and incapable of depicting effectively the alternate lights and shades of benevolence and irascibility

as they fluctuate in *Lear's* agitated mind; nor, do
I fancy Mr. Forrest's *tread* of the stage with his toes
inclined somewhat inward like that of an Indian;
for the reason that it renders *Lear's* personal carriage undignified: there is a want of keeping too in
the paralytic action of his head and limbs, which at
times exhibit too firm a repose for a man "fourscore
and upwards," and then at others a shaking so violent and overdone as to verge closely upon carica-
ture.

At the close of the following dialogue, namely—

" *Lear*. Dost thou know me, fellow ?
Kent. No, Sir! but you have that in your countenance
which I would fain call *master*.
Lear. What's that ?
Kent. Authority !"

Mr. Forrest paused here some seconds, wagged
his head about and smiled very significantly as
though *Lear's* vanity was particularly pleased that
his features had indicated to a poor-service-beggar,
an *autocratic rule*—one to which *Lear* (be it remembered!) had been born, ever been used, and then
had never yet had disputed.

In the last scene of the first act Mr. Forrest
adhered to Nahum Tate's injudicious omission of the
bit of pathos with which Shakespeare has interposed
before the curse-direct.

" *Lear*. What, fifty of my followers at a clap!—within a
fortnight ?

Albany. What's the matter, sir?

Lear. I'll tell thee! (*Then, with falling tears and choking utterance, turned to Goneril.*) Life and death! I am asham'd
That thou hast power to shake my manhood thus;
That these hot tears which break from me perforce,
Should make thee worth them.—Blasts and fogs upon thee!
The untented woundings of a father's curse
Pierce every sense about thee! &c."

Though it may be judicious to transpose some of this matter, as Tate has done—making it antecedent instead of subsequent to that terrific invocation which begins "Hear, Nature, hear!" and at the end whereof, according to Shakespeare, *Lear* "rushes out" for a few moments and "returns" exclaiming as above (quoted in parenthesis), I decidedly disapprove of Tate's rejection of the pathetic portion, and have restored it; because, first, it bespeaks the sympathy of the audience, breaks the continuity of cursing, mitigates the shock and averts its abhorrent quality when *Lear* vents the bitterness of his bursting heart; and secondly, because it discovers that malevolence, though provokable, is neither uppermost, nor wanton, nor gratuitous, nor unremitted in *Lear's* nature.

In the curse, after falling upon his knees, Mr. Forrest exhibited *Lear's* nervous system so relaxed, that from the commencement to the climax he shook constantly and from head to toe; not unlike some poor fitful victim of what is called St. Vitus's Dance— whereas, according to my observation of Nature, old and ordinarily nervous men, during a fit of excessive anger, become comparatively firm and strong in their bodily faculties, which sink again as the temporary excitement subsides into a proportionately lower state of debility; that Shakespeare himself thus regarded man's physique in old age, be it remembered that he has made *Lear*, just before breathing his last, recover strength enough to "kill the slave that was hanging Cordelia;"—having "seen the time he could have make them skip;"—a circumstance not impossible for such an old man, but which however Shakespeare's good taste preferred *Lear's description*, but which Tate has undertaken to bring into *effective* action upon the stage, where I have always seen it fail: indeed, it seemed so ludicrous to the spectators that many have laughed outright whenever a *representation* of that *conceivable* feat was attempted.

> "*Kent.* (*In the stocks.*)   Hail, noble master!
> *Lear.* How!   Mak'st thou this shame thy pastime?"

It struck me here that Mr. Forrest descried *Kent's* condition from his own distance too readily for the "dull sight" of which *Lear* complains afterwards; nor did Mr. Forrest attempt, when *Lear* discovered *Kent's* disgraceful pastime, to make manifest through his features and manner the surprise and indignation occasioned by such a palpable insult as he esteems it according to his expressions of resentment.

Mr. Forrest made no point, nor seemed to attach any characteristic value to the line,

——"The KING would speak with Cornwall!"

of which it is susceptible. It can be made to tell with an audience, particularly by *Lear's* making a short *pause* before uttering the sentence, gradually straighten himself up to his full height, and, with majestic pride and bearing, dwell, with deep intonation and powerful emphasis, upon the word "KING."

In the menace which *Lear* orders *Gloster* to convey—

> ——"bid them come forth and hear me,
> Or, at their chamber door I'll beat the drum,
> 'Till it cry sleep, to death!——"

The actor of *Lear* should remain prominently forward, near the footlights, as *Gloster* brings the excuses of the Duke and his wife for not deigning to *speak with* him, and, at the climax of *Lear's* threat, let *Cornwall* and *Regan* come hastily forward, and appear suddenly at *Lear's right* hand (*Gloster* being on his left side), when, with mingled surprise and mock courtesy, and in a loud ironical tone, his gibe can be made most effectively:—

> "Oh! Are you come!"

but Mr. Forrest, having finished the threat which he had commanded *Gloster* to convey to his reluctant son-in-law and delinquent daughter, instead of awaiting the effect of his message, walked *up* the stage and *met* them in their gateway; a situation which precluded *Lear* the opportunity for a strong point—afforded by Tate's arrangement of the break and exclamation.

Mr. Forrest, in articulating the letter "O" in "*bones,*" allowed so little quantity that it sounded like "*buns;*" also, the double "O" in "*food*" was given short, as in "*foot.*"

There was no pungency in Mr. Forrest's tone or manner when he taunted *Goneril,*—

> "I will not trouble *thee,* my child; farewell!"

nor in the rebuke,—

> "But, I'll not *chide* thee;
> * * * * * I can stay with *Regan,*
> I and my hundred knights."

Now, be it observed, that the more boastfully *Lear* is made to utter this last line of his invective, the greater must be his confusion, the deeper his mortification, and the more intolerable his sense of disappointment and degradation, when *Regan* abruptly checks his confident expectations, with—

> "Not *altogether* so, sir;
> I looked not for you yet, nor am provided
> For your fit welcome: Give ear to my sister," etc.

Lear, then, with a spirit quite subdued, inter-jects—

"Is this well spoken, *now?*"

also, when *Regan* concludes,

"If you *will* come to *me*,
(For now I spy a danger) I entreat you
To bring but five-and-twenty · to no more
Will I give place or notice,"

it makes *Lear's* distress and utter helplessness the more apparent, and his heart-breaking recollection and expression—

"*I* gave *you* ALL ! "—

the more natural and sympathy-winning to an audience. *Lear*, now humbled and embarrassed by his reduced condition and forlorn situation, implores *Regan* to reconsider her edict, and, at the same time, deprecates a confirmation of her degrading decree—thus—

"What, must I come to you
With five-and-twenty, Regan?   *Said* you *so?* "

Regan answers :—

"And speak it again, my lord; no more with *me !*
Lear. Those wicked creatures yet do look well-favor'd,
When others are more wicked; not being the worst,
Stands in some rank of praise: I'll go with *thee*.
[*Turning to Goneril."*

Mr. Forrest here went *unhesitatingly* and put his hand upon *Goneril* rather *affectionately*, which I think morally impossible with such a nature and under the circumstances, for *Lear* to persuade himself to do; because, though he says to *Goneril*—

> " Thy fifty yet doth double five and twenty,
>   And *thou* art *twice* her love—"

his is only a choice of two evils, and an alternative forced by his necessity ; in fact, so poor is the quality of *Goneril's* love, though " twice " that of *Regan*, it could not renew his affection, nor even paternal regard for *Goneril* most particularly, having *cursed* her most bitterly, and so recently, and on *three several* occasions; for this reason, instead of saying readily or cordially—

> " I'll go with *thee!* "

as Mr. Forrest does to *Goneril*, I prefer that *Lear* should hesitate a little—as if self-debating his own extremity—and then, only half-turning his person towards *Goneril*, utter the line (" I'll go with *thee!* "), *constrainedly* and in a tone of painful repugnance ; because, after all, *Lear*, though shorn of his autocratic sway and pride of power, in his heart cared less about the number of his retinue than these insulting proofs of his two daughters' grudging and ungrateful spirit, in thus reducing his individual consequence, and an appearance becoming—

which only remained to him after partitioning his
kingdom.

" *Goneril.*   Hear me, my lord!
     What need you five and twenty, ten or five,
     To follow in a house where twice so many
     Have a command to tend you?
 Regan.   What need one?
 Lear. [O, reason not the need: our basest beggars
     Are, in the poorest thing, superfluous:
     Allow not *Nature* more than Nature *needs.*
     Man's life is cheap as beast's: thou art a lady:
     If only to go warm were gorgeous,
     Why Nature needs not what thou gorgeous wear'st
     Which scarcely keeps thee warm.   But for true need,
     You Heavens! give me *patience! that, I need ;*]
     You see me here, you gods, a poor old man,
     As full of grief as age; wretched in both,
        &c., &c., &c.   Oh, fool, I shall go mad!"

The portion of *Lear's* words, quoted above and
written within my brackets, contains so much of
poetry, philosophy, and character, that in studying
the part of *Lear*, I determined to restore what Tate
had omitted, and render it on the stage in the hope
that it might please some lover of Shakespeare in
his integrity.   Apropos, what can be more graphic,
and at the same time more beautifully poetic, than
the following description given by the " Gentleman," met by *Kent* upon the heath and inquired of
by him when searching for *Lear* amid the storm.
I esteem it an exquisite morceau—

" *Kent.*   Where's the king?
  Gentleman. Contending with the fretful elements.
     Bids the wind blow the earth into the sea,
     Or swell the curled waters 'bove the main,
     That things might change or cease : tears his white hair :
     Which the impetuous blasts with eyeless rage,
     Catch in their fury, and make nothing of :
     Strives in his little world of man to outscorn
     The to-and-fro conflicting wind and rain.
     This night, wherein the cub-drawn bear would couch,
     The lion and the belly-pinched wolf
     Keep their fur dry, unbonneted *he* runs,
     And bids what *will* take *all.*"

According to my idea, in the defiance of the
storm,

      ——" Blow, winds, and crack your cheeks !"

Mr. Forrest seemed deficient in that wild energy
implied by the text and demanded by the circumstances ; also, Mr. Forrest addressed to *Kent* the
passage—

  " What, so kind a father—ay, there's the point," &c.,

which, I think, should be uttered *abstractedly.* Instead of the original text—

      " The tempest in my mind
       Doth from my senses take all feeling else
       Save what beats *there,*"

Mr. Forrest substituted the word *here* (for Shakespeare's " *there*") and pointed to his *heart,* whereas,

I take it, *Lear* refers to his *brain*, an organ which beats as sensibly as the heart under violent mental excitement, and mentions elsewhere—"lest my *brain* turn"—"I am cut to the *brain*." Characters in other plays of Shakespeare speak of a "troubled brain," and "perturbation of the brain," and of the "brain fuming."

Mr. Forrest gave with a smile of idiotic pleasure,

> "The little dogs and all,
> Tray, Blanch, and Sweetheart, see—they bark at me,"

whereas, I understand *Lear* to be annoyed by some *disagreeable* fancy, which would cause him to start and *shrink* back from the imaginary objects named. The context convinces me that Shakespeare intended *Lear* to exhibit great uneasiness just then ; because, it is *Lear's* answer to *Kent's* question when animadverting upon *Lear's* ravings—

> ("*Kent*. O pity !—Sir, where is the *patience*, now,
> That you so oft have boasted to retain ?")

besides that, Edgar evidently understands *Lear* to be troubled by such imagined *barking* of those dogs ; else he would not have taken such pains to humor *Lear's* deranged fancy, and to scare the dogs away ; thus—

> "*Edgar*. Tom will throw his head at them :
> Avaunt, you curs ! &c., &c.
> *Lear*. Thou hast seen a farmer's dog bark at a beggar ?
> *Gloster*. Ay, Sir !
> *Lear*. And the *man* ran from the *cur ?*"

Mr. Forrest, instead of articulating as antitheses
"*man*" and "*cur*," laid the strongest possible
emphasis upon the preposition "FROM."

When *Lear*, in a paroxysm, attempts to tear off
his clothes, saying—

> "Off, off, you lendings:—Come *unbutton* here!"

Mr. Forrest tore open his dress from his neck to his
chest and discovered a naked body, without any
sign of there being or having been a *shirt* worn
between, which I consider an unreasonable omission ; because, whatever the proper costume of those
rude times wherein the action of the play is laid
may have been, and even supposing that history
could establish a shirt to be a more *modern* refinement, Shakespeare makes the absence of a shirt
upon *Lear* an inconsistency ; forasmuch as, Edgar,
a son of one of *Lear's* dukes and his subject, boasts
of having formerly rejoiced in half a dozen among
his wardrobe, viz.—

> "*Edgar*. Poor Tom, &c., who hath had three suits to his
> back, *six shirts to his body*, horse to ride," &c.

In *Lear's* dying speech over the dead *Cordelia*,

> "And my poor fool *is* hang'd! No, no, no life:
> Why should a dog, a horse, a RAT have life,
> And *thou* no breath at all? O, thou wilt come no more.
> Never, never, never, never, never!
> Pray you, undo this button : thank you, Sir.
> Do you see this? Look on her—look—her lips—
> Look *there*, look there!—(*Dies.*)

Mr. Forrest, instead of uttering—

> "And my poor fool *is* hang'd!"

By way of an apostrophe to *Cordelia's* fate, turned from the contemplation of the lifeless object of his all-absorbing solicitude and spoke the line interrogatively to *Kent*, as though *Lear* could abstract his thoughts then from *Cordelia* to inquire about the fate of his professional "fool" or jester, whereas, I am confirmed by a careful re-consideration of my original conception that by "*poor fool*" in this place *Lear* refers to his *Cordelia*, whom he in his madness just before has refused to believe *dead*, and whom until that moment he has been trying to arouse, by saying in the ear of her corpse—

> "I kill'd the slave that was a hanging thee."

But, at this juncture, having exhausted his ingenuity in efforts to discover a sign of life in her, concludes—

> "And my poor fool *is* hang'd!"

or in other words—'After all, I find that my poor innocent is indeed strangled to death. There is "no life" in her!' For my part, I cannot imagine how any careful student or judicious reader of Shakespeare's context here (and elsewhere in connexion with the epithet) can doubt that *Lear*, by "poor fool" refers to his unwise in her beginning and unfortunate in her ending-daughter, *Cordelia*, or how, if any candid mind had doubted at first, but had read and reflected upon the strong and lucid arguments of Steevens and of Malone, in opposition to the fanciful, but solitary-thoughted, Sir Joshua Reynolds upon this very point, a conviction could be avoided that Steevens and Malone were in the right; Sir Joshua was evidently a clearer-sighted genius in the art of painting, than in his penetration into the mind's eye of Shakespeare in drawing his pictures of humanity.

When *Lear* in the storm, uses the same words in speaking to "his poor" shivering *Jester*, he adds another epithet which characterizes his vocation, viz. :

" My poor fool *and knave !*"

N.B.—The foregoing is copied from my original M.S. Notes upon *Mr. Forrest's* performance of *Lear* in *Philadelphia, Dec.* 1, 1840.

Mem. New York, Oct. 26, 1860.—I saw Mr. Forrest again in this character at Niblo's theatre. I noticed no material difference except that he was in his physical efforts comparatively a little less vigorous.

MACREADY.

By the way, apropos of *Lear's* "fool," when Mr. Macready and myself chanced to sojourn together at New Orleans, in 1844, and were taking a walk for

exercise one day, that eminent artist observed to
me—

"Mr. Hackett, a common friend (David Cadwa-
lader Colden of New York), has intimated to me that
you have been a particular student of *Lear*, and I
should like you much to *see my Lear ;* in order to
have your judgment upon my taste in *adapting* the
original to the stage, and most especially upon *my*
idea of causing the *fool* to be personated by a
woman, who can *look like a boy of eighteen* and also
sing to the king upon the heath and during his madness those occasional couplets which Shakespeare
has put into the *Fool's* mouth, to *divert Lear* in his
misery."

I did seize the first opportunity to see his performance ; one occurred only a few nights afterwards.
When Mr. Macready and myself met next, he
inquired how I liked his idea of having *Lear's* Fool
thus represented.

I replied—

"It is a pretty and ingenious conceit, and not
ineffective at times; but, *I* have imagined that this
Fool was introduced by Shakespeare, not only in
conformity with the usages of primitive times as an
attendant of a king, but, in *this* play and *occasion*, as
a sort of *practical cynic ;* in order that such Fool
might *extract* and *point the moral* of the passing
scene to the *understandings* of the *audiences* of
Shakespeare's day, composed as they must have
been mostly of the uneducated populace of an

unlettered and unrefined Age—such scraps of moral
caustic as a king's "fool and knave" was privileged
to interject at intervals must reasonably be supposed
to have originated in the fool's mind *naturally*, and
to have been the result of an acute observation,
with previous opportunities and much *experience* of
the *world;* but, Mr. Macready, it seems to me that
such wisdom in thought, and aptitude in expression
and of *application* to passing events, from the mouth
of '*a boy of eighteen,*' would be more than prodi-
gious: to the reflecting and judicious of the
audience such wisdom and satire would seem *preternatural*, or to have been derived from nothing short
of *Inspiration.*"

Mr. Macready listened to me very attentively,
and without the least interruption; and, when I had
concluded, uttered not a word in defence or support
or justification of his innovation.

Mr. Macready's *King Lear* was in *conception* very
generally in accordance with my own, and his performance scholarly and highly artistic; the main
defects, which I detected in his attempt to personate
Lear and which frequently destroyed the illusion,
arose from his too-often forgetting, in the carriage
of his body, and by the quickness and the vigor of
his movements and action, as well as the occasional
strength of his lungs, that *Lear* was "fourscore and
upwards and *a weak and infirm old man.*"

I saw the *King Lear* of Edmund Kean repeatedly
when in America, in 1826. His performance of the

character was very uneven. He seemed to have contented himself with searching for *points* susceptible of brilliant effect in each of *Lear's* scenes, and in making their splendor great enough to either blind the mass of his audience towards, or make them forgetful of his *intervening*, and *frequent*, and *palpable deficiencies*. Mr. Kean evidently possessed the ability, but had not had, originally, either the will or the industry necessary, in both study and practice, to make his impersonation of *Lear*—like his *Othello*—as a *whole*, transcendent.

The history and traditions of the stage, to this day, point to David Garrick as the greatest actor of *Lear* that has ever lived. Murphy, his biographer, has preserved to us a remarkably full description of that performance, and records—" *King Lear* was Garrick's most perfect effort;—in this part he has remained without equal or rival. He was transformed into a feeble old man, still, however, retaining an air of royalty. He had no sudden starts, no violent gesticulations; his movements were slow and languid; misery was depicted in every feature of his face; he moved his head in the most deliberate manner; his eyes were fixed, or, if they turned to any one near him, he made a pause, and fixed his look on the person after much delay, his *features at the same time expressing what he was going to say before he uttered a word*." Then Mr. Garrick did not think it necessary—" as many of our players do "—to cover up with thick white hair his fea-

tures: they may thus be made picturesque, but
rigid and incapable of expressing occasional alternations of the countenance. The late Charles
Young, of Covent Garden, London, for such reasons wore for *Lear* a thin and scattered beard upon
his cheeks, and proportionately short from the chin.

ACTORS OF HAMLET.

ACTORS OF HAMLET.

Hamlet may justly be called one of those beings who " resolves and re-resolves, yet dies the same."

Some analytical and instructive notices of the character may be found in the following literary works, viz. :—

> Schlegel's *Lectures.*
> Goethe's *Wilhelmeister's Apprenticeship.*
> Davies' *Life of Garrick.*
> Boaden's *Life of John P. Kemble.*

I have become fully convinced of the truth of what Schlegel says of the character of *Hamlet*, viz. "Many of his traits are too nice and too delicate for the stage, and can only be seized by a great actor and understood by an acute audience."

A critic, contemporary with Garrick, remarks :— " Among the requisites for a perfect delineation of this difficult character are—the ease of a gentleman, the dignity of a prince, symmetry of features, expression of countenance, and flexibility of voice —to give proper variety to the vehement passions, weight to the declamation, and poignancy to the spirited and satirical parts—joined with originality and sound judgment."

Among the various performers of any pretension to eminence in the character of *Hamlet*, whom I remember in my youth, the earliest was

Thomas A. Cooper,

From 1816 to 1818, at the Park Theatre, New York.

Mr. Cooper was noted, at that time, for a handsome face and a commanding and an Apollo-like figure, and his *Hamlet* was a favorite and particularly attractive with the public ;—indeed, he was generally popular in many if not most of the characters wherein John Philip Kemble had become famous upon the London stage, and Mr. Cooper was said to have modelled his own after the *style* of that great actor, with which he had become familiar in his youth, and prior to his first visit, his early marriage into one of the first families at New York, and his subsequent life-long residence in the United States.* After the death of George Frederick

---

* Mr. Cooper married Miss Mary Fairlie, a daughter of Major Fairlie, of the American Revolution ; and Mr. Cooper's daughter

Cooke, in 1812, and until the first advent of Mr. Wallack, in 1818, and of Edmund Kean, in 1820, Mr. Cooper was the only theatrical star in our Western hemisphere, and New York had—and continued to have until 1824—only the *Park Theatre.*

I was too young when I first saw Mr. Cooper's *Hamlet* and had too vague a conception of the character to criticise that performance; though I well remember that his voice was full and of considerable compass, and his articulation was very distinct; his eyes, which were of a pale blue, and habitually—perhaps owing to near-sightedness—somewhat contracted, were not effective in his art, and his countenance had little flexibility; his gestures were usually formal and sometimes stiff, and the carriage of his body was generally heavy and sluggish, and occasionally, in action or movement, clumsy and ungraceful; his style was cold and declamatory, and sometimes turgid or bombastic; yet, in some other parts, and particularly in Shakespeare's *Mark Antony,* and as *Brutus,* in J. Howard Payne's adaptation of *The Fall of Tarquin,* and also in Sheridan Knowles's *Virginius,* and his *Damon,* when Mr. Cooper first performed the latter characters, and yet retained enough of his *natural impulse* to break

Priscilla, who had been favorably received by the public as an actress, left the stage to become the wife of Mr. Robert Tyler, a son of ex-President John Tyler.

away from the trammels of his *original schooling,*
he exhibited some very touching and highly effective *bits* of acting.

Note.—When Mr. Washington Irving, to whom I had
loaned for perusal, in 1818, my manuscript volume respecting
my own reminiscences of by-gone actors of *Hamlet,* returned
it, I found that he had done me the favor to *note* in pencil
upon the margin as follows:—

"At this time Cooper had lost the fire and flexibility of his
earlier style of acting. He grew cold, formal, and declamatory
as he passed his meridian."

W. I.

JAMES W. WALLACK.

New York, 1818–19.

Mr. Wallack then seemed not more than twenty-
five years of age, came directly from Drury Lane,
London, where he had already attained a high rank
in a profession then graced by many eminent
artists; and the season of 1818 was Mr. Wallack's
first in America. His figure and personal bearing
on or off the stage were very *distingué;* his eye was
sparkling; his hair dark, curly, and luxuriant; his
facial features finely chiselled; and together with
the natural conformation of his head, throat, and
chest, Mr. Wallack presented a remarkable speci-

men of manly beauty. He at once became, and
continued to be, during visits which were repeated,
occasionally protracted, and were seldom separated
by intervals longer than a theatrical season or two
each, and for a term of more than twenty years, one
of the greatest and most invariably attractive
favorites furnished the American by the British
stage.

With particular reference to Mr. Wallack's *Hamlet*, which as it has happened I have not had an
opportunity to witness since my *youth*, when my
ideas of the character were crude and superficial,
and which, therefore, it would be unjust in me now
to criticise retrospectively, I did then very well note
that Mr. Wallack's action was easy and graceful;
his voice and articulation were clear and distinct;
and though from the impression it made, and which
I still retain of that early-seen performance, it
might according to my later and more matured
ideal have lacked a sufficiency of *weight* in the
philosophical portions, and also of depth and intensity of meditation in the soliloquies, it was then
unanimously approved and a special favorite with
the New York public.

Mr. Wallack, besides being popular in a number
of leading tragic parts, was esteemed without an
equal as *Don Felix* in the comedy of *The Wonder*,
and throughout the range of genteel and high-
spirited comedy generally, as also in a number of
melodramatic characters. His *Martin Heywood* in

The Rent Day, Massaroni in *The Brigand,* and his *Don Cæsar de Bazan* in later years, manifested a high and exquisite order of art; whilst those who in Mr. Wallack's early days saw his *Rolla* in the play of *Pizarro* can never forget that it was unapproached by any other performer, and the most remarkably picturesque, fascinating, and continually attractive performance then known to the American stage. In versatility of talent, probably the stage has never had any other actor capable of satisfying the public in such a *variety* of prominent characters : his costumes, too, were remarkably characteristic, and always in admirable taste, and Mr. Wallack, in every respect, has proved himself a complete master of the histrionic art.

WILLIAM AUGUSTUS CONWAY.

New York, 1825.

Mr. Conway came from England to America during the season of 1823. He had been a great favorite whilst *Miss O'Neil* shone at Covent Garden, London, as a tragic star of the first magnitude ; he having supported that famous actress in the principal male characters of the dramas wherein she appeared. It was reported that " Mrs. Siddons had pronounced him superior in several respects to any actor of that day;" and it was also said and generally believed, too, that "the popularity he was fast acquiring had raised up against him a host of enemies in his own profession, and that the celebrated critic Hazlitt by a course of persistent ridicule had successfully conspired with them to drive him from his position soon after Miss O'Neil had left the stage." Mr. Conway being of a retiring and very sensitive nature suddenly and spontaneously resigned in disgust his situation as an *actor* with a good salary upon the London stage, and accepted that of a *prompter* at the Haymarket theatre, until he resolved to withdraw altogether from the turmoil and cabals of the London theatres, and come over professionally to the United States. Mr. Conway was well received in New York, and also in Philadelphia and Boston, and for a season or two was respectably without being at any time greatly attractive. His most approved parts were Hamlet, Coriolanus, Cato, Jaffier in *Venice Preserved* and Lord Townly in *The Provoked Husband*.

Mr. Conway was a very tall man, stooped a little in the shoulders and had a large foot, the heel of which, being habitually put first to the ground in stepping, made his tread of the stage rather unseemly; otherwise his proportions, though inclined to the colossal, were good; he was remarkably classic in his style and read *Hamlet* with nicety and strict propriety, and evidently had a good idea of the character; its melancholy and morbid sensitiveness were rendered very prominent, but he lacked

the occasional lightness and gaiety required by the
satire and also the warmth necessary for the spirited
parts; his chief defect consequently was a heavi-
ness, with occasional monotony. His *Cato* and
Coriolanus I liked best of all his performances seen
by me in our country.

About the year 1826, Mr. Conway resolved to
quit the stage and study Divinity; and about three
years thereafter, meeting with some personal opposition from the then Bishop (Hobart) of New York,
"*from the fact of his having been an actor,*" and
whilst on his voyage to Savannah for the purpose of
obtaining of Bishop White there, leave to "take
orders in the church," in a sudden fit of despondency
of a fine afternoon when his fellow passengers were
below at dinner, Mr. Conway jumped from the deck
of the ship into the sea off Charleston Bar, and,
refusing to avail himself of the means thrown over-
board to save him, was drowned.

THOMAS S. HAMBLIN.

New York, 1825.

Mr. HAMBLIN was in height above the ordinary
stature of men, and his frame was more bony than
fleshy; his head was remarkable for its covering by
a shock of thick and curly dark-brown hair; his nose
was high and thick, and long like his visage; his

voice husky; his breathing asthmatic; his manner stiff and formal; his eyes were of a dark hazel, small, sunken, and set very close to each other and not either penetrating or effective, and his other facial features were more rigid than plastic.

Mr. Hamblin was announced " from Drury Lane, London," where he had held for a season or two a respectable but subordinate situation in that Company. Rumor, however, said that "upon some recent occasion he had obtained an opportunity to act *Hamlet* at the Haymarket, where the audience received his performance with great favor, and regarded it as a very respectable copy of John Kemble's, *from which it appeared to have been studied.*" Mr. Hamblin's ideas of the character were strictly conventional. He was always noisy without passion, and always seemed to me not unlike a piece of animated machinery—incapable of any spontaneous impulse. Mr. Hamblin, however, had made himself familiar with all the mechanism of tragic art in the Kemble school; and with his tall figure, which he costumed to much advantage, as Shakespeare's *Brutus* and *Coriolanus*, and adapted to such artificial bearing as has become consonant with our modern ideas of the manner of those ancient Romans, Mr. Hamblin acquired and maintained many years a respectable stand among the tragedians of the city of New York.

EDMUND KEAN.

*New York, 1826—the year of his second and last
advent to the United States of America.*

Of all the attempts to act *Hamlet* which I have
seen, Mr. Kean's pleased me most.   He was a little
below the middle stature, and not as near the ideal
"glass of fashion and the mould of form" in person
as some of his competitors, though he had rather a
compact and not disproportioned nor ill-formed
figure ; but his face beamed with intelligence, and
its muscles were plastic and suggestive of the passions ; his eyes were black, large, brilliant, and
penetrating, and remarkable for the shortness of
their upper lid, which discovered a clearly-defined
line of white above the ball, rendering their effect
when fixed upon an object very searching ; his
action and gesticulation, though ever easy and
natural, were generally quick and energetic, and
very earnest-like ; his style in colloquy was "familiar but by no means vulgar :" it conformed to the
dignity of the occasion, and was most signally conserved in the last scene of John Howard Payne's
play, where, as *Lucius Junius Brutus, the Tribune,*
he struggles with the nature of the father and con-
demns his son, and himself gives the signal for the
axe of the executioner ; his manner, indeed, throughout the character, indicated the soul of the patri-

cian unalloyed by that of the plebeian ; his voice, when raised or strained, was harsh and dissonant, but in level speaking, and especially in poetic measure, its undertones were charming, musical, and undulating ; verily, the ensemble of Kean's physical features was well adapted to depict the

——"flash and outbreak of a fiery mind."

In *Hamlet's* advice to the players and in the strictly declamatory portions of the character, Mr. Kean did not particularly excel, but he seemed to me to have inspired and more ably to illustrate the soul of *Hamlet* than any actor whom I have seen in the part ; its intellectuality and sensitiveness were wrought into transparent prominency ; every particle of its satire was given with extraordinary pungency ; its sentiment was upon each occasion very impressively uttered, and the melancholy was plaintively-toned and sympathy-winning ; the action was free and natural and never ungraceful, the passion heart-stirring, and the poetry was read with correct emphasis and a nice ear to rhythmical measure : yet, Kean's *Hamlet*, which surprised and enraptured me, I discovered, to my surprise, chagrin, and vexation, was not *particularly* appreciated by the most intelligent of our New York audiences. Mr. Kean's most popular and invariably-attractive part was *Richard the Third ;* but his *Othello* was a far more exquisite and intellectual, as also meritorious performance ; his *Sir Giles Over-reach* a more terribly-energetic, and his *Shylock* his most unexceptionably-perfect character.

One of Kean's most enthusiastic admirers was Lord Byron. He pronounced " Kean's third act of *Othello* the perfection of tragic art," and said that " acting could go no farther." His Lordship, too, is said to have remarked that he " pitied those who were not near enough—as he had made it a rule to be (seated in the third row of the pit)—to *see* the *constant alternations* and *bye-play* of *Kean's countenance*" during the dialogue.

After Lord Byron had left England, and reached Italy, he sent Kean a snuff-box, with the following lines :

> ——" Thou art the Sun's bright child !
> The genius that irradiates thy mind
> Caught all its purity and light from Heaven.
> Thine is the task with mastery most perfect
> To bind the passions captive in thy train.
> Each crystal tear that slumbers in the depth
> Of feeling's fountain, doth obey thy call.
> There's not a joy or sorrow mortals prove
> A feeling to humanity allied
> But tribute of allegiance owes to thee.
> The shrine thou worshippest is Nature's self,
> The only altar Genius deigns to seek :
> Thine offering—a bold and burning mind,
> Whose impulse guides thee to the realms of fame,
> Where crown'd with well earn'd laurels all thine own,
> I herald thee to Immortality."

I happened to be in London and was in the stage box of Covent Garden Theatre the evening of the

25th of March, 1833. The play was *Othello*. Mr. Kean, who was announced to act *The Moor*, had been so advertised recently, and having proved too unwell to appear, fearing another disappointment, comparatively few of the admirers of this " the greatest theatrical genius of the Age," had confidence enough in the report of his convalescence and ability to act again, to attend the theatre on this occasion, though it offered them an extraordinary inducement, viz. " his son, Mr. Charles Kean, would for the first time in London appear with him on the stage and sustain the character of *Iago* to his father's *Othello*." The curtain rose to an evidently intelligent but only about a half-filled auditorium.

When Kean the father and Charles Kean his son, as *Othello* and *Iago*—entered upon the second scene of the tragedy, they were greeted with vociferous manifestations of welcome which continued until each had reached his respective stage-position, right and left centre, and had turned and faced and bowed once to the audience, whereupon the Pit and Boxes rose simultaneously ; the gentlemen cheering and clapping their hands, and the ladies waving their handkerchiefs ; Mr. Kean, who was on the left side of the centre, seemed to appreciate highly the compliments, and grasping his son's left within his own right hand advanced firmly to the footlights and gracefully presented his son Charles, by a gentle wave of the other hand, and then a grateful smile, and their united and modest obeisance. The whole

audience seemed wild with delight at this little incident, and doubly redoubled their significant expressions of enthusiasm at the occurrence, and the father
and son were for an uncommonly long interval compelled to bow their acknowledgments accordingly
before they were allowed to return to their relative
stage-positions, and resume their respective characters and open the dialogue of the scene.

Mr. Kean appeared physically feeble and indis-
posed to make any special efforts even where he had
long been wont in the first and second acts, and I
inferred therefrom that he had not confidence in the
extent of his recovered strength, and was reserving
that which he thought he could command for the
first exigency in the third act.

The same feebleness, however, continued manifest
to every one until he uttered that famous apostrophe, *Act* 5, *Sc.* 1, " Now for ever farewell," &c.

I had often heard him deliver this favorite apostrophe, and seldom receive less than three or four
rounds of applause. On this occasion the applause
was prolonged and renewed, and seemed to occupy
at least a minute's time by the watch. I never
before had heard him utter the words with half the
intense and heart-rending effect, and I remarked to
my companion in the stage box :—" Poor fellow ! I
fear that a consciousness of the applicability to his
own individual self of ' *Othello's occupation's gone!*'
has unnerved him. I now realize the great critic
Hazlitt's observation that ' this apostrophe and its

termination'—as Kean delivered it in his earlier days—'lingered upon the ear like an echo of the last sounds of departing Hope.'"

During this long protracted applause, Mr. Kean stood motionless, his eyes closed, and his chin resting upon his chest. When it had quite subsided, and some fifteen or twenty seconds of time had elapsed, and Mr. Kean still remained motionless and statue-like, loud whisperings prevailed among the spectators—"Why don't he proceed? He must be ill again? What can be the matter with him?" The very silence around him seemed suddenly to arouse him to a sense of his own condition. He raised his head languidly, blinked repeatedly, and turning feebly towards *Iago* on his right, instead of that articulate vehemency usual with the words, Mr. Kean tottered visibly and muttered indistinctly —and *inaudibly beyond the orchestra*—"Villain—be—sure you—prove—" here he hesitated in his approach towards *Iago*, but stretched out both hands and ejaculated, "Oh, God! I'm dying! Speak to them, Charles!" Whereupon his son sprang forward and caught him in his arms. Several voices from the auditorium cried, "Oh, take him off! Send for a surgeon!" &c. Some one from the stage entrance on Mr. Kean's left came and assisted, and with either arm resting upon those two persons, Mr. Kean partly stepped or was borne out of sight of the audience whilst bowing his head feebly in token of his sense of their kind indulgence.

The curtain was dropped, and after a few moments Mr. Bartley, the stage-manager, came forward and observed that though Mr. Kean was faint, he hoped he might be restored by a surgeon who had been sent for, and be able to finish his part, and craved their indulgence accordingly for fifteen minutes. When the time had expired, Mr. Bartley re-appeared, and regretted to inform the audience that the surgeon had pronounced Mr. Kean utterly incapable of resuming his part, which *Mr. Warde* would undertake with the consent of the audience to finish in Mr. Kean's stead, and the play was continued to its conclusion without further interruption.

Mr. Kean was carried to the nearest hotel, and after a few days removed to his home at Richmond, where he lingered about three weeks, and expired 15 April, 1833.

CHARLES MAYNE YOUNG.

Covent Garden Theatre, London, 1827.

It was impossible not to be pleased with Mr. Young's *Hamlet,* as a *whole.* He had a full, compact, and a well-proportioned figure, a little above the medium height, an intellectual cast of countenance, with straight, dark hair. His features were not remarkable, unless for a Roman nose, which, though well formed, was in length a little beyond its proportion, and contributed to make the face rather fixed and inflexible; but his voice was full and of great compass, and he seemed to be aware and proud of it, inasmuch as he would frequently seize occasion to practise it in a sort of chanting when delivering poetry; his articulation and declamation were good, though a slight lisp could occasionally be detected in his speech; his action was easy and graceful, indeed very gentleman-like; his readings were sensible, and generally accorded with my taste, and his conception of the character of *Hamlet* seemed pretty just in the main—though I am bound to take particular exception to Mr. Young's marked hauteur in receiving the players, and to his dictatorial bearing whilst conversing with them; his utterance especially of, " Com'st thou to beard me in Denmark?" was characterized by a tone of rebuke instead of that of a jocose and condescending familiarity, such as *Hamlet* would be likely to use in welcoming " the tragedians of the city in whom he was wont to take such delight, and who had come expressly to offer him their service."

Mr. Young's general demeanor in the part, however, might be said to conform more to the conventional idea of what is termed "*princely*" than did Mr. Kean's, but it did not indicate as open a nature nor as innate a nobility of soul as Kean's manner conveyed, and notwithstanding that Mr. Young had greater advantage in personal appearance, and was more classic in his style, the impulse of Mr. Kean's genius gained for him, in my esteem and com-

parison, the transcendency in the performance of
Hamlet.

Mr. Young, however, was generally a most admirable tragic-artist. I saw with unmixed pleasure and satisfaction his *King John*, *Brutus* (in *Julius Cæsar*), and his *Mr. Beverly* in the tragedy of *The Gamester*. His *Iago* (1827) was very highly estimated by the London public, and its rendering was indeed very *artistic;* but, though I could not but admire Mr. Young's talent in filling his particularly gay, bold faced, and broadly conceived outline, my judgment resisted the conviction of the *justness* of his peculiar notions of the character. 'Tis true, his jollity of manner created much laughter, and was greeted with loud and frequent applause, and he capitally worked up his points to his theory, and artfully hid its unsoundness; and *applause* is the meed, the goal, the capital every aspiring and unscrupulous actor seeks: because it is generally considered the test of merit, and whoever has been able to obtain repeatedly and continuously the greatest quantity in any popular character, has seldom failed to become its most attractive and consequently best remunerated representative. An actor, however, may occasionally succeed in surprising the senses, suspending the judgment of the few who *think* in a theatre, or in confounding their faculties, whilst he secures the ready applause of the excited many who do not stop to consider the *premises* or might discover that the actor was

shamefully perverting his author's most obvious
design ; but the actor in the meantime has become
assured of his booty, and revels in a demonstration
in his favor which will not be restrained and cannot
be recalled, and also in the consoling conclusion
that *should* any of his victims detect the actor's *dis-
honesty* in acquiring his own inconsiderate approbation, such an one would surely lose any vexatious
sense of his robbery, in *admiration* of the *adroitness*
of such *moral thief*.

Mr. Young made *Iago* seem constitutionally gay
and lightsome, and too *heartily* joyous in certain portions of his dialogue, and not apparently wretched
enough in particular soliloquies, where he expresses
pent up grievances, the cause real and imaginary of
his secret but malignant hatred to the *Moor*—for one
complaining of hating that " which like a poisonous
mineral gnawed his inwards," and of course had
cankered all joy in his soul or any *sincere* inclina-
tion for gaiety and merriment. *Iago* should indeed
assume a blunt but *cynical* humor ; certainly not
provocative in the acting of as much mirth among
the audience as it would be if rendered in a *jolly*
manner, though much more consistent with the
nature and the circumstances of the character ; but
these nice and delicate distinctions are very difficult
for an actor to signalize intelligibly or render transparent to an audience, yet are worthy of an artist's
studious efforts. *Iago's* manner should naturally
differ when alone with either *Othello,* or *Cassio,* or

Roderigo, or in his general intercourse with those around him, and appear *assumed* accordingly; but, in his *soliloquies*, the actor should portray his *real* and *absolute* misery and sufferings without disguise; they constitute the key which unlocks and exposes to the audience the secret motives of his envious, jealous, cruel, wretched, and revengeful nature, and of his mean, base, dishonorable, hypocritical, and detestable actions. Mr. Young neglected to display in strong colors the rancor at heart and its original complex causes, leaving his villany to seem too gratuitous and his humor too easy and spontaneous instead of forced and unnatural.

A few days after I had seen *Mr. Young* perform *Brutus* in *Julius Cæsar*, I met that gentleman at dinner and took occasion to express to him the effect his acting that part had had upon me. I observed that his manner, after the quarrel with *Cassius* had been ended and when *Cassius* said—"I did not think you could have been so angry!"—of slowly turning and facing *Cassius* and in a melancholy tone uttering—"Oh, *Cassius*, I am sick of many griefs!" and then slowly approaching him, taking one hand within his own and resting the other on *Cassius's* shoulder and pausing a little and fixing his gaze upon the face of *Cassius*, and then with a faltering voice, and a suffused eye and choking utterance, which seemed to me to indicate that he was nerving himself in order to impart without emotion a heart-rending fact to one whose sympathies would be strongly moved and his shock would else *re-act* upon *himself* and shake his own fortitude before he added—" *Portia—is—dead!*" and closed his eyes, had so overcome *my* sensibilities, as his auditor and spectator in the stage-box of Covent Garden, that I involuntarily fell backwards among those behind me—my heart seeming to heave into my throat and stop my breath, and, sobbing audibly, I became for a few moments quite a spectacle to those immediately about me, and had felt quite ashamed of my own weakness afterwards.

Mr. Young thanked me for the compliment I had paid to his own *art*, but modestly remarked that "he *deserved no credit for its original conception*, inasmuch as he had taken it from the late Mr. Kemble's performance of *Brutus*, whilst he himself had frequently acted *Cassius* with him."

WILLIAM CHARLES MACREADY

as Hamlet, New York, 1826 *and* 1843.

Mr. Macready, in propria persona, minutely surveyed, is above the middle height; his port rather stiffly erect; his figure, not stout but very straight, and at the hips quite the reverse of *en bon point;* his ordinary or natural gait is not dignified; he steps short and quick with a springy action of the knee joints, which sometimes trundling his stiff bust—as in a rush from the centre to a corner of the stage—

reminds one of the recoil of a cannon upon its carriage; in his slow and measured tread of the stage,
he seems somewhat affected: he sags his body alternately on either leg, whilst his head waves from side
to side to balance it: his head, however, is not un-
proportioned, and his hair is of a dark brown; his
face, though occasionally lighted up by a pleasing
smile, can hardly have beauty predicated of it: his
forehead is good, but his *brow* does *not*—

———"like to a title leaf
Foretell the nature of a tragic volume;"

being rather high, vacant, and irregularly arched
though not inflexible; his eyes are blue, of good
size, widely set and tolerably effective in his acting;
though he has a trick of turning them upward rather
too frequently and dropping his chin upon his breast;
half covering the eye-balls with the upper lids and
leaving the whites below well-defined, looks too
much aghast when he would express reverential
awe; his nose is of ordinary length, rather low and
straight from his forehead down to beneath its
bridge, where it abruptly rises; his mouth is not
remarkable and his chin is prominent; his voice is
tolerably strong, but without volume or much compass; when sunk it is sometimes monotonous, and
when raised often becomes quite reedy; it rarely
breaks by accident, but does for effect occasionally
by intention in the course of his *Richelieu* and also
in the utterance of *Lear's* curse; his articulation is

generally distinct and his enunciation clear and pure, excepting some rare specimens of what seem the remains of an early or slight Irish brogue; his legs are rather long and thin by *nature*, but being straight are proportioned on the stage by his *art*, and his arms are more bony than brawny; his actions are generally formal and sometimes more angular than graceful; many of his attitudes are good, but he has a habit of sinking his body by bending both knees, as though his breast was o'erfraught with a heavy weight of matter which he was impatient to discharge or utter loudly; a favorite station of his is formed by reclining his weight upon one leg whilst his body is steadied by the other leg dragging extendedly behind and resting upon its toes: one posture of his is particularly uneasy and ungraceful, not to say painful, to behold: in his gladiatorial combats, when preparing to give or receive a blow, he throws his head and chest so far backward as to make himself appear in danger of losing his equilibrium: but, with all Mr. Macready's personal disadvantages, his discerning mind and untiring industry have so disciplined his physique, that, "take him for all in all," I consider him by far the most intellectual and generally effective actor of the time; indeed, I doubt whether stage-history can furnish another instance of such a signal triumph of *Mind* over the impediments involved in a very imperfect physical material. He seems, when forming his style of acting, to have taken as models and compounded the classical dignity of John Kemble with the intense earnestness and colloquial familiarity of Edmund Kean.

The difference between Kean and Macready struck me to be this:—*Kean* seemed to have far greater genius for the stage than Macready, and having once fully imbibed the spirit and carefully committed to memory the words of his author, appeared not to have bestowed much forethought in his closet upon the precise way in which he would *act* it; but, aware of his usual power of self-abandonment, risked the event before his audience, trusting mainly to his ready *impulse* to inspire him with all the other requisites to produce effect. Kean's early and irregular life, too, favors the conjecture that in such manner, when, amidst poverty and obscurity, after performing his characters in the English Provinces, his genius was sometimes quickened by his natural ardor, and at others by the bowl of Bacchus, and he originated and accumulated on such occasions, many of those bold, novel, and splendid points which afterwards were transplanted in the metropolis and electrified the London public. *Macready*, by his acting, impressed me with the idea of one who had begun *secundum artem*, by reading and pondering well his author, formed his corporate conception of the entire character he would play, dissected and elaborated its points, and then had recourse to his utmost art to re-unite and incorporate the several particles into a unique, complete, and harmonious impersonation, but never permitted himself to appear in a part before an *audience* until it had been long practised in his closet and sufficiently rehearsed upon the stage to become almost *second-nature* to him; upon such an hypothesis, his pictorial and mechanical portions having been duly considered by himself and thoroughly understood by the corps of performers employed to support his scenes in the play, his *art*, not impulse, his reliance, and the *degree* of earnestness only left to his nature to acquire whilst acting, *Macready* could differ little in the quality of his performance of the same character though frequently repeated: whilst *Kean*, who depended more upon the excitability of his nature and the inspiration of the occasion to arouse his impulses and to aid him before an audience, being consequently ever more or less in the vein, was sometimes dull, flat, or uneven, but at others was gay, energetic, or impetuous, and then his genius often became highly inflamed and burst like a meteor; its sparks seeming to ignite the sympathetic bosom of every spectator, until pit, boxes, and gallery reflected one grand blaze of enthusiasm.

It was in reference to one of these occasions, namely, the closing scene of his first performance of *Sir Giles Over-reach* (in *A New Way to Pay Old Debts*,) at Drury Lane (1814,)

——" When all were fir'd—"

that upon returning home immediately afterwards

in his carriage, and without waiting to change his stage-costume as *Sir Giles*, Kean proudly related to his impatient and expectant wife the victory just obtained over a whole theatre, crammed, as it was that night, with literati, nobility, and gentry, and among which, of course, figured his new but charmed friend, enthusiastic professional admirer, and most zealous and distinguished patron, the *Earl of Essex*—the foremost of the several nobles conspicuous then for their desire to cultivate a social intimacy with "the brightest genius" of the stage. Mrs. Kean seemed still unsatisfied, because her husband had neglected even to mention the name of an acquaintance of which she was most proud, and restlessly interjected :—

"But, Ned, dear ! what did *Lord Essex* say ? "

Kean's abrupt and emphatic, but very significant response was—

"Oh, d——n Lord Essex !—The Pit rose at me !! "

Macready's *Richelieu* I regard, as a whole, his most artistical assumption of character : his *Werner*, in his own adaptation of Byron's, is truly *sui generis*, a masterpiece of that class of tragedy ; but, though it may be termed "comparatively faultless," it reflects less credit upon him as an artist ; because, the manner demanded by the character assimilates so closely to his own natural style, that it requires but little if any degree of assumption in that respect. Mr. Macready being "elder and abler" than myself, great deference is due from me to his discernment and judgment or conclusions; therefore, I have reconsidered my own conception of *Hamlet*, and, finding that I cannot overcome my original objections to many portions of that representation, I will venture to record the following reasons.

Mr. Macready continues, after *Hamlet's* opening scene, to weep and whine too much, and resorts to his handkerchief too often; it is true that the memory of his father, then "not two months dead," may keep open "the fruitful river in the eye," amongst other "forms, modes, shows of grief," which he describes, but *Hamlet* claims to "have that within which passeth show;" therefore an actor should observe a nice discretion in his weeping: because, tears are a rare relief in nature to one who has

> ——" something in his soul,
> O'er which his melancholy sits on brood;"

besides, with dejected patients in real life weeping is an end and an attainment studiously sought by their physicians; because, if it can be superinduced *copiously*, it is known to relieve the o'erfraught heart, and to furnish the readiest antidote to "the poison of deep grief."

Mr. Macready moves about the stage too often and too briskly, and in too clerklike a gait for one of a princely education, leisurely habits, and a contemplative turn of mind; his manner, also, is generally too hurried and restless, and he imparts to the features of his countenance a spasmodic expression in many of their variations; indeed, sometimes their transitions are as sudden and their contractions as violent as though the muscles of his face were acted upon by a galvanic battery; his limbs, too, seem incapable of any just medium between moderate exercise and a paroxysm of action;—these violent contractions and expansions occasionally may serve to indicate a very nervous temperament, but, if too frequently practised, destroy a chance to depict neatly the variety of delicate lights and shades which belong to a mind naturally sensitive and meditative; in speaking he seldom used his left arm, but kept it under his cloak; in short, his manner generally wanted ease, was seldom graceful, and never exhibited the repose characteristic of a philosophic mind.

His arrangement of the scenes wherein *Hamlet* appears denoted generally much forethought and a nice taste; but amongst the exceptions I would instance his mode of rendering—

"Arm'd, say you?"—

which, following next in the order of the text to the answer given to *Hamlet's* previous inquiry, "Hold you the watch to-night?" was given in such a pauseless manner as at least to confuse the auditor's understanding that *Hamlet's* thoughts had reverted

to and had special reference to the peculiar appearance of the *Ghost*—

——" armed at point, exactly cap-à-pié ; "

for example; after *Horatio* had finished his description of the apparition and attendant circumstances,
and added :—

> " And we did think it writ down in our duty
>   To let you know it : "

Mr. Macready darted up the stage, turned suddenly
and rushed down to his starting place, and uttered

> " Indeed, indeed, sirs, but this troubles me ; "

then, standing between *Horatio*, on his left hand,
and *Marcellus* and *Bernardo* on his right, he inquired
of those two officers—

> " Hold you the watch to-night ? "

who reply—

> " We do, my lord."

At this juncture Mr. Macready, without turning his
face or changing his attitude, tone of voice, or
expression of countenance, or waiting a single
second of time, proceeded rapidly—

> " Arm'd, say you ?
> *All.* Arm'd, my lord !
> *Ham.*   From top to toe ?
> *All.* From head to foot.
> *Ham.* Then saw you not his face ?"

Up to this period, these questions and answers were pronounced with the utmost rapidity consistent with distinct articulation, and their more immediate antecedent having been " Hold you the watch to-night?" an auditor, though well acquainted with the text, might be in the hurried interim misled by such a manner of delivery to suppose that by the following interrogatory—" Arm'd say you?"—*Hamlet* meant to inquire connectedly whether those who should hold the watch would be *arm'd*, until the closing part of the context—

" Then saw you not his face ?"

brings the listener's thoughts necessarily back to the Ghost, to whose appearance " in arms" the inquiry refers : whereas, if, instead of the manner Mr. Macready adopted, after addressing the two soldiers then on his *right* hand with—" Hold you the watch to-night?" he had made a short *pause*, and with the fixed eye of abstract and profound consideration turned his face from them towards *Horatio* standing at his left, and sinking his voice into a musing and an under tone inquired of *Horatio* particularly, " Arm'd say you?" the most uninformed auditor could not have been for a moment misled from this special reference to the *Ghost*.

In the *First Folio* and in the early *Quarto* editions, the *answers* to *Hamlet's* particular inquiries are printed differently ; being in one copy ascribed to " *both*" and in another to " *all ;*" but, whether

these answers properly belong to the *two officers*
only or to *all three who were witnesses* is quite
immaterial; because, in the *acting* of the scene it is
right and proper to use the most obvious method to
convey to an audience and the spectators the dramatist's meaning, and to remove as far as possible
any obstacle to their ready and perfect comprehension, when it may be involved in some obscurity by
an author's style. In this case, however, there can
arise no just cause of any confusion in a spectator's
understanding if the actor of *Hamlet* will only confine his questions concerning the *Ghost* to *Horatio*,
as he ought to do for the reasons that *Horatio* is
Hamlet's confidential friend who has sought him for
the express purpose of communicating these particulars, and has already premised that " these gentlemen, *Marcellus* and *Bernardo*," had stood dumb
from fear and spoke not to the apparition; the last
fact being in itself a sufficient motive with *Hamlet*
for not seeking out nice particulars from *them* whose
" fear-surprised eyes" might render their report
subject to his suspicion of exaggeration; though it
would be quite natural that those soldiers should
join Horatio in his answers to questions specially
directed to him by *Hamlet:* because they had become privileged, having been eye-witnesses too of
the " dreaded sight," and also because they would
naturally be ambitious of an opportunity to confirm
such important information to one of so high rank
as *Prince Hamlet.*

> "His beard was grizzled? No?"

Mr. Macready after "grizzled" allowed the witnesses not a moment for reflection, but impatiently and rather comically stammered, "N'—n'—no?"

Instead of the usual entrance of the *Ghost* with *Hamlet* following, Mr. Macready's arrangement for their discovery in relative positions was new, effective, and picturesque.

> "*Polonius.* Will you walk out of the air, my lord?
> *Hamlet.* Into my grave!"

Mr. Macready uttered *Hamlet's* reply *interrogatively*, which was new to my ear upon the stage; but, though it is the punctuation of the Folio of 1623, I would prefer that it should be given as an *exclamation*.

Mr. Macready's style wanted the philosophic sententiousness requisite for an harmonious delivery of the analysis of "Man;" besides which he adopted the late John Kemble's omission of the indefinite article "*a*" before "*man*;" an omission not warranted by any of the original and authentic editions: the true text is when *Hamlet* would analyse God's animated machine,

> "What a piece of work is a man?"

The article "a" prefixed to the word "man" is essential here, because *Hamlet* descants particularly upon the male sex and their attributes as constitut-

ing the " paragon of animals" and in contra-distinc-
tion to the female portion of human kind enumerates
the peculiar and highest order of *men's* intellectual
gifts combined with a perfection of personal forma-
tion, and when he has summed them all up, he
adds—

" Man delights not me l"

The courtier then smiles, and he rebukes him with—

" Nor *woman* neither," &c.

Now had *Hamlet* begun with " What a piece of
work is *man ?*" such a general term—*man*—in his
premises would have signified the *genus homo*, and
been understood by the courtier as comprehending
woman also, and thus the point of *Hamlet's* rebuke
at this imagined impertinence been lost.

Like every other actor of *Hamlet* whom I have
seen, Mr. Macready's emphasis and intonation of
the word " *Southerly* "—" I am but mad North,
Northwest ;—when the wind is Southerly I know a
hawk from a handsaw"—were such as to imply to a
listener that when the wind may be from the South
the atmosphere is clearer than when from the North,
Northwest ; whereas the very reverse according to
Shakespeare elsewhere is the fact ; for example, see
" *As You Like It*," Act 3, Sc. 5.

> " You foolish shepherd, wherefore do you follow her,
> Like *foggy South*, puffing with wind and rain."

Hamlet, as I understand the passage, means to reflect gently upon the conceited cleverness of those clumsy spies, *Rosencrantz* and *Guildenstern,* whose ill-concealed designs are transparent to him, by intimating to them that their employers are deceived in respect to the point or direction of his madness; that, figuratively, his brain is disordered only upon one of the clearest points of the compass, to wit, North, Northwest; but that even when the wind is *Southerly,* and his intellectual atmosphere in consequence most befogged and impenetrable, his observation is not so mad or erratic as to be unable to distinguish between two such dissimilar objects—for example—as "*a hawk and a handsaw.*" Whether the form of a handsaw in Shakespeare's time may have including its teeth borne some remote resemblance to that of a hawk when his wings were extended, and the ends of the long feathers of his tail also apparently *notched,* and suggested the comparison, may seem a far-fetched as well as absurd idea; but if Shakespeare wrote "*hernshaw*"—as has been suggested—this would have been the only occasion of his use of that word throughout his works, whereas he has once elsewhere introduced *handsaw*—"My sword hack'd like a *handsaw.*"

In the soliloquy on suicide, Mr. Macready lacked that semblance of profound abstraction and of deep meditation—that absence of action and motion— I may say that almost statue-like station which is natural to a mind absorbed in philosophical and metaphysical self-debate, whilst the general physique of the man seems in a state of complete repose, all of which outward shewing appears to me indispensably necessary to give the language intensity in its delivery upon the stage. It was very inferior in effect to the manner of Edmund Kean or of Charles Young.

In the sentence—

———" To die ?—to sleep,

No more !"

Mr. Macready, to my surprise but not satisfaction, punctuated by his tone of voice the words—" No more," (?) as an interrogatory and as though they involved the *continuity* of a question, instead of that denoting an emphatic and responsive exclamation (!) of a *conclusive reflection* upon his own preceding answer to his self-inquiry: in common prose, I understand the course of Hamlet's reasoning to be thus :—" To live or to die is now the question with me! which of the two is the more noble? To put up with the stunning *slings* and heart-piercing *arrows* of that blind and fickle goddess, outrageous *Fortune*, or to take arms against *myself* and end them by suicide? What is *death ?* It is merely a sleep: nothing more! Admitting then, that, by thus terminating my existence I could put an end to an aching heart and the thousand natural shocks to which humanity is subject, would not such a termination of our accumulated miseries be a most devoutly-desirable attainment? Stay, let me pause and reconsider this hypothesis! Granted, that to die is merely to sleep; pursuing the analogy it may be to *dream* also, which is often incidental to a sleep, or the steeping of our natural senses in *temporary* oblivion and a *suspension* of the faculties! Ah, in that view of the subject a restraining cause is presented; for, in that *everlasting* sleep, when all hope of awaking—as in the body—and the possibility of retracing our rash and suicidal experiment are lost in fate, what *kind* of dreams may absorb us— whether happy or miserable ones—must make us hesitate; that uncertainty it is which reconciles us to endure the rather a long continuance of calamity: otherwise, who would bear a load of heart-sickening griefs and unmerited annoyances oft-recurring or protracted, when it is in his own power to silence and to rid himself quickly of them all, by taking the most handy of *arms*, "*a bare bodkin*" (the unsheathed dagger) and plunging it into his *heart*, the fountain of life?

Observe Shakespeare's sublime and beautiful concordance in the sentiments expressed in his play of *Measure for Measure, Act* 3, *Sc.* 3.

"*Claudio.*   Oh, Isabel!
Isabella. What says my brother?
Claudio.   Death is a fearful thing.
Isabella. And *shamed* life, a hateful.
Claudio. Aye, but to die and go we know not where;

> To lie in cold obstruction, and to rot;
> This *sensible warm motion** to become
> A kneaded clod   *   *   *   *   *   *   *
> *   *   *   *   *   *   'tis too horrible!
> The weariest and most loathed worldly life,
> That age, ache, penury or imprisonment
> Can lay on nature, is a paradise
> To what we fear of death."

Mr. Macready, therefore, by uttering " No more !' not with the natural cadence of a response to his own inquiry but as a further interrogatory—destroys the harmony of Hamlet's course of reflection, and prematurely supersedes the enumeration of the many consummated conquests promised himself until the link in his chain of reasoning is arrested whilst he returns to and reconsiders and analyses his crude and incipient ideas of suicide.

With special reference to this soliloquy and to that portion of *Dr. Goldsmith's XVIth Essay*, animadverting upon it as a composition, I remember having in 1828 examined the whole subject and dissected its component parts, and forming my own conclusion, that this British Classic's objections were hypercritical and founded in a singular misconception of Shakespeare's intention.—*See p.* 58.

That which Goldsmith complained of as an " incongruous metaphor " and proved a stumbling-block to Pope and to some other noted critics, viz. :

* The heart.

7*

——" To take arms against a sea of troubles,"

I understand thus:—the " arms " which Hamlet proposes to take and end his troubles withal are the common implements of suicide; of which he afterwards specifies the *kind* in his disquisition of the subject to be " *a bare bodkin*," a bodkin being the ancient name for a *dagger ;* the " *sea* of troubles " referred to, is figurative of his own *heart's* swelling and unceasing commotion. The integrity of the metaphor consists in the particular *arm* which he thought of " *opposing*," in order thus " to *end the heart-ache*" being no other than " a bare bodkin " (unsheathed dagger) wherewith he " *might* " put an end to *this* life's troubles. Upon searching Shakespeare's works I find the word " *Sea*," often used as figurative of a vast quantity ; for examples, " a sea of blood—of air—of glory—of joys—of sorrows ;" and, in *The Two Gentlemen of Verona*, in immediate connexion with the *heart*, thus :

> ——" a heart
> As full of sorrows as a sea " (is) " of sands."

In *Othello* the *Moor* refers to the *heart* as—

> " The fountain from the which my current runs
> Or else dries up."

In the *Second Part of King Henry IV.*—

> " The tide of blood in me
> Hath proudly flowed in vanity till now,
> Now doth it turn and ebb back to the *sea*."

That the word "sea" in this sentence specially alludes to the *heart* is indisputable; because the "blood" can "turn and ebb back" to no other "sea."

The analogy between the functions of the heart and the sea is obvious. The action of the *heart* continually propels the blood, and receives it again through the "channels" (or arteries) and the veins of the body, as in like manner does the commotive power of the *sea*, the flux and reflux of its tides, through its estuaries, its rivers, and smaller tributaries. A more direct and poetic aptitude to me seems inconceivable. My theory removes the occasion for Pope's substitute of *siege*, and of Warburton's suggestion of the word *assail* for "*sea*," and permits the whole of *Hamlet's* reasoning faculties to flow in a regular and unbroken and undeviating course, from the beginning to the end of this incomparable soliloquy.*

Respecting the propriety of Mr. Macready's conception of causing both the *King* and *Polonius*, after their hiding themselves behind the arras, to reappear for a moment, and by their sudden retreat to their covert be supposed to make some noise or momentary exposure of their persons, in order to afford *Hamlet* a pretext for his evident suspicion that *Ophelia* is in a plot against him, which his sudden change of manner and his severe invective

---

* See *Comments on Dr. Goldsmith's XVI. Essay*, pp. 14–59.

seem to imply,* it strikes me that it might be expedient, for the sake of stage-illustration, that *Polonius* only should show himself, stealthily and for an instant; because his so doing would be quite in keeping with his obsequiousness to the *King*, and his characteristic officiousness; but the juncture of his affording *Hamlet* such a glimpse would seem more opportune just when *Ophelia* is tendering to *Hamlet* his "gifts again," and for the reason that it is immediately thereafter that *Hamlet* changes his tone and language from delicate tenderness to bitter irony and personal animadversion; whereas, Mr. Macready selects a time when *Hamlet* has half finished his severity upon *Ophelia* and her sex generally, and has arrived at the point of asking his pungent question—

"Where's your father?"

Admitting, however, that Mr. Macready's selection of the particular time for *Hamlet* to catch a sight of *Polonius* might be the most fitting, would it not be unreasonable that the *King* should show himself at all? Would he not be too cautious to risk *Hamlet's* discovery of his espionage, and whilst, too, he could, without even peeping, hear through the arras every syllable of their conference? But, above all, it was very inconsistent in Mr. Macready to make *Hamlet*, who has been striving in various ways to

* See my letter to Mr. Adams.

divert the *King* from any suspicion that he was watching his proceedings, walk up close to the *King's* place of concealment, and there *vociferate* his parting speech ;—one evidently intended to be but partly heard even by *Ophelia*—the threat respecting the *King*, contained in the natural parenthesis, being to realize to *himself* what dramatic soliloquists are designed to share with an audience, a *secret thought*, namely—

"I say, we will have no more marriages: those that are married already (*all but one*) shall live; the rest shall keep as they are. To a nunnery go.

[Exit."

Mr. Macready, in the *advice to the players*, wanted the familiarity of courteous condescension; it was not easy and graceful, but stiff and formal. The piquant sentence—

" If his occulted guilt
Do not itself unkennel in one speech,"

was not pronounced with the particular and requisite emphasis upon the words which imply that it is some speech which *Hamlet* has interpolated where the blank verse had been made to "halt for it," or one wherein he had expected to "catch the conscience of the *King*."

" *Hamlet.* They are coming to the play; I must be *idle :*
    Get you a place."

By " *idle* " I understand *Hamlet* to signify to *Horatio* that he himself must seem to have no fixed object by or during the performance; his policy dictating that he should appear listless and unoccupied, in order that the *King* might disregard his presence, confine his attention closely to the play, and thus become entrapped into some exhibition of compunction or remorse. Mr. Macready, however, construes the word " *idle* " very differently; inasmuch as he immediately assumed the manner of an idiot, or of a silly and active and impertinent booby, by tossing his head right and left, and walking rapidly across the stage five or six times before the foot-lights and switching his handkerchief—held by a corner—over his right and left shoulder alternately, until the whole court have had time to parade and be seated, and *Hamlet* finds himself addressed. Such behavior was ill-calculated to indicate an " *idle* " spectator.

" *Hamlet.* It was a brute part of him,—to kill so capital a calf there!"

Instead of availing *Hamlet* of the privilege of his assumed madness, as a screen behind which to insult the old *courtier* and *lord chamberlain* in presence of the *court*, would it not have been in better taste if Mr. Macready had spoken the latter part of the sentence (aside) as though muttered to himself?

" *Hamlet.* Oh, they do but *jest*,—POISON in jest! No offence in the world!"

Mr. Macready, under a comic guise, brought out that interjection with great pungency and admirable effect.

" *Guildenstern.* The King, Sir, is in his retirement, marvellously distempered;
Hamlet. With drink, Sir ?"

Mr. Macready instead of as an interrogation uttered the words rapidly and in a tone of exclamation denoting an *unquestionable conclusion.* It was good and not objectionable for the reason that the sneer at the habits of " the bloat king " is practically conveyed to the listener by either punctuation.

Like every other actor of *Hamlet* seen by me, Mr. Macready infused no petulancy and seemed to attach no special importance to the REPETITION of the irritable answer when he is interrupted by Polonius's unwelcome entrance and abrupt delivery of his mother's message. *Hamlet's* situation at the juncture is suggestive.

Whilst suffering already from the intrusion of the courtiers Rosencrantz and Guildenstern, whom he rebukes with—" Call me what instrument you will, though you may *fret* me, you cannot *play* upon me !" he is subjected to another infliction by the unexpected and equally unwelcome approach of Polonius, whom he salutes with ironical courtesy—

" God bless you, Sir !
Polonius. My lord, the queen would speak with you, and presently.

Hamlet. Do you see yonder cloud that's almost in the shape of a camel?

Polonius. By the mass, and '*tis* like a camel, indeed!

Hamlet. Methinks, it's like a *weasel.*

Polonius. It is *backed* like a weasel.

Hamlet. Or like a whale?

Polonius. Very like a whale!

Hamlet. Then I will come to my mother by and by. They fool me to the top of my bent!—I will come by and by!

Polonius. I will say so.   [*Exit Polonius.*

Hamlet. (As Polonius is departing.) By and by is easily said! (Then turning to the Courtiers he dismisses them with marked irony.) Leave me, friends!"

My idea of the proper *stage*-manner of *Hamlet,* when giving *Polonius* his answer, is derived from the fact that *Hamlet* is particularly nettled, as his words imply; he thinks *Polonius* " a foolish, prating knave," and when pestered at this unseasonable time by his officious entrance and offensive self-importance, abruptly assumes to be busily engaged in reconnoitring some object aloft, which he describes and asks *Polonius* whether he, too, sees it; *Polonius* readily veers about with the wind of what he supposes *Hamlet's* diseased imagination, and humors his crafty whims in three distinct appearances of the same impalpable object; *Hamlet,* upon finding that *Polonius* will agree to every thing he suggests, reciprocates the courtesy and dismisses him with,—

" Then, I will come to my mother by and by !"

and turning away from him, and walking towards

the other side of the stage, soliloquizes respecting his own vexation—

"They fool me to the top of my bent;"

and naturally supposing that *Polonius*, to whom he had already given an answer, had gone with it in haste to his mother, *Hamlet* is about to resume his invective against the Courtier when he turns and perceives *Polonius* still standing just where he was when he had given him his answer, and also still gaping at him in stupid amazement; whereupon, as I conceive, *Hamlet* ought to approach *Polonius* and *repeat loudly*, and *peevishly* and syllabically-distinct, the words :—

"*I will* COME *by and* BY !"

in order that *Polonius*, now no longer unable to comprehend *Hamlet's* desire for his departure, may withdraw, as he does presently, saying—"I will *say* so!" upon which *Hamlet* abruptly remarks—"By and by is *easily* said!" in a tone and with a brusquerie, denoting in plain prose,—

"If you understood my answer, which is so simple and *easily* carried, why do you continue here instead of dispatching it ?"

Finally, as respects these delicate traits of *Hamlet's* character, which I have described as I understand them, I reiterate that Mr. Macready's negligent manner in pronouncing—"I will come by and by!" wanted motive. He delivered the next sen-

tence—" They fool me to the top of my bent !" without walking away, or even turning his face enough
from *Polonius*, to realize to the audience the abstraction due an "aside" speech, and then hurriedly full-
facing him again, *repeated*—" I will come by and
by !" not only without a point but with a listlessness
which he carried into the subsequent remark, viz.—
" By and by is easily said !" as though he was quite
unconcerned whether his words were emphatical, or
even heard by *Polonius* whom he is rebuking.

'Tis true, that very few individuals among even a
large assemblage might recognise such nice distinctions in an actor's performance; but a great artist
owes it to his own pretensions to study closely,
discern and try to penetrate, and to *develop with
fidelity in his portraiture*, the most delicate recesses
in *Hamlet's* mind.   No word or line of the language
put by Shakespeare in the mouths of any of his leading characters is unworthy of the best actor's careful consideration, or of his art to utter effectively.

A most thoughtless but outrageous license with
Shakespeare seems to have become invariable with
the actors of *Hamlet* in the *application* of the lines—

> " I must be cruel only to be kind,
> Thus bad begins and worse remains behind."

This couplet in every *stage*-edition of the play is
arranged to conclude the closet-scene, and every
actor of *Hamlet* whom I have seen, has more or less
perverted the bard's true meaning and more in

ignorance than cunning, as I hope, joined in casting
a moral blot upon the character of *Hamlet*, totally
unwarranted by the text or context; the atrocity
consists in the reigning fashion of rendering this
couplet upon the *stage*, which is as follows:—After
the termination of the dialogue between *Hamlet* and
his mother, as it is abridged and arranged for representation, when *Hamlet* utters the words—

"So again, good night!"

the Queen is required to approach *Hamlet* and to
offer a parting *embrace*, at which *Hamlet* seems
shocked, and shudders, and shrinks back with
averted palms, and pharisee-like *refuses to allow
her;* the Queen then seems convulsed, bursts into
tears, and rushes off one way whilst *Hamlet* goes in
the opposite direction, expressing first as an apparent excuse for such unrelenting hard-heartedness
the couplet—

"I must be cruel only to be kind:
Thus bad begins and worse remains behind."

Whereas, if we carefully examine the original scene
and the order of Shakespeare's language we find
that this same couplet does not come in next after
the *last* time of *Hamlet's* saying—"Good night,
mother!" but, in the *midst* of his advice, reflections, and varied expostulations with his mother,
and when the *Ghost* of his father—conjured to his
imaginative vision by the heat of his distemper, in

"the very witching time of night"—had been dispelled by some sprinkling of cool patience, and his reasoning faculties had again resumed their sway. In the *third* line of the speech wherein this couplet occurs—after which he utters some fifty more lines before he separates from her—he has interjected, "Good night!" as if for the purpose of hurrying her away, and with the object of securing a chance to secrete the body of *Polonius;* then adding some dozen lines of sentiment about "Virtue," &c., says—

> "Again good night!"

and—as an inducement for a mother to become virtuous, and be in a condition to bless her son with a good grace—remarks in substance—

"When you by a reformation evince an anxiety to deserve a blessing of Heaven, I will beg a blessing of you!"

He then alludes to the fate of *Polonius*—

> "For this same lord,
> I do repent: but Heaven hath pleased it so,
> To punish me with this, and this with me,
> That I must be their scourge and minister.
> I will bestow him, and will answer well
> The death I gave him. So again, good night!
> I must be cruel only to be kind,
> Thus bad begins and worse remains behind.
> But one word more, good lady.
> *Queen.*   What shall I do?
> *Hamlet.* Not this, by no means, that I bid you do:
> Let the bloat king tempt you again to bed,
> &c.,   &c.,   &c.,   &c.,   &c."

From the foregoing context, then, the obvious meaning of

> "I must be cruel only to be kind,"

is, "I must 'wring your heart,' as I premised to you at the opening of this interview would be necessary when I peremptorily bade you so 'let me,' and added—

> "Come, come, and sit you down; you shall not budge;
> You go not, till I set you up a glass
> Where you may see the inmost part of you;"

" this seeming *cruelty* of mine, in ripping up and exposing to your own censure your conduct, *must* be committed in order to prove to you by its effect the essential kindness of my ulterior object, which is *your reformation;* when I began and put it to you roundly you became alarmed, and cried out for 'Help!' and I—mistaking the voice behind the arras for that of another person—slew *Polonius* unintentionally:" "Thus bad begins and worse remains behind," *id est*, "Thus, you should perceive, your own bad or wicked beginning, in being won to the shameful lust of your husband's brother, my uncle, ended in worse consequences, to wit: my uncle's murder of my father." (To which murder *Hamlet* must at least have suspected her to have been accessory when in reference to her calling his killing of *Polonius* "a rash and bloody deed!" *Hamlet* remarks—

   " Almost as bad, good mother,
  As kill a king and marry with his brother,")

" and now here is another consequence following
that, to wit, my own unhappy mistake here in my
homicide of *Polonius.*"

In reply to the Queen's inquiry

    " What shall I do ?"

Hamlet ironically puts her upon her guard against
the probable attempts of his uncle to disclose—

  " That I essentially am not in madness,
   But mad in craft; 'twere good you let him know," &c.

The Queen thereupon assures *Hamlet,* on her life,
that she will not *breathe* what he has said to her.
He then reminds her of what she " had forgot,"
namely, that it has been concluded by a resolve of
the King that " *Hamlet* must be sent to England ;"
acquaints her with the plot against himself in which
his two schoolfellows conspire, &c., and of his design to outwit them ; that this fate of *Polonius* will
necessarily precipitate his departure ; again he
says,

    " Mother, good night !"

as he commences to drag the corpse of *Polonius*
into an adjoining room, and moralizes upon his
character, and then goes off the scene one way
hauling the dead body after him, and reiterating—

"Good night, mother!" whilst the Queen departs simultaneously in another direction.

Therefore, I contend for the absolute correctness of my interpretation of the aforesaid couplet—

> "I must be cruel only to be kind,
>   Thus bad begins and worse remains behind;"

—and to *whom* and to *what* the words refer; and furthermore that they have not only no connexion with any imaginary refusal on the part of *Hamlet* to permit his mother to *embrace* him, but, that, after a minute examination of every link in the entire chain of the colloquy, there can be discerned *no warranty whatever* anywhere for the Queen's *offer* to *embrace Hamlet*, either expressed or implied by the words or the several situations: but, supposing for argument's sake that the Queen, conscience-stricken and seeking her son's counsel, *would* offer to embrace *Hamlet*, would it be consistent with his previous character, his frequent acknowledgment of his own imperfections, his pre-determination when sent for and obediently going to his mother—

> "Let me be cruel, not unnatural,"

and now especially, having just slain by mistake, in his rash haste, the unlucky *Polonius*, to *refuse* an embrace to his unhappy mother at parting and upon the Pharisee's pretext? "Stand off, I am holier than thou!" whenever I have seen this atrocity committed upon the stage, I have invoked the shade of Shakespeare to forgive the *ignorance* of the actor who could not be aware of what he was doing, when thus constructively libelling *Hamlet's nature.*

" That skull had a tongue in it and could sing once ;"

Mr. Macready, like every other actor seen by me, by his emphasis rendered " tongue " and " sing " antithetical, which fails to point to the listener the *moral* intended.   *Hamlet* begins moralizing to *Horatio* as they enter the grave-yard, upon the grave-digger's habit of *singing* whilst engaged in so melancholy an employment ; when they have approached him more nearly the grave-digger sings a *second* verse, and with his spade at the same time throws up *a skull ; Hamlet* then remarks—"That SKULL had a tongue in it and could sing ONCE !" to convey the idea that the *skull* now so mute and knocked about by the rude clown, ONCE had a tongue in it and could do that which he (the grave-digger) is *then* doing, namely, SINGING ; this *moral*-pointing of *Hamlet's* reflection can be most clearly conveyed to an auditor's comprehension by special emphasis and intonation, rendering the words, " *skull* " and "*once*," strongly emphatical as *antitheses*, thus— " That SKULL—had a tongue in it and could sing ONCE ;" but as pronounced by Mr. Macready and others, the point of the sentiment is not prominent enough, and *Hamlet* might with equal effect have referred to either of the *other* faculties once possessed by that now *speechless* skull in common with the grave-digger's, as, " that it had an *eye* and could *see* once, or an *ear* and could *hear* once, &c. ;" however, Mr. Macready's voice, or his ear, seems not very well suited to intonate some of Shakespeare's *prose* with the most appropriate effect, and evidently is incapable of regulating the utterance of his *poetry* with harmonious variety ; his voice seems least disqualified where his subject affords scope for strong physical excitement, or discordant fury ; his taste or his ear must be bad, because he frequently destroys the rhythm of the line; sometimes by omitting necessary syllables, and at others by adding to a word what is not in the text.

In conclusion, to leave Mr. Macready's personation, and to treat of the character of *Hamlet* only, it recurs to my mind that much irrelevant learning has been displayed, as also abstract and unnecessary argument indulged by eminent critics, in attempts to prove whether Shakespeare intended that *Hamlet* should be really mad, or throughout only affecting insanity. A mature digestion of his text is quite sufficient to furnish me abundant and conclusive evidence upon *that* point, and I was very much gratified, after our correspondence respecting the character, to hear my honorable and learned friend, Mr. Adams, express his coincidence in my opinion.

After *Hamlet's* first interview with the apparition, that he *feigns* madness—to conceal his secret design

—cannot be disputed; because, he adjures his companions who shared the sight, that—   •

> " How strange or odd soe'r I bear myself,
>   As I, perchance, hereafter shall think meet
>   To put an antic disposition on————,"

they never shall in any way intimate or signify to another that they "*know* aught" of him. That *Hamlet*, however, actually becomes after the play-scene the victim of temporary aberration of mind, I think a very reasonable inference; because, his violent excitement in the closet-scene with his mother—his short soliloquy prior to proceeding thither and including—

> " Now could I drink hot blood
> And do such bitter business as the day
> Would quake to look on ;"

his rash slaughter of *Polonius*, there, and the conjuration of his father's spirit through the medium of his heated imagination, indicate a gradual tendency towards and the reaching of a *climax* of *delirium*.

During *Hamlet's* short cruise his senses seem to have been tranquillized, and his ingenuity precipitated; but when he was landed stealthily and walks casually into the grave-yard he moralizes to *Horatio* sensibly enough until the incidental news of the death and his presence at the actual obsequies of *Ophelia* shock his sensitive and susceptible nature, put a period to his *reasoning* interval, and produce a

fresh outbreak of madness; a predisposition to which
is accelerated by the ravings and frantic conduct of
Laertes before he joins him by leaping into *Ophelia's*
grave: for, *Hamlet* says calmly afterwards in conversation with *Horatio* in reference to *Laertes* and
the occasion—

> " But, sure, the bravery of his grief did put me
> Into a towering passion."

After *Hamlet's* phrensy in that scene had reached
the height of verbal and practical extravagance, his
mother interjects—

> " This is mere madness,
> And thus awhile the fit will work on him;
> Anon, as patient as the female dove
> When that her golden couplets are disclos'd,
> His silence will sit drooping."

Hamlet's wild and indecorous behavior, during
Ophelia's obsequies, I regard as stronger and more
intrinsic proof of his absolute derangement than
even his own *admission;* because, it might be
argued against *that*, that he has still an object in
keeping the fact unknown of his then or upon any
occasion *feigned* madness; and it also might be
consistently urged that his mother's having then
pronounced him " mad " was but in virtue of the
promise he exacted of her in her closet, to keep
his secret: but, in the denouement, when his madness is not doubted by any one and he can have no

motive for deception, when the king puts the hand
of *Laertes* into that of *Hamlet* after saying—

"Come, *Hamlet*, come, and take this hand from *me*,"

if *Hamlet* is not *honest* in his voluntary apology
and gratuitous explanation to *Laertes*, and does not
really believe himself "punished with a sore distraction," such meanness, cowardice, insincerity,
and inconsistency, should furnish conclusive evidence that he *must* be *mad without being aware
of it.* Mark his words to *Laertes*—

> "Give me your pardon, Sir, I have done you wrong,
> But, pardon it, as you are a gentleman.
> This Presence knows, and you must needs have heard,
> How I am punish'd with a *sore distraction.*
> What I have done,
> That might your nature, honor, and exception,
> Roughly awake, I here *proclaim was madness.*
> Was't Hamlet wrong'd Laertes? Never, Hamlet;
> If Hamlet from himself be ta'en away,
> And, WHEN HE'S NOT HIMSELF, does wrong Laertes,
> Then Hamlet does it not; Hamlet denies it.
> Who does it then? His madness: if't be so,
> Hamlet is of the faction that is wrong'd;
> His *madness* is poor Hamlet's enemy."

Hamlet then appeals to the feelings of *Laertes*, who
hypocritically professes to be "satisfied."

> "Sir, in this audience,
> Let my *disclaiming* from a *purpose* evil,
> Free me so far in your most generous thoughts,
> That I have shot my arrow o'er the house,
> And *hurt my brother.*"

From these premises, then, one of two conclusions I deem unavoidably to be drawn by every candid and strict investigator of the character, namely: either that Shakespeare intended to depict in *Hamlet* an unhappy and distracted but honorable gentleman, or a base, degenerate, and contemptible prince.

NOTE.—Only three or four nights prior to Mr. Macready's final performance and retirement from the stage, he played *Cassius* in *Julius Cæsar*, at the Haymarket, London, the season of 1851–52. Sir Thomas Noon Talfourd was seated by my side in a stall during the play, and afterwards we walked thence together to the Garrick Club. Sir Thomas was a great admirer of Macready, and seemed very much gratified when I observed to him that "I had been surprised and delighted at witnessing his personification of *Cassius*, which I considered to be *perfectly Shakespearean*, and that acting could not more completely represent such a character."

CHARLES KEMBLE.

Park Theatre, New York, 1832.

His style of reading *Hamlet*, though artistical, was prosy and measured; his action and gestures were graceful, but never seemed impulsive, and his manner—wherein "*ars est celare artem*" appeared throughout—studied and mechanical; his voice was tenor-like, and never descended into any profundity of tone, and whenever elevated was thin and reedy, and sometimes became quite shrill; and notwithstanding a characteristic wig, his features denoted his age to be far in advance of the "thirty years" which the grave-digger reports *Hamlet* to have attained, at the time when the *fifth* act of the tragedy has commenced.

Mr. Kemble was tall, and had rather a good but fixed and elongated visage, and prominent features, and his profile particularly partook mostly of the Grecian order; his figure was fine and commanding, and the carriage of his person remarkable for ease, grace, dignity, and for elegance in high-comedy and characters like *Lord Townly* in *The Provoked Husband*, which I saw him personate at Covent Garden in 1827 (during my first visit to England), to the *Lady Townly* of the celebrated and beautiful *Miss Foote*, who became afterwards *Countess of Harrington*. Briefly, I can conceive of no more refined and admirable personations than Mr. C. Kemble gave, in those days, of *Benedick* in *Much Ado about Nothing*, *Charles Surface* in *The School for Scandal*, *Don Felix* in *The Wonder*, *Doricourt* in *The Belle's Stratagem*, and of each of the other characters in elegant-comedy wherein Miss Foote was then the great feature of the British stage.

I had often heard Mr. Charles Kemble's *Cassio* highly commended by Londoners, but never had an opportunity of seeing him in that part. I saw him play *Othello* once to Charles Young's *Iago*, but it seemed to me passionless, and too stately and courtly for the Moor, who deprecates his own deficiencies in social and refined education and manners, by observing that he has not "those soft parts of speech that chamberers have," and that—

> " Since these arms of mine had seven years' pith
> Till now some nine moons wasted they've used
> Their dearest action in the tented field."

Mr. C. Kemble's *Romeo* was a very acceptable performance, and his *Mercutio* gay, spirited, and thoroughly Shakespearean ; his *Falstaff* of *King Henry IV.* (First Part) was chaste and sensible, but showed no mellowness, nor unctuosity, or rich humor—it was very dry and hard ; his *Mark Antony* in *Julius Cæsar* was popular, effective, and excellent ; but, of all the characters of the Bard of Avon, his personation of *Falconbridge* (*The Bastard* in *King John*) was the greatest, most perfect, and admirable.

JUNIUS BRUTUS BOOTH.

Chestnut Street Theatre, Philadelphia, 1831.

Mr. Booth read *Hamlet* with a good degree of understanding, and he had a fine intellectual eye and cast of countenance ; but his voice was nasal, the action of his arms awkward—they seemed as though they were pinioned at the elbows ; he was below the medium stature and had very bandy legs, and his gait and bearing were not susceptible of

depicting any personal dignity; indeed such were
Mr. Booth's natural impediments, that no human
genius could surmount or blind an intelligent spectator, or cause him to forget them, and esteem his
personation of *Hamlet satisfactory*—or tolerable.
As *Richard the Third*, however, Mr. Booth was
generally popular; and had been originally brought
to Covent Garden Theatre, London, from the provinces, and pitted as a rival to Edmund Kean, after
the latter had made a stand and proved so attractive
in that character at Drury Lane. By many of the
critics of London Mr. Booth, whose conception and
manner of representing *Richard* seemed very similar to Kean's, was regarded as an imitator of that
then new and popular actor, and not allowed the
credit of that original genius which he appeared to
me at intervals subsequently to display clearly.
Some, however, considered his performance of
Richard quite as meritorious as Kean's, and Mr.
Booth's tent-scene, *particularly*, was pronounced
"superior;" and when I had had an opportunity,
years afterwards, at New York, to see both and
compare them, despite my decided preference for
Kean's *general* performance, I was bound to esteem
Booth's *tent-scene* the most startling and effective:
but, upon research and reflection in after years, I
found I had—like a large portion of play-goers—
derived my first impression and general conception
of *King Richard the Third*—not from received
history, nor from Shakespeare's genuine dra-

matic portrait, but that I had caught it from that popular actor's peculiar and fascinating style in rendering *Cibber's stage-adaptation* of the play; and, much as I admired Edmund Kean, and closely as I had studied his manner when I first adopted the stage, and applauded as I had been both in London and New York, in the year 1827, for my avowed *imitation* of him throughout that arduous part, subsequent examination and comparison of reports and imitations by contemporaries of the *departed* but famous Cooke's style, convinced me that, though Mr. Kean's genius and tact had enabled him to withdraw my consideration from many of *Richard's* proper and authentic characteristics, and surprise and charm me with his own substituted peculiarities, yet the late *George Frederick Cooke's* performance of that part—at New York as late as 1810—must have been much nearer Shakespeare's intention.

JOHN VANDENHOFF.

New York, 1838.

Mr. Vandenhoff was not gifted by nature with a fine face, its features were so hard as to be incapable of any *variety* of expression; his figure was indifferent; his action not remarkable for grace, and his step tardy and gait heavy; his blood seemed to be too cold and temperate, and his occasional enthusiasm too *palpably* artificial; his delivery of the text of *Hamlet*, though indicating sound sense and careful study, was generally prosaic and monotonous, and sometimes smacked strongly of the conventicle; he had also a catarrh-like and seemingly-organic impediment in his speech, and looked altogether *too old* to represent the character.

In the play-scene, whilst *Lucianus* was reciting his last speech and preparing to poison the *player-king*, Mr. Vandenhoff, who had made *Hamlet* conspicuous enough by his behavior to withdraw the eyes of the whole *court* from the play, and to fix them upon himself—notwithstanding that *Hamlet* had just previously and confidentially observed to his friend *Horatio* that his policy in this play-scene dictated his own seeming to be " *idle*," or listless and inattentive to the performance, that he might, *unnoticed*, watch and rivet his own eyes upon his *uncle's face*—began to creep, cat-like, across the stage, and, thus approaching the footstool of his *uncle-king*, just as the actor-murderer had finished pronouncing his infernal invocation, and commenced pouring the poison into his victim's ear, struck *Claudius* a smart blow upon his knee with *Ophelia's* fan, and, rising simultaneously, with violent gesticulations vociferates—

" He poisons him in the garden for his estate," etc.

which sent the *King* packing—as well it might. Yet how so discerning and judicious a student as

Mr. Vandenhoff could feel himself justified in innovating such an "*ad captandum vulgus*" display, by making *Hamlet* at this stage of the character assault with such gross and personal rudeness the reigning majesty of Denmark, whilst he was seated quietly at a play which had been ostensibly gotten up to divert him, and in the midst of his *court*, I am quite puzzled to imagine. *Hamlet*, prior to the approach of the *King* and his *court*, privately communicates to *Horatio* his object in reference to "one action" of the play to be represented, and begs his "heedful note" of its effect upon his *uncle;* remarking that if his hidden *guilt* may not betray and expose *itself*, particularly when the *player* shall utter "ONE speech,"—alluding of course to those "lines" which *Hamlet* himself had arranged to "*insert*" in the play—he would conclude that it must have been—"a damned Ghost that we have seen, and my imaginations are as foul as Vulcan's stithy:" whereas, by such practical rudeness as Mr. Vandenhoff made *Hamlet* exhibit, the *King's* evident surprise and abrupt departure might not unreasonably have been imputed rather to the offence his *person* had taken than his "conscience had caught;" besides being highly exceptionable. That *Hamlet's* manners *could* not have been so absolutely outrageous on the occasion may fairly be inferred from his dialogue with *Horatio* afterwards, when they compared notes, and "both their judgments joined in censure of the *King's* seeming."

——"Didst perceive,—upon the *talk* of the *poisoning?*"

But I regret, for the sake of my estimate hitherto of the taste and intelligence of a large audience in my native city, to record that Mr. Vandenhoff, instead of meeting with that *silence* which his own intelligence would have interpreted into their gentle rebuke for his temerity, was "most tyrannically clapp'd" for this unaccountable innovation.

Mr. Vandenhoff, however, in *Cato, Brutus, Coriolanus*, and some other characters, was excellent, and proved himself to be a highly-accomplished tragedian.

CHARLES JOHN KEAN.

Theatre, Haymarket, London, 1839.

Charles Kean evidently possesses remarkable talent and considerable *genius*, though of an order quite secondary when compared with that of his late father, Edmund Kean, and is also inferior in the capabilities of the face, and in the lower tones of the voice to those of his progenitor; his hair is as dark but straighter and less luxuriant than was his father's; his forehead broader; his eyes, though black and full, and effective upon the stage, not near so piercing and brilliant; in no other respect do I perceive any physical resemblance between him and his famous and departed sire. Charles has a face which is unusually wide across the eyes but tapers down to a narrow chin; his mouth is wide, and he has very white teeth irregularly set forward in the lower jaw and which impart a sibillating sound to his enunciation; his nose is low at its bridge, and rather pouty and broad at the end; his figure is less compact, and his height a little greater than were those of his father, and his brows are thicker and not so flexible: the *Elder* Kean had a straight and well-proportioned nose, and mouth which was regular and with lips which were often remarkable for their close muscular compression and strong expression whenever great firmness or determination of purpose were to be indicated. Charles Kean's general manner is easy and graceful; his gait, owing to his legs being longer and not so straight, but bending slightly outward, and to his frame not being so well knit together as was his father's, is not so *firm*, but the style of his most acceptable points, made in either of the characters wherein I have seen his father, makes it plainly apparent that, by Art or Nature, he follows, as far as he is able, in the still well-remembered footsteps of his deservedly illustrious predecessor.

Charles Kean's *Hamlet*, I regret to record, discovers various proofs of a defective ear, by sundry false emphases, bad cadences, and misplaced pauses; his personation was remarkable also for clap-trap effects with which it superabounds; in short, it was a tissue of bustle, rant, and posturing; his person

underwent unceasing locomotion, and was not in
repose even during the profoundest meditation of the
metaphysical soliloquies ; he has evidently discovered
that which pleased best the demonstrative ground-
lings and truckles to it accordingly, and successfully ;
he seems less bent on trying to inform and convince
their understandings, than to " amaze their very
faculty of eyes and ears ;" his philosophy evidently
teaches him to seek plenty of applause, not by the
rugged path of patient merit, but by a recourse to
surprises and slippery tricks in questionable shapes
and places, and which he may eventually find to be
as quicksands where he would establish the base of
his fame as a *classic* artist, though they may seem
evidence of growing popularity and be of temporary
advantage.

One of his most admired and applauded points
was, his manner of rendering, " *Is it the King ?*"
which effect was produced by Mr. C. Kean by making *Hamlet*, after he had thrust violently through
the arras in 2nd stage entrance left, *slide* ten or
twelve feet upon the floor-cloth down to the right-
centre of the stage, and then and there utter those
words, " Is it the king ?" with his loudest possible
shout of exultation.   His tone and manner denoted
unmistakably an *undisguised intention*, and betrayed
his *would-be-secret and concealed purpose*, and was
utterly at variance with the pretext he had the
instant before adopted to mislead his mother in
respect to the person he presumed to be listening

behind the arras, when, whipping out his rapier and thrusting through them, he had " killed the unseen good old man," crying out simultaneously—

> " How now ! a rat ?
> Dead, for a ducat, dead !"

Of course, when *Hamlet* searches and finds afterwards that he has slain *Polonius*, and apostrophizes—

> "Thou wretched, rash, intruding fool !
> I took thee for thy better,"

he admits to himself that he thought *Polonius* to be the king ; but then in order to preserve his consistency previously, his remark and question—

> " I know not.   Is it the king ?"

and that the horror-stricken queen may still be kept in ignorance of his sinister purpose, should be uttered with a tone of surprise, natural to a sense of one's commission of some incidental *and unintentional* mischief; the inquiry of *Hamlet* should seem to his mother to have been caused by her sudden and apparent anguish, as though the idea but then had suggested itself, that it might be the *king*, whom he had killed by accident, but who could have had no *honorable* motive for hiding there.

But I have heretofore had ample evidence that any strong effect produced upon the stage will be certain to be greeted with loud applause by the "barren spectators" who constitute the great majority of any audience, and who are ever ready for excitement and never stop to reflect whether the acting, however good in *itself*, is not inapplicable, misplaced, and quite *inconsistent* under the circumstances with the *character* to be represented.

GEORGE VANDENHOFF.

Park Theatre, New York, 1842.

MR. G. VANDENHOFF (son of Mr. John Vandenhoff, the tragedian) made his *debût* in America as *Hamlet.* His complexion is fair, his eyes blue, and his natural countenance is pleasing, but not capable of much variety of expression, and he had a habit, whenever he would appear grave, earnest, or severe, of arching and contracting his brows into a sort of lacrymose frown, that seems quite artificial, and as though it might have been studied before a looking-glass. His person is a little above the middle height, rather lightly but neatly and proportionately framed, and his whole appearance prepossessing ; his voice was pure, sonorous, and indicated considerable depth, but was too monotoned in level speaking ; his gestures were easy and rather redundant, though they never seemed to mark particularly the sentiment ; and many of his attitudes were graceful and somewhat picturesque, as though they had been carefully studied and much practised ; his emphasis and readings denoted intelligence and a nice articulation, but his qualities generally seemed more suited to the highest order of sentimental comedy; his manner wanted weight and dignity on occasion, and he uttered *Hamlet's* philosophic sentences not as though they were spontaneous expressions of thoughts originating in his own meditative mind, but the sentiments of another which he had learned and conned by rote, and scanned in his head rhetorically, but wherein his own heart did not participate, nor could his own judgment adopt and assume. The declamatory portions of the character were acceptably recited, but as a whole, whilst it secured general and patient attention and occasional approbation from the audience, it pretended *no new and original idea*, but proved at all points *thoroughly conventional*.

I saw Mr. G. Vandenhoff a few years later perform *Mark Antony* in *Julius Cæsar* very creditably throughout; whilst the oration over the dead body of Cæsar particularly was pronounced in the master-like spirit of one evidently confident of his own abilities, but nevertheless a truly accomplished elocutionist.

EDWIN FORREST.

Bowery Theatre, New York, 1829.

I was present at Mr. Forrest's original *début* as *Hamlet*, but he seemed out of his element; his spirit seemed incapable of being subdued to the normal quality and meditative propensity of *Hamlet's* philosophic mind; his iron nerve and powerful physique appeared to pant continually for opportunity or pretexts to display themselves; his evident uneasiness suggested to me such as I would conceive natural to a young but full-grown and newly-caged lion: indeed, it struck me that could Mr. Forrest's *Hamlet* have been, through some accident, allowed to ventilate his own impulses for a few moments, as soon as his father's ghost had bidden him—"Adieu! Adieu! Remember me!" he would have bounded unceremoniously into the presence of his uncle *Claudius*, and with the impetuosity of an enraged and sinewy athlete have driven his rapier through and through his heart, and by such foreclosure have ended the tragedy with his *first* act: in fact, Mr. Forrest's performance of *Hamlet*, though it obtained the applause of the large majority of the audience, was very unsatisfactory to me.

Mr. Forrest's own *propria facies* is what may be classed in its *ensemble* "handsome," though the nose is a little too small, crooked, and short, to be symmetrical; Nature has given him pleasing black eyes, too, which, however, he seems not to have acquired the art to make specially effective on the stage—possibly because his inflexible brows, which arch low and near the bridge of the nose, impart when pursed together a grim severity to his countenance, thus seemingly rendering it incapable of

much variety, or of sudden alternations, or of lightness of expression ; his person generally, with his
ample chest, long body, short and Herculean-pro-
portioned arms and legs, does not conform to
the ideal of an Apollo ; nor is his ease, or grace
of action, or carriage of body, remarkable or conventionally well-adapted to represent "the glass of
fashion and the mould of form."   Mr. Forrest's
voice is strong, but appears not susceptible of much
modulation, though his articulation is good, and his
general physique denotes extraordinary animal
strength.

Though Mr. Forrest's and my own notions of the
character of *Hamlet* differ widely, I have, since the
date of his original *début* therein, repeatedly seen
portions of his performance of *Othello* with great
satisfaction.   I rank it as a whole, and excepting
the late *Edmund Kean's*, the best I have ever seen
in either hemisphere.   Mr. Forrest may even be
said to be more "terribly in earnest" in giving effect
to the *fiercer* passions, but is Kean's inferior in portraying the *tender* qualities of the Moor's nature.
Mr. Forrest inspires more terror than pity ; though
I remember on one occasion particularly, at the
Park Theatre, noticing to a friend that " Mr. Forrest
had infused into his *last* act of *Othello* a degree of
manly tenderness, refined sensibility, and touching
melancholy, so true to Nature and Art, that his performance therein afforded me exquisite and unalloyed gratification."

PART V.

SHAKESPEREAN SUBJECTS.

UPON SHAKESPEREAN SUBJECTS.

---

*From the Hon. John Quincy Adams, of the House of Repre-
sentatives, and an ex-President of the United States.*

HAMLET.

WASHINGTON, Feb. 19, 1839.

To James H. Hackett, Esq., New York :—

DEAR SIR :—I return herewith your tragedy of
Hamlet, with many thanks for the perusal of your
manuscript notes, which indicate how thoroughly
you have delved into the bottomless mine of Shakespeare's genius. I well remember the conversation,
more than seven years by-gone, at Mr. Philip Hone's
hospitable table, where, at the casual introduction
of the name of *Hamlet the Dane*, my enthusiastic
admiration of the inspired (muse inspired) Bard of
Avon, commenced in childhood, before the down
had darkened my lip, and continued, through five
of the seven ages of the drama of life, gaining upon

the judgment as it loses to the imagination, seduced me to expatiate, at a most intellectual and lovely convivial board, upon my views of the character of *Hamlet*, until I came away ashamed of having engrossed an undue proportion of the conversation to myself. That my involuntary effusions and diffusions of mind on that occasion were indulgently viewed by Mr. Hone, so as to have remained with kindness upon his memory to this day, is a source of much gratification to me, and still more pleasing is it to me that he should have thought any of the observations which fell from me at that time worthy of being mentioned to you.

I look upon the tragedy of *Hamlet* as the master-piece of the drama—the master-piece of Shakespeare—I had almost said, the master-piece of the human mind. But I have never committed to writing the analysis of the considerations upon which this deliberate judgment has been formed. At the table of Mr. Hone I could give nothing but *outlines* and *etchings*. I can give no more now—snatching, as I do, from the *morning lamp*, to commune with a lover and worthy representative of Shakespeare upon the glories of the immortal bard.*

What is tragedy? It is an imitative representation of human action and passion, to *purify* the heart of the spectator through the instrumentality

---

* It was Mr. Adams's custom to rise at 4 a.m., and dispatch all his *private* affairs, that they might not interfere with his *duties* of the day in the *House of Representatives.*   J. H. H.

of *terror* and *pity*. This, in substance, is the definition of Aristotle ; and Pope's most beautiful lines,
in the prologue to *Cato*, are but an expansion of the
same idea.

Hamlet is the personification of a *man*, in the
prime of life, with a mind cultivated by the learning
acquirable at an university, combining *intelligence*
and *sensibility* in their highest degrees, within a
step of the highest distinction attainable on earth,
crushed to extinction by the pressure of calamities
inflicted, not by nature, but against nature—not by
physical, but by moral evil. *Hamlet* is the heart
and soul of man, in all their perfection and all their
frailty, in agonizing conflict with human crime, also
in its highest pre-eminence of guilt. *Hamlet* is all
heart and soul. His ruling passions are, filial affection—*youthful love*—manly ambition. His commanding principles are, filial duty—generous friendship—love disappointed and subdued—ambition and
life sacrificed to avenge his father.

Hamlet's right to the throne has been violated,
and his darkest suspicions roused by the marriage
of his mother with his uncle so speedily succeeding
his father's death. His love is first trammelled by
the conflicting pride of his birth and station operating upon his ambition, and although he has " made
many tenders of his affection" to *Ophelia*, and
" hath *importun'd* her with love in *honorable*
fashion," yet he has made no proposal of marriage
to her—he has promised her nothing but love, and,

cautioned both by her brother and her father, she meets the advances of *Hamlet* with repulsion. Instead of attributing this to its true cause, he thinks she spurns his tenderness. In his enumeration of the sufferings which stimulate him to suicide, he names " the pangs of *despised* love," and his first experiment of assumed madness is made upon her. He treats her with a revolting mixture of ardent passion, of gross indelicacy, and of rudeness little short of brutality—at one moment he is worshipping at her feet—at the next, insulting her with coarse indecency—at the third, taunting her with sneering and sarcastic advice to go to a nunnery. And is this the language of splendid intellect in alliance with acute feeling? Aye—under the unsupportable pressure of despised love, combined with a throne lost by usurpation, and a father murdered by a mother and an uncle, an incestuous marriage between the criminals, and the apparition, from the eternal world, of his father's spirit, commanding him to avenge the deed.

The revelation from the ghost caps the climax of calamity. It unsettles that ardent and meditative mind—you see it in the tone of levity instantly assumed upon the departure of the " perturbed spirit " —you see it in the very determination to " put on an antic disposition." It is the expedient of a deadly, but *irresolute* purpose. He will execute the command of his father, but he will premeditate the time, the place, the occasion, and to fore-arrange the most convenient opportunity, will feign occasional madness with intervals of clear and steady rational conversation. And thus it is that "the native hue of resolution is sicklied o'er with the pale cast of thought."

This perpetual action and reaction between the mind and the heart; the feeling spurring him on, and the reflection holding him back, constitute that most admirable portrait of human nature, in its highest estate little lower than angels, little above the Hottentots of the African cape, which pervades every part of the character of *Hamlet*. The habitual turn of his mind is to profound meditation. He reflects upon life, upon death, upon the nature of man, upon the physical composition of the universe. He indulges in minute criticism upon the performance of the players; he reads and comments upon a satire of Juvenal; he quibbles with a quibbling grave-digger; commemorates the convivial attractions of an old jovial table companion, whose bones the good man Delver turns up in digging the grave for *Ophelia*, and philosophizes upon the dust of imperial Cæsar, metamorphosed into the bung of a beer barrel. During all this time he is charged with the command of his father, rising from the dead, to take the life of his murderer, to execute divine justice, in the punishment of his crime. He is firmly resolved to execute this command—has frequent opportunities for the execution of it, which he suffers to escape him, and is constantly reproaching himself for his delays. He shrewdly detects and ingeniously disconcerts the practices of the murderers against his life; discloses to his mother his knowledge of her guilt. Kills *Polonius* most rashly, *pretending* to kill a rat, and *intending* to kill the king, whom he supposes to be the person behind the arras, and to have been there listening and overhearing his terrible expostulations with his mother. When he discovers that the person he has killed was not the king, but *Polonius*, instead of compunction and remorse, he begins by a cruel joke upon the dead body, and finishes by an apologetic burst of indignation at the wretched, rash, *intruding* fool, who had hidden himself behind the arras to overhear the interview with his mother. Yet the man whom he has killed is the *father* of *Ophelia*, whom he loves to distraction, and whose madness and death are immediate consequences of this murder of her father. Shakespeare has taken care not to bring *Hamlet* and *Ophelia* into the presence of each other after this event. He takes no notice at the grave-digging scene, that the grave over which he so pathetically and humorously disserts upon the bones of Yorick, the king's jester, was about to receive the corpse of OPHELIA.* Afterwards, at the funeral scene, he treats *Laertes* as roughly, but finally apologizes to him, and desires him to attribute his violence and unkind treatment to his mad-

---

* Hamlet did not then know of it.—J. H. H.

ness. The reasoning faculty of *Hamlet* is at once sportive, sorrowful, indignant, and melancholy. His reflections always take the tinge of the passion under which he is laboring, but his conduct is always governed by the *impulse* of the moment. Hence his madness, as you have remarked, is sometimes feigned, and sometimes real. His feigned madness, *Polonius*, without seeing through it, perceives has *method* in it. His real madness is *towering passion*, transient—momentary—the *furor brevis* which was the ancient definition of anger. It overwhelms at once the brightest genius, the soundest reason, and the kindliest heart that was ever exhibited in combination upon the stage. It is *man* in the ideal perfection of his intellectual and moral nature, struggling with calamity beyond his power to bear, inflicted by the crime of his fellow man—struggling with agonizing energy against it—sinking under it to extinction. What can be more terrific? What can be more piteous?

This is the hasty outline of my view of the character of *Hamlet*. I regret that time will not allow me to fill the canvas with lights and shades borrowed from the incidents and dialogue of the play. But after bestowing so much of my own tediousness upon you, I can only repeat my thanks for the perusal of your own very ingenious comments upon this incomparable tragedy, and add the assurance of my best wishes for your health and happiness, and of my cordial sympathies with your devotion to the memory of the immortal bard.

John Quixcy Adams.

N. B. When the foregoing reached my hand, I was preparing to embark for England.

Immediately upon receipt of Mr. Adams's letter I sent it to Mr. Philip Hone (ex-Mayor of New York), and received from him the following :—

Thursday, 7th March, 1839.

Dear Sir :—I herewith return to you the delightful letter of Mr. Adams, of which (anticipating your consent) I have kept a copy. I am fortunate in having been, incidentally, the means of furnishing you with such a treasure. What an astonishing man this is ! Engaged in all important public measures—never out of his seat in Congress—working more laboriously in anything he undertakes than any other person I ever knew, acquainted with all subjects, and thoroughly with most; and trifling like a youthful poet when he first begins to "lisp in numbers" with subjects that other wise men disdain to stoop to ; such are the pursuits of this truly great man. It is like the lordly eagle coming down from his "pride of place" to sip with the humming-bird the sweets of every flower. But such subjects as this treated of in your letter constitute the relaxation of Mr. Adams's mind. I wish he would give us more of *Hamlet* and "such like things!"

Your friend and servant,
PHILIP HONE.

James H. Hackett, Esq.

Mr. Hackett to Mr. Adams.

22 CHARLOTTE STREET, BEDFORD SQUARE, }
LONDON, 24th July, 1839. }

To the Hon. John Quincy Adams, Boston:

DEAR SIR—I have at length an opportunity to acknowledge your obliging favor of 19th Feb. last, which was duly received by me at New York, prior to my sailing thence for this country. That you should have esteemed me worthy of such pains will remain graven on my memory as one of the most gratifying incidents of my life, and your autograph document shall be treasured in my archives.

The elements of which that matchless character, Shakespeare's *Hamlet*, is compounded, are generally as justly analyzed by you, as they are throughout beautifully described; but there are some causes you impute as contributing essentially to his madness, about which I beg leave to differ, and quote here and there a sentence of yours, the better to refresh your memory. "*Love disappointed and subdued.*" Now I have always considered *filial piety*, in both *Hamlet* and *Ophelia*, the most prominently developed trait of character; a father's fate, in both cases, operates so powerfully on their sensitive natures, as finally to overthrow the seat of reason; their love for each other was quite secondary; in pursuance of his voluntary oath to the *Ghost*, that "thy remembrance all *alone* shall live," &c., unmixed with baser matter, *Hamlet's* first scheme is to feign madness, and he begins "to put an antic disposition on" in the presence of *Ophelia*, for whom he was reputed to entertain a tender affection, in order, as it seems to me, that she may (as she does) tell her father, and that *Polonius's* garrulity may advertise the whole court of his being mad for her love—a cause and effect calculated to mislead and calm the apprehensions of the guilty *usurper*, and better enable *Hamlet* to scrutinize his unguarded behavior thereafter.

Had *Ophelia's* love for *Hamlet* been strong, she would naturally not have yielded so readily to become the medium of assisting the espionage of her parasitical father and the complotting king, when it is proposed, in her presence, to "let her loose to *Hamlet*," whilst they watch them behind the arras; and here let me remark upon your sentence—"*he treats her with a revolting mixture of ardent passion, of gross indelicacy, and of rudeness little short of brutality*"—that from his previous conduct "when she was sewing in her chamber," he knows she esteems him *mad*, and will not feel wounded at anything he may say. For example, when he is most censorious of her father, she prays, "Oh, help him,

you sweet heavens!"   Further extenuation may be
found in another, and not unreasonable *supposition*,
that, at the *time*, *Hamlet* had some lurking suspicion of her unfair position; else, why change his
tone so suddenly from the incipient complimentary
supplication, "Nymph in thy orisons be all my sins
remembered!" to such pointed rebuke.   When
asked—"Are you *honest?*" she evades a categorical
answer by "My lord!" then he follows—"Are you
fair?" and explains to her why, if she is both, and
would preserve her honesty from the contaminating
influences of beauty, she should not admit them to
any discourse with each other, "because the power
of *beauty* will sooner transform honesty from what
it is into a [corrupt] bawd, than the force of honesty
will translate beauty into his [honesty's] likeness,
now the time gives proof."   (As here is she herself,
for instance, allowing the effect of her *beauty* upon
him to be used by her father for a sinister purpose,
and at the expense of her *honesty*.)   He "did love
her once," but upon consideration "loved her not,"
finding that she has inherited so much of her "old
stock" (viz. her father's courtier-like insincerity), as
to render her nature incapable of thorough honesty;
"for virtue cannot so inoculate our old stock but
we shall relish of it."   "We are arrant knaves
all!"   The aptitude of his epigrammatic sentiments,
whether from accident or design, evidently embar-
rasses and betrays her into an absolute falsehood;
for when questioned, "Where is your father?" she

answers, "At home!" knowing *Polonius* to be a covert listener to them at that moment; and, by the way, be it remembered of this scene, that the *king*, who witnessed it, and was a keen observer, remarks—"Love!—his affections do not that way tend!" and also of her when mad, he says, "This is the poison of deep grief; it springs all from the father's death." In short, *Ophelia* never in her madness alludes to *Hamlet*, nor does *he* but once, subsequently, refer to his love for *her*, and then only when chance informed him of her death, and had brought him to her burial, where, in a fit of temporary derangement, he lets the bravery of *Laertes'* grief "put him into a towering passion," which he afterwards, by way of apology to him, "proclaims —was madness."

Permit me to quote you further :—

"*His love is first trammelled by the conflicting pride of his birth and station operating upon his ambition.*"

As regards *Hamlet's* ambition—in the course of what he stigmatizes to the courtiers "as their trade" with him, he certainly pretends to them his cause of madness is, "I lack advancement!" but this he says *after* he has discovered the necessity of having an eye of them, and a determination to "trust them" only as he would "adders that have fangs;" for in his *first* interview on their arrival, and before he inquires whether they have not been "sent for," he welcomes his old schoolfellows with "Excellent good friends!" and unreservedly scouts their notions of his being ambitious because he esteems Denmark a prison; and when they suggest, "it is too narrow for your mind," adds—"oh, God! I could be bounded in a nutshell, and count myself a king of infinite space, but that I have had bad dreams"—in fact, had he not had "bad dreams" concerning his father's fate, I doubt if disappointed ambition had ever caused him to express regret, much less urged him to any active measures about his deferred succession to the throne of Denmark. You continue —*"and although he has made many tenders of his affection to Ophelia, and hath importuned her with love, in honorable fashion, yet he has made no proposal of marriage to her—he has promised her nothing but love."*

To the consummation of his love by *marriage*, his queen mother refers when scattering flowers during *Ophelia's* obsequies—

> "I hop'd thou should'st have been my Hamlet's *wife*,
> I thought thy bride-bed to have deck'd, sweet maid!
> And not have strew'd thy grave;"

the inference is, that the only reason for a truce to his love pursuit was its interference with a paramount consideration—the performance of his *vow* to his *father's unrevenged* and *perturbed spirit.*—

But you say, "*cautioned both by her brother and her father, she meets the advances of Hamlet with repulsion.*"

Her brother's caution arose, not from a suspicion that *Hamlet's* ambitious pride of " birth and station" would hinder their *marriage*, but that the " state " on which it depended might not confirm his choice, and adds,

> " Then weigh what loss your honor may sustain,
> If with too credent ear you list his songs;
> Or *lose* your *heart;* or your chaste treasure open
> To his unmaster'd importunity."

Her father's command, as he afterwards confesses, sprang from his " fear that *Hamlet* did but trifle, and meant to wreck thee," therefore his " love in honorable fashion and countenanced with all the holy vows of heaven," *Polonius* calls " springes to catch woodcocks," and charges her, " Do not believe his vows," to which she replies, " I shall obey, my lord," and so she does—making it evident that *both* their *loves* were subservient to *filial duty;* but the nicest search cannot detect a line indicating that his heart contained a scrupulous thought that *Ophelia* was beneath his *station*, nor that the repulsion of his letters, or denial of his access, or attempted return of his gifts, was a source of any serious disappointment to him, or, as you think, "*of acute feeling—under the insupportable pressure of despised love;*" inasmuch as he never subsequently refers to either circumstance;—you also say, "*instead of attributing his repulsion to its true cause, he thinks she spurns his tenderness; in his enumeration of the sufferings which stimulate to suicide, he names the pangs of despised love.*"

"The pangs of despised love," in my humble opinion, have no more immediate reference to his own case than "the law's delay, the insolence of office," and the spurns and other vexations to which all "flesh is heir;" and one fact that particularly weakens his self-application of this line is, that the folio edition of 1623 (now received as the best authenticated) reads, not "*despised*," but "disprized love:" a distinction, to my thinking, not without a difference, though corrupters of the text since have not even deigned an excuse for their license;—for as love begets love, and hate, *his* kind, so love that finds itself *despised* instead of returned by its object soon flies the human breast, and its *void becomes supplied* by rank *hatred;* but the pangs of *disprized* love are those of one whose spirit sinks and writhes under the pride-stung consciousness that the being towards whom their own heart yearns, *disprizes* their strong affection;—it is this species of love which, unvalued or entertained with indifference, cannot be diverted or superseded, or, as if *despised*, find a relief in *hatred*—but brooding over its own subtile mortification, produces that poignant melancholy which, rankling in a proud soul, may stimulate to suicide.

A marked characteristic from the outset in *Hamlet*, is, self-dissatisfaction—

> "The time is out of joint—O cursed spite,
> That ever I was born to set it right."

He is a creature of impulse; he cannot take the life of the Regicide when in his power; his heart revolts at so *cold-blooded* a deed, though just; he puts up his sword, and tries to find an excuse to himself in the refined notion that it would be "hire and salary, not revenge," to kill his uncle whilst "praying and purging his soul," who took his father's, unprepared, "with all his crimes broad-blown;" without excitement, his nature is prone to meditation, and all his philosophical reasoning is upon his wrongs and their villanous causer. The player, whose whole function readily yielded to his conceits—the equanimity of *Horatio,* in whose nature the "blood and judgment" are so enviably "co-mingled"—all contrasts serve but to paralyze his own energies, and almost blunt his very purpose, instead of arousing him to indignant action. Thus "conscience makes a coward" of *Hamlet,* who possesses the *moral principle* of a hero, but is deficient in *physical nerve* requisite to avenge *coolly* and *resolutely* his father's murder—an attainment he seems to despair of, after discovering his fatal mistake in killing *Polonius;* and it is *after that event,* that the tumult created in his sensitive soul reaches its climax; and the mind, which though hitherto predisposed has exhibited but *counterfeit frenzy,* breaks forth at intervals of *subsequent excitement,* into paroxysms of *decided madness.*

But the only excuse I can offer to you, for permitting my love of the subject to render me so *diffuse*, is, that I, too, "from boyhood," have been "enthusiastic" in relation to this character, and have habituated myself for years to ponder over its merits—as a miser would over his gold—collating the earliest editions of this play, and searching the *accumulated* annotations of its numerous critics—many of whom, in attempting to explain, have often only mystified the meaning of a *clear original* text, by alterations, omissions, and substitutions, and shown themselves "ignorant as vain," and as wide of the author's design, and as *vexatious* to every *true* lover of the bard, as *must* be some of the actors of our time, who exhibit to audiences, seemingly "capable of nothing but inexplicable dumb show and noise," a sort of *conventional, stage-beau-ideal* of *Hamlet*, *overflowing* with *bustle, starts*, and *rant*, and *entirely destitute* of that *meditative* and *philosophic repose*, which *Shakespeare* has made the *leading feature* of the *character*.

Hoping at no distant day to have the pleasure of a "large discourse" with you, *in person*, about *Hamlet*, and that your useful life, with continued health of body and vigor of mind, may be prolonged for many years,

I remain, honored sir,

Your humble servant, ever,

JAS. H. HACKETT.

I was in the habit of meeting daily at the Garrick Club, London, Mr. James Smith, one of the brothers who were authors of the celebrated "*Rejected Addresses.*" I submitted to his perusal Mr. Adams's letter, dated 19th February, 1839, together with my reply, dated 24th July ensuing, which he returned with a note of which what follows is a copy.

27 Craven Street,
Thursday, 15th August, 1839.

Many thanks, my dear sir, for the Lithographic Correspondence between yourself and the ex-President, Mr. Adams, upon the subject of *Hamlet.* That gentleman's notion of the character is ingenious : but yours is (to quote the words of *Osric*) " a palpable hit."

Yours very truly,
James Smith.

Mr. Smith intimated his desire that I should forward to his brother *Horatio* at *Brighton*, where he resided, copies also of the same correspondence, which I did accordingly, and received from him the following letter :

12 Cavendish Place, 26 September, 1839.

Dear Sir—I feel much flattered by your obliging letter and its very interesting inclosures, which will be preserved with care as a valuable addition to the contents of my portfolio. How inexhaustible are the pleasures afforded by our Immortal Bard, since the most attractive portions of our current literature are the endless study of his characters, and the expansion of his illimitable ideas. You must have bestowed much thought indeed upon the character of *Hamlet*, and I incline to side with you, wherever you are opposed to the views of the enlightened and venerable Mr. Adams. Schlegel's critique upon *Hamlet* is perhaps the most original and conclusive that has yet been published, and how happy is his image of the delicate vase being shattered by the expansion of the plant committed to it !

As an ardent admirer of America and its noble institutions, I am ever proud to make acquaintance with your countrymen, and I much regret that my absence from Brighton prevented my paying my respects to Mr. Willis during his visit.

Pray command my services here if they can be made available, and believe me with many thanks,

Your obliged and obedient servant,

HORATIO SMITH.

James H. Hackett, Esq.

I was indebted to my friend Mr. James Fenimore Cooper, in 1844, for an introduction (by letter from New York) to the *Hon. Charles Augustus Murray*, then Master of the Queen's household. Mr. Murray had visited America whilst I was abroad, and by his intelligence and very agreeable social manners

had made many strong personal friends in the
United States. He made a tour through the Western States, and afterwards wrote his "*Prairie
Bird.*"

He is a younger son of the Earl of Dunmore. I
loaned him for perusal my notes and comments
upon *Hamlet* and *Lear*, and upon some of their
stage-representatives, which he returned with a letter, of which the following is a copy.

BUCKINGHAM PALACE, January 30, 1845.

My DEAR SIR :—I beg to return you your notes
on *Lear* and *Hamlet* with many thanks: it would
be impertinent in me to pretend to any opinion on
the professional peculiarities of most of the parties
referred to, as I have had few if any opportunities
of seeing them on the stage; but I can truly say
that many of the thoughts and reflections on the
intention and conception of the Great Dramatist
seem to me extremely just, discriminating, and well
defined: I only regret that my early departure*
will prevent my having the pleasure of seeing them
embodied in the person of their author next month
on the boards of Covent Garden.

Believe me, my dear sir,

Very truly yours,

CHAS. A. MURRAY.

---

* Mr. Murray had just been appointed by the Queen Her Britannic
Majesty's *Consul to Egypt*, and had resigned his position as *Equerry
to Prince Albert.*

I originally made the personal acquaintance of *Serjeant* (afterwards *Sir Thomas Noon*) *Talfourd* at the Garrick Club, London, where we used to meet often and chat familiarly, and whence we occasionally proceeded together to one or other of the theatres to witness any extraordinary performance. He had frequently referred to my correspondence with ex-President Adams respecting *Hamlet*, and I loaned him my volume of notes, comments, and criticisms upon the actors, which, as I knew his engrossing professional occupation, I requested him to retain and look through at his entire convenience and intervals of leisure. Upon its return it was accompanied by a note, whereof the following is a copy.

SERGEANT'S INN, 23d June, 1845.

MY DEAR SIR:—I return your manuscript with my best thanks. I regret that the very anxious trials in which I am engaged at this season has not permitted me to contemplate with the attention the subject deserves your delightful recollections; but I have seen enough of them to feel that they are among the most intellectual the stage can give a nation.

Believe me I remain, my dear sir,
Very truly yours,
T. N. TALFOURD.

J. H. Hackett, Esq.

ORIGINAL IN MY PORTFOLIO.

Copy of the last Letter received from the Honorable John Quincy Adams, Ex-President of the United States.

QUINCY, 4 Nov. 1845.

To James H. Hackett, Esq.

TREMONT HOUSE, *Boston.*

MY DEAR SIR—I return herewith the very interesting volume of your manuscript notes upon Shakespeare, and upon the representation of several of the persons of his Drama by sundry eminent performers of our cotemporaries.

I thank you for the privilege of perusing these notes and for your letter, and, in conformity with your request, I inclose herewith and ask your acceptance of a few scattered leaves, containing remarks of mine upon *Othello, Romeo and Juliet,* and *Lear.** They were written in letters to a friend who thought them worthy of publication with my consent, although by many of their readers they have been deemed paradoxical, perhaps heretical. The remarks upon the character of *Desdemona* have been thought by many of her admirers, unreasonably severe, and perhaps the opposition they have encountered may have tended to confirm me in my own opinions. Mrs. Inchbald's almost adoration of

* Since *bound* hereinafter.—J. H. H.

the cunning ————* that's "married to *Othello*," and Dr. Johnson's grave admiration of the artless simplicity of the "super-subtle Venetian," are strangely at variance with my estimation of the sound canons of criticism. The same Dr. Johnson, in his life of *Dryden*, says, that when hard pressed by the critics of his time, upon the immorality of his comedies, as a last resort he turned upon his accusers and denied that a comic poet was under any obligation to preach morality. Pope, however, is not of the same opinion, with regard to tragedy.

> " To wake the soul by tender strokes of art,
>   To raise the genius and to mend the heart.
>   To make mankind in conscious virtue bold,
>   Live o'er each scene and be what they behold.
>   *For this*, the Tragic Muse first had the stage,
>   Commanding tears to stream thro' every age.
>   Tyrants no more their savage nature kept,
>   And foes to virtue wondered why they wept."

Tragedy, then, is, in its nature, pre-eminently devoted to Morals; but when, in one of the inclosed papers, I said that in the days of manhood I had studied Shakespeare chiefly as a teacher of morals, I was answered, after the manner of Dryden, that this was degrading Shakespeare to the level of Esop.

In France, the theatre is sometimes made the school of Politics, and in England it would have

---

* A *word* which his *daughter* could not be expected to *write*—therefore omitted.

been made so, but for the counter-check of the Lord Chamberlain's license. In the month, I think, of April, 1785, I was present in the Cathedral church of Notre Dame, and witnessed a solemn procession of Louis the Sixteenth, then called "Louis le bien faisant," with all his Court to return thanks to Almighty God in His Holy Temple for the birth of the Duke of Normandy, his second son, who, not long afterwards, by the decease of his elder brother, became the Dauphin of France, and was the hapless child, who, a few years later, perished an apprentice to a shoemaker, under the discipline of Revolutionary France. The Bourbon family and their adherents call him " Louis the Seventeenth," and his fate, in the vicissitudes of human life, closely resembles that of the person called " Edward the Fifth," in the History of England. The solemn procession of the absolute monarch of France to the Te Deum of that day, made a deep impression upon my mind. More than six years before I had witnessed the most splendid illumination of Paris that my eyes ever beheld, upon the birth of the first child of the same Louis the Sixteenth, the Duchess of Angoulême. On both these occasions it seemed as if there was one universal burst of joy throughout the whole kingdom of France. But, not many days after the Te Deum at the Cathedral church of Notre Dame, I saw performed at the Theatre Français, the tragedy of Rhadamisthe et Zénobie, by the elder Crébillon. In that tragedy, the principal character, being himself king of Armenia, appears as an ambassador from Rome at the Court of his own father, King of Iberia, and, after complaining, in the name of the Roman Republic, of certain preparations for war on the part of the King of Armenia,* which had excited the jealousy of the Roman Republic, he says in a tone of insolent menace—

> " Rome, de tant d'apprêts qui s'indigne et se lasse,
>   N'a point accoutumer *les Rois* à tant d'audace."†
>   [*Crebillon's Tragedy of Rhadamisthe et Zenobie.*

Never in the course of my attendance upon theatrical performances throughout my life, did I hear a more deafening and universal shout of applause, than upon the delivery of these two lines, marked by the peculiar emphasis with which the actor dwelt upon the words "*les Rois.*" I shall never forget the effect of this incident upon my reflections at the time. Louis the Sixteenth was yet an absolute king—he seemed still seated in the affections of his people, who still boasted of their attachment beyond all other nations to the persons of their sovereigns. His reign had been successful and glorious! How often since the Te Deum for the birth of the Duke of Normandy and the perform-

---

* *Iberia*, I think Mr. Adams intended, and dictated to his daughter, who at that date was his social amanuensis.—J. H. H.

† Rome, outraged and weary of such preparations,
  Has never accustomed *Kings* to such audacity.—J. H. H.

ance of Crébillon's tragedy—occurring so nearly at the same time—have those two incidents reminded me of the lines of Gray's bard—

> " Fair laughs the Morn, and soft the Zephyr blows,
>   While proudly riding o'er the azure realm
> In gallant trim the gilded vessel goes;
>   Youth on the prow and Pleasure at the helm;
> Regardless of the sweeping Whirlwind's sway,
> That, hushed in grim repose, expects his evening prey."

Let me return to Shakespeare. As a teacher of morals, you will perceive that, in the inclosed papers, I have expressed the opinion that he was not sufficiently so considered by the performers of his personages upon the stage. I excepted Mrs. Siddons, whose—

> " I say, take heed, my lord!"

I shall never forget. When these remarks were written, I had never seen you upon the boards, and had not the pleasure of your acquaintance. I hope that, upon the character of *Desdemona*—upon the absurdity of restoring *Lear* to his Crown, and upon the age of *Juliet*, I shall not find myself so wide from the coincidence of your judgment as I have from that of many other admirers of the Swan of Avon.

Not intending to try your temper with a sermon in return for the pleasure which I have received from your manuscript, I will close with the assurance of my grateful and respectful esteem.

(Signed) JOHN QUINCY ADAMS.

NOTE.—Mr. Adams was born July 11, 1767. Died *in the Capitol* at Washington, Feb. 23, 1848.

MISCONCEPTIONS OF SHAKESPEARE, UPON THE STAGE.

BY J. Q. ADAMS.

My admiration of Shakespeare, as a profound delineator of human nature and a sublime poet, is but little short of idolatry. I think he is often misunderstood, as performed on the stage.

The character of *Juliet*, for example, is travestied almost into burlesque, by the alteration of the text in the scene where the nurse, with so much precision, fixes her age (*Act* 1, *Scene* 3). The nurse declares she knows it to an hour, and that next Lammas eve (which Lady Capulet says will be in a fortnight and odd days) she will be *fourteen*. Upon this precise age, the character of *Juliet*, her discourse, her passion, and the deep pathos of the interest that we take in her fate, very largely repose. Born under Italian skies, she is at the very moment of transition from the child to the woman. Her

10

love is the pure impulse of intelligent, sensitive
nature—*first love*—unconscious and undissembled
nature, childhood expanding into maturity, physical
and intellectual—all innocence, all ardor, all ecstasy.
How irresistibly are our sympathies moved at seeing
the blossom blasted at the very moment while it is
opening to the sun!   As the play is performed on
the stage, the nurse, instead of saying that *Juliet*, at
the next Lammas eve, will be fourteen, says she will
be *nineteen*.   Nineteen!   In what country of the
world was a young lady of nineteen ever constantly
attended by a nurse?   Between the ages of thirteen and fourteen, a nurse, in a noble Italian family
of the middle ages, was not yet an unnatural companion.   On the verge of nineteen, the nurse is not
only supernumerary, but very much out of place.
Take away the *age* of Juliet, and you take away
from her all her individuality, all the consistency
of her character, all that childish simplicity, which,
blended with the fervor of her passion, constitutes
her greatest charm.   In what but in that, and in
everything which she does and says, congenial to
that age, does she differ from *Viola*, from *Miranda*,
from *Ophelia*, and indeed from all the lovely daughters of Shakespeare's muse?   They are all in love,
but you can never mistake one of them for another.
The peculiarities of *Juliet* all have reference to her
age; and that which in her mouth is enchanting,
would seem but frothy nonsense from a woman five
years older.   *Juliet* says—

> " And when Romeo dies,
> Take him and cut him up in little stars,
> And he shall make the face of Heaven so fine,
> That all the world shall grow in love with night,
> And pay no worship to the garish sun."

In the incomparable beauty of this passage, as spoken by a girl under fourteen, there is something too childish for a woman of nineteen, however desperately in love.　One, who has been accustomed to personate *Juliet* as a young woman of nineteen, may see no incongruity with that age in her character; yet that one, who has herself passed through both those stages of life, should not understand the difference of maturity between the ages of fourteen and of nineteen in the female sex, is scarcely conceivable.　That Shakespeare should have confounded them, is impossible.　That he intended to make the *age* of Juliet an exposition of her character, is evident from the special care he has taken to make the nurse announce it.　If the meanest of dramatists were to undertake to write a tragedy, and to draw the character and to repeat the discourse of a girl of fourteen, attended throughout the play by a nurse, can we imagine that he would change the age to nineteen and yet retain the nurse, and give to the full-formed woman the same character and the same tone of dialogue which he would to the ripening child of fourteen?　Such a writer would prove himself as poor a proficient in the school of human nature as in that of Shakespeare.*

In that ever memorable delineation of the Life of man, and its division into "seven ages," by Jaques, in the comedy of "As you Like it," the meditative moralist says that each man in his turn plays many parts. He says, too, that all the men and *women* are merely players. In coming to the details, he exhibits only the seven ages of the *man;* but there was certainly in the mind of the poet a corresponding division in the ages of the *woman;* and Juliet, at any age short of fourteen, and yet under the care of a nurse, partakes at once, in the relation of her sex, of the school-boy with his satchel and shining morning face, creeping like a snail unwillingly to school, and of the lover sighing like a furnace, with a woful ballad made to his mistress's eyebrow. Shakespeare was not the observer and painter of

---

* The history and traditions of the stage do not furnish a single instance of an *actress* who by Nature or Art seemed not more than *nineteen* years of age, and yet was able to perform with adequate effect the latter portion of the character of *Juliet.* The most *famous* representatives have attained to an age of twenty-five or thirty years *prior* to an acquirement of the pre-requisites of mind, art, and *experience upon the stage.* It has been generally in an actress asking quite indulgence enough of an audience to *suppose* her age not more than "*nineteen;*" whereas, had any called it "*fourteen,*" instead of a passing wink of silent consent, she would have been very apt to cause a general titter, and among the rude spectators some derisive laughter. The alteration of "fourteen" to nineteen, is one of the absolute necessities of stage representation. Mrs. Siddons is said to have continued acceptable as *Juliet* when over forty-three years of age.—*J. H. Hackett.*

nature, to confound them together. If *he* had exhibited in action a school-boy of between thirteen and
fourteen, think you that he would have given him
the features, or inspired him with the language and
ideas of a lover at nineteen? Our youth at fourteen
are yet under the age of passing from the school to
the university; at nineteen, many of them have
already closed their career at the university and
passed into the busy scenes of active life. The
female mind and person hastens also to maturity in
advance of the male; and a woman at nineteen is
generally more completely formed than a man at
twenty-one.

Shakespeare, with his intuitive sagacity, has also
marked the characteristics of the *change* between
these two of his "seven ages." In the "Merchant
of Venice," when Portia proposes to Nerissa that
they should assume male attire and go to Venice,
she says—

> "I'll hold thee any wager,
> When we are both apparell'd like young men,
> I'll prove the prettier fellow of the two,
> And wear my dagger with the braver grace,
> *And speak between the change of man and boy*
> With a reed voice; and turn two mincing steps
> Into a manly stride; and speak of frays
> Like a fine bragging youth; and tell quaint lyes
> How honorable ladies sought my love,
> Which I denying, they fell sick and died.
> I could not do withal: then I'll repent,
> And wish, for all that, that I had not kill'd them—

> And twenty of these puny lyes I'll tell,
> That men shall swear *I've discontinued school*
> *Above a twelvemonth.*"*

Tragedy, according to the admirable definition of Aristotle, is a poem imitative of human life, and the object of which is to purify the soul of the spectator by the agency of terror and pity. The terror is excited by the incidents of the story and the sufferings of the person represented; the pity, by the interest of sympathy with their characters. Terror and pity are moved by the mere aspect of human sufferings; but the sympathy is strong or weak, in proportion to the interest that we take in the *character* of the sufferer. With this definition of tragedy, "Romeo and Juliet" is a drama of the highest order. The incidents of terror and the sufferings of the principal persons of the drama arouse every sympathy of the soul, and the interest of sympathy with Juliet. She unites all the interest of ecstatic love, of unexampled calamity, and of the peculiar tenderness which the heart feels for innocence in childhood. Most truly, then, says the Prince of Verona, at the conclusion of the play—

> "For never was a story of more wo
> Than this of Juliet and her Romeo."

The age of Juliet seems to be the key to her character throughout the play, an essential ingredient

---

* Act 3, Scene 5.

in the intense sympathy which she inspires; and Shakespeare has marked it, not only in her discourse, but even in her name, the diminutive of tender affections applied only to childhood. If Shakespeare had exhibited upon the stage a woman of nineteen, he would have dismissed her nurse and called her Julia. She might still have been a very interesting character, but the whole color and complexion of the play must have been changed. An intelligent, virtuous woman, in love with a youth of assorted age and congenial character, is always a person of deep interest in the drama. But that interest is heightened and redoubled when, to the sympathy with the lover, you add all the kind affections with which you share in the joys and sorrows of the child. There is childishness in the discourse of Juliet, and the poet has shown us why; because she had scarcely ceased to be a child. There is nonsense in the alteration of Shakespeare's text upon the stage.

There are several of the most admired plays of Shakespeare which give much more pleasure to read than to see performed upon the stage. For instance, *Othello* and *Lear*; both of which abound in beauty of detail, in poetical passages, in highly-wrought and consistently preserved characters. But, the pleasure that we take in witnessing a performance upon the stage, depends much upon the sympathy that we feel with the sufferings and enjoyments of the good characters represented, and upon the punishment of the bad. We never can sympathize much with *Desdemona* or with *Lear*, because we never can separate them from the estimate that the lady is little less than a wanton, and the old king nothing less than a dotard. Who can sympathize with the love of *Desdemona?*—the daughter of a Venetian nobleman, born and educated to a splendid and lofty station in the community. She falls in love and makes a runaway match with a blackamoor, for no better reason than that he has told her a braggart story of his hair-breadth escapes in war. For this, she not only violates her duties to her father, her family, her sex, and her country, but she makes the first advances. She tells *Othello* she wished Heaven had made her such a man, and informs him how *any* friend of his may win her by telling her again his story. On *that* hint, says he, I spoke; and well he might. The blood must circulate briskly in the veins of a young woman, so fascinated, and so coming to the tale of a rude, unbleached African soldier.

The great moral lesson of the tragedy of *Othello* is, that black and white blood cannot be intermingled in marriage without a gross outrage upon the law of Nature; and that, in such violations, Nature will vindicate her laws. The moral of *Othello* is not to beware of jealousy, for jealousy is well founded in the character and conduct of his wife, though not in the fact of her infidelity with *Cassio*. *Desdemona* is not false to her husband, but she has been false to the purity and delicacy of her sex and condition when she married him ; and the last words spoken by her father on parting from them, after he has forgiven her and acquiesced in the marriage, are—

> " Look to her, Moor; have a quick eye to see:
> She has deceived her father, and may thee."

And this very idea is that by which the crafty villain *Iago* works up into madness the jealousy of *Othello*.

Whatever sympathy we feel for the sufferings of *Desdemona* flows from the consideration that she is innocent of the particular crime imputed to her, and that she is the victim of a treacherous and artful intriguer. But, while compassionating her melancholy fate, we cannot forget the vice of her character. Upon the stage, her fondling with *Othello* is disgusting. Who, in real life, would have her for a sister, daughter, or wife? She is not guilty of infidelity to her husband, but she forfeits all the affection of her father and all her own filial affection for him. When the duke proposes, on the departure of *Othello* for the war, that she should return during his absence to her father's house, the father, the daughter and the husband all say " No!" She prefers following *Othello*, to be besieged by the Turks in the island of Cyprus.

The character of *Desdemona* is admirably drawn and faithfully preserved throughout the play. It is always deficient in delicacy. Her conversations with

Emilia indicate unsettled principles, even with regard to the obligations of the nuptial tie, and she allows *Iago*, almost unrebuked, to banter with her very coarsely upon women. This character takes from us so much of the sympathetic interest in her sufferings, that when *Othello* smothers her in bed, the terror and the pity subside immediately into the sentiment that she has her deserts.*

We feel a similar want of interest in the character and fortunes of *Lear*, as represented upon the stage. The story of *Lear*, as those of *Othello* and *Romeo* and *Juliet*, was ready-made to the hand of Shakespeare. They were not of his invention. *King Lear* and his three daughters form a part of the fabulous history of England. The dotage of an abso-

---

* I must differ materially with Mr. Adams in his estimate of the character of *Desdemona*. She had frequently seen *Othello* when invited by her father to his domicile—she was struck by his valiant parts, and became so infatuated that she saw *Othello's* visage only in his mind, and eventually resolved to consecrate to him her life and fortunes as his wife.

I agree with Mr. Adams respecting the *moral* which Shakespeare designed to convey so far as it involves a caution to fathers that they should " never introduce to their domestic hearths where they have a daughter, young, warm-hearted, and very susceptible of impression, any man, who, from his nature or his conditions in life, might, if such daughter happened to fancy him, prove an unsuitable husband for her." Because, there is no accounting for differences of taste, and often the obstinacy of some women's natures will induce them to entertain a man's professions of love and admiration, and yield to his fascinations, the more readily from being *put upon their guard* against him as " an *improper* suitor;" especially certain *young* girls, with whom passion is often stronger than reason.—*J. H. Hackett.*

lute monarch may be a suitable subject of tragedy;
and Shakespeare has made a deep tragedy of it.
But, as exhibited upon the stage, it is turned into a
comedy. *Lear*, the dotard and the madman, is
restored to his throne, and *Cordelia* finishes with a
wedding. What can be more absurd!

Dotage and madness, in the person of a king, possessed of the power to give away his kingdom at
his pleasure, afford melancholy contemplations of
human nature. They are not fit subjects for comedy.
Lear is no more fit to be restored to his kingdom
than *Christopher Sly* is to be metamorphosed into
a lord.* *Lear* is a dotard and a madman from the
first scene in the play, and his insanity commences
with such revolting injustice to his only affectionate
daughter, that we feel but little *compassion* for
whatever may afterwards befall him. The interesting character of the play is *Cordelia;* and what a
lovely character it is! But the restoration of a
dotard from old age to his senses is as much out of

* After seeing *Edmund Kean* perform *Lear* at New York in 1826,
I expressed to him my surprise at his choice of Nahum Tate's alteration to the *great Original's* conclusion of the tragedy. Mr. Kean
observed:—"I do not prefer it, but I first studied Tate's alteration
and acted accordingly, because it was popular. Afterwards I restored
Shakespeare's text and conclusion, and acted *that;* but, when I had
ascertained that a large majority of the public—whom we live to
please, and must please to be popular—liked Tate better than Shakespeare, I fell back upon his corruption; though in my soul I was
ashamed of the prevailing taste, and of my professional condition that
required me to minister unto it."

nature as the restoration to his throne is preposterous. *Lear*, as Shakespeare painted him, is the wreck of a mighty mind and proud spirit, sunk from despotic power into dotage, and maddened by the calamitous consequences of his own imbecility. His madness, with lucid flashes of intellect, is incurable. It is terrible! it is piteous! But it is its effect on the fortunes and fate of *Cordelia* that constitutes the chief interest of the spectator; and *Lear* himself, from his first appearance, loses all title to compassion.*

The chief import of these objections to the manner in which Shakespeare's plays are represented upon the stage, is to vindicate the great " master of the drama " from the liberties taken by stage-managers with his text. In *Romeo and Juliet*, the alteration of a single word—the substitution of nineteen for fourteen—changes the whole character of the play—makes that, which is a perfect imitation of nature, incongruous absurdity, and takes from one of the loveliest creations of Shakespeare half her charm.

* Shakespeare has pointed the moral the more strongly by letting *Cordelia* find suffering in life and eventually share death with her father; when the doting and imbecile Octogenarian despot was in the act of dividing his kingdom, and coveted, and expected, and exacted of each of his daughters their warmest expressions of filial affection, *Cordelia*, instead of gently and innocently humoring her weak but loving and *partial* father, showed the slight but only fault in her character, by obstinacy and reserve. To her truth and coldness, and her father's rashness and folly, *then* may be traced the primary causes of the sad catastrophe.—*J. H. Hackett.*

PERSONATIONS OF THE CHARACTERS OF SHAKESPEARE.

(EXTRACTS FROM THE MS. LETTERS OF A CELEBRATED PERSONAGE.)

I HAVE been, man and boy, a reader of Shakespeare at least three score years. A pocket edition of him was among the books of my mother's nursery-library, and at ten years of age I was as familiarly acquainted with his lovers and his clowns, as with Robinson Crusoe, the Pilgrim's Progress, and the Bible. In later years I have left Robinson and the Pilgrim to the perusal of the children; but have continued to read the Bible and Shakespeare, always recognising the precedence of veneration due to the holy Scriptures.

I have read Shakespeare as a *teacher of morals*—as a student of human nature—as a painter of life and manners—as an anatomical dissecter of the passions—as an artificer of imaginary worlds—as at once the sublimest and most philosophic of poets.

When I say that my admiration of Shakespeare is little short of idolatry, I mean to be understood that it is *not* idolatry—that I hold him amenable to the common laws of criticism, and feel at liberty to censure in him, as well the vices of his age, which abound in all his plays, as his own faults, from which he is by no means exempt. Yet, admiring him as I do, with all his blemishes, I take no pleasure in dwelling upon them. My remarks were confined to the different impressions made upon me by the true Shakespeare in my closet, and by the spurious Shakespeare often exhibited upon the stage.

I had been more than seven years a reader of Shakespeare before I saw any of his plays performed. Fifty-two years have passed away since I first saw John Kemble, in the vigor of early manhood, personate, upon the boards of Drury Lane, the character of *Hamlet*. It was the first play that I ever saw performed in England—the first of Shakespeare's plays that I had seen performed anywhere—and I was disappointed. I had been much accustomed to the theatres of France—far advanced beyond those of England in the art of dramatic representation—and although John Kemble was then in his prime, and *Hamlet* was one of his favorite parts, in the comparison which crowded upon my mind, between Drury Lane and the Theatre Français at Paris, and between the *Hamlet* of John Kemble and the *Hamlet* which I had by heart from Shakespeare, the Prince of Denmark himself, the most admirable of all Shakespeare's *portraits of man*, became to me a weary, flat, stale, and unprofitable personage. Such was the impression left upon me by the first exhibition that I ever witnessed of Shakespeare upon the stage; and that impression, after the lapse of more than half a century, remains uneffaced, and, while memory holds her seat, uneffaceable from my mind.

I have since then seen almost all the plays of Shakespeare that are ever exhibited upon the stage —Mrs. Siddons, in the character of *Isabella*, of *Queen Catharine*, of *Hamlet's Mother*, and of *Lady Macbeth;* Mrs. Jordan in the characters of *Viola* and of *Ophelia;* Miss Wallace and Miss O'Neil in that of *Juliet;* Mrs. Abington in that of *Beatrice;* Miss Foote in that of *Imogen;* and the parts of *Hamlet, Lear, Othello, Macbeth, Coriolanus, Richard 3d, Falstaff, Mercutio, Benedick, Shylock, Iago, Romeo,* and *Petruchio* by John Kemble, Palmer, Kean, Cooper, Fawcett, Lewis, Macklin, and Booth; besides the parts of *Hamlet* and *Cardinal Wolsey* by Henderson, and the grave-diggers and clowns by Parsons, Quick, Munden, and Liston. There was scarcely an eminent performer at Drury Lane or Covent Garden, for the space of thirty-five years, from 1783 to 1817, but I have seen grapple with some of the persons of Shakespeare's drama. The female parts I have thought generally well performed, though that of *Juliet* was always disfigured by the substitution of that age of nineteen for the original fourteen. The consequence of which has been that the enchanting mixture of childish frailty and innocence, with her burning and hopeless love, which constitute the profound pathos of the tragedy, is entirely lost. Of all the performers that I have ever seen presuming to speak the language, and to convey the thoughts of Shakespeare, Mrs. Siddons has appeared to me to understand them best. Henderson's *Hamlet* and *Wolsey*, Macklin's *Shylock*, Lea Lewis's *Mercutio*, John Kemble's *Lear* and *Macbeth*, Kean's *Richard*, Parsons's *Grave-Digger*, Liston's *Launcelot Gobbo*, Mrs. Jordan's *Viola*, and Mrs. Abington's *Beatrice*, have been among the most renowned of personations of Shakespeare's parts since the days of Garrick. But in my, perhaps eccentric, judgment, no person can deliver the words and ideas of Shakespeare who has not been accustomed to study them as a *teacher of morals*— the *first* of the capacities in which I have looked up to him since, in my career of life, I have passed the third of his seven ages. As a school-boy, I delighted in him as a teller of tales and a joker of jokes. As a lover, I gazed with ecstasy upon the splendors of his imagination, and the heart-cheering, heart-rending joys and sorrows of his lovers. Never as a soldier; but in the age of active manhood, which he allots to that profession, I have resorted to him as a pilgrim to the shrine of a saint, for moral, ay, and for religious instruction. I have found in the *story* of most of his plays, in the *characters* of most of his personages, in the *incidents* of his fables, in the *sentences* of unparalleled solemnity and magnificence, delivered as part of the dialogue of his speakers, nay, in the very conceits and quibbles of his clowns, lessons of the most elevated and comprehensive morality. Some of them have

at times almost tempted me to believe in them as
of more than poetical inspiration. But, excepting
John Kemble and Mrs. Siddons, I never met with a
player who appeared to me to have thought of
Shakespeare as a moralist at all, or to have inquired
what were the morals that he taught; and, as I
have said, John Kemble did not appear to me to
understand the character of *Hamlet.** Garrick
himself attempted to strike out the grave-digger
scene from the tragedy of *Hamlet*, and the very
rabble of London, the gods of the galleries, forced
him to restore it. There is not, in the compass
of the drama, a scene of deeper and more philosophical morality.

* Oh, how I would that Mr. Adams had expressed his reasons!
John Kemble died at Lausanne, in Switzerland, some six years prior
to my first visit to England, and therefore having never had an opportunity of seeing him, I can only form an idea of his claims to pre-
eminence in personating *Hamlet* from tradition or through his contemporary critics; but, I can more readily impute to Mr. Adams
hypercriticism or an eccentric taste, than I can believe that John
Kemble could have been so popular for forty years, and yet not had
at least a *generally good understanding of Hamlet's character.—J. H. H.*

THE CHARACTER OF DESDEMONA.

BY JOHN QUINCY ADAMS.

THERE are critics who cannot bear to see the virtue and delicacy of Shakespeare's *Desdemona* called in question; who defend her on the ground that *Othello* is not an Ethiopian, but a Moor; that he is not black, but only tawny; and they protest against the sable mask of *Othello* upon the stage, and against the pictures of him in which he is always painted black. They say that prejudices have been taken against *Desdemona* from the slanders of *Iago*, from the railings of *Roderigo*, from the disappointed paternal rancor of *Brabantio*, and from the desponding concessions of *Othello* himself.

I have said, that since I entered upon the third of Shakespeare's seven ages, the first and chief capacity in which I have read and studied him is as a *teacher of morals;* and that I had scarcely ever seen a player of his parts who regarded him as a *moralist* at all. I further said, that in my judgment no man could understand him who did *not* study him pre-eminently as a teacher of morals. These critics say they do not incline to put Shakespeare on a level with Æsop! Sure enough *they* do not study Shakespeare as a teacher of morals. To *them,* therefore, *Desdemona* is a perfect character; and her love for *Othello* is not unnatural, because he is not a Congo negro but only a sooty Moor, and has royal blood in his veins.

My objections to the character of *Desdemona* arise not from what *Iago*, or *Roderigo*, or *Brabantio*, or *Othello* says of her; but from what she herself does. She absconds from her father's house, in the dead of night, to marry a blackamoor. She breaks a father's heart, and covers his noble house with shame, to gratify—what? Pure love, like that of *Juliet* or *Miranda?* No! unnatural passion; it cannot be named with delicacy. Her admirers now say this is criticism of 1835; that the color of *Othello* has nothing to do with the passion of *Desdemona.* No? Why, if *Othello* had been white, what need would there have been for her running away with him? She could have made no better match. Her father could have made no reasonable objection to it; and there could have been no tragedy. If the color of *Othello* is not as vital to the whole tragedy as the age of *Juliet* is to her character and destiny, then have I read Shakespeare in vain. The father of *Desdemona* charges *Othello* with magic arts in obtaining the affections of his daughter. Why, but because her passion for him is *unnatural;* and why is it unnatural, but because of his color? In the very first scene, in the dialogue between *Roderigo* and *Iago*, before they rouse *Brabantio* to inform him of his daughter's elopement, *Roderigo* contemptuously calls *Othello* " the thick lips." I cannot in decency quote here—but turn to the book, and see in what language *Iago* announces to her father his daughter's shameful misconduct. The language of *Roderigo* is more supportable. *He* is a Venetian gentleman, himself a rejected suitor of *Desdemona ;* and who has been forbidden by her father access to his house. Roused from his repose at the dead of night by the loud cries of these two men, *Brabantio* spurns, with indignation and scorn, the insulting and beastly language of *Iago ;* and sharply chides *Roderigo*, whom he supposes to be hovering about his house in defiance of his prohibitions and in a state of intoxication. He threatens him with punishment. *Roderigo* replies—

> " *Rod.* Sir, I will answer any thing. But I beseech you,
>   If't be your pleasure, and most wise consent,
>   (As partly, I find, it is), that your fair daughter
>   At this odd-even and dull watch o' the night,
>   Transported—with no worse nor better guard,
>   But with a knave of common hire, a gondolier,—
>   To the gross clasps of a lascivious Moor,—
>   If this be known to you, and your allowance,
>   We then have done you bold and saucy wrongs;
>   But if you know not this, my manners tell me,
>   We have your wrong rebuke. Do not believe,
>   That, from the sense of all civility,
>   I thus would play and trifle with your reverence:
>   Your daughter—if you have not given her leave,—
>   I say again, hath made a gross revolt;
>   Tying her duty, beauty, wit, and fortunes,
>   To an extravagant and wheeling stranger,
>   Of here and every where : Straight satisfy yourself:

> If she be in her chamber, or your house,
> Let loose on me the justice of the state,
> For thus deluding you."

Struck by this speech as by a clap of thunder, *Brabantio* calls up his people, remembers a portentous dream, calls for light, goes and searches with his servants, and comes back saying—

> " It is too true an evil : gone she is :
> And what's to come of my despised time,
> Is nought but bitterness."

The father's heart is broken ; life is no longer of any value to him ; he repeats this sentiment time after time whenever he appears in the scene ; and in the last scene of the play, where *Desdemona* lies dead, her uncle Gratiano says—

> " Poor Desdemona ! I am glad thy father's dead,
> Thy match was mortal to him, and pure grief
> Shore his old thread in twain."

Indeed ! indeed ! I must look at Shakespeare in this, as in all his pictures of human life, in the capacity of a teacher of morals. I must believe that, in exhibiting a daughter of a Venetian nobleman of the highest rank eloping in the dead of the night to marry a thick-lipped wool-headed Moor, opening a train of consequences which lead to her own destruction by her husband's hands, and to that of her father by a broken heart, he did not intend to present her as an example of the perfection of female virtue. I must look first at the action, then at the motive, then at the consequences, before I inquire in what light it is received and represented by the other persons of the drama. The first action of *Desdemona* discards all female delicacy, all filial duty, all sense of ingenuous shame. So I consider it—and so it is considered by her own father. Her offence is not a mere elopement from her father's house for a clandestine marriage. I hope it requires no unreasonable rigor of morality to consider even *that* as suited to raise a prepossession rather unfavorable to the character of a young woman of refined sensibility and elevated education. But an elopement for a clandestine marriage with a blackamoor! That is the measure of my estimation of the character of *Desdemona* from the beginning ; and when I have passed my judgment upon it, and find in the play that from the first moment of her father's knowledge of the act it made him loathe his life, and that it finally broke his heart, I am then in time to inquire, what was the deadly venom which inflicted the immedicable wound :—and what is it, but the color of *Othello ?*

> " Now, Roderigo,
> Where did'st thou see her ?—Oh, unhappy girl !—
> *With the Moor, say'st thou ?*—Who would be a father ?"

These are the disjointed lamentations of the wretched parent when the first disclosure of his daughter's shame is made known to him. This scene is one of the inimitable pictures of human passion in the hands of Shakespeare, and that half line

> " With the *Moor*, say'st thou ?"

comes from the deepest recesses of the soul.

Again, when *Brabantio* first meets *Othello*, he breaks out :

> " O, thou foul thief, where hast thou stow'd my daughter?
>   Damn'd as thou art, thou hast enchanted her :
>   For I'll refer me to all things of sense,
>   If she, in chains of magic were not bound,
>   Whether a maid so tender, fair, and happy,
>   So opposite to marriage that she shunn'd
>   The wealthy *curled* darlings of our nation,
>   Would ever have to incur our general mock,
>   Run from her guardage *to the sooty bosom*
>   Of such a thing as thou ; to fear, not to delight."

Several of the English commentators have puzzled themselves with the inquiry why the epithet " curled" is here applied to the wealthy darlings of the nation ; and Dr. Johnson thinks it has no reference to the hair ; but it evidently has. The *curled* hair is in antithetic contrast to the sooty bosom, the thick lips, and the woolly head.*   The contrast of

---

* " *Wealthy curled darlings.*"

  The negro's hair curled like *wool* naturally ; the Venetians' locks of hair were curled artificially, and betrayed vanity and effeminacy in their desire to become the " darlings" of the *ladies*, whose curls adorn their countenance, and in many of the sex are not produced by nature, but also by the art of the toilette.—*J. H. H.*

color is the very hinge upon which *Brabantio* founds his charge of magic, counteracting the impulse of nature.

At the close of the same scene (the second of the first act), *Brabantio*, hearing that the duke is in council upon public business of the State, determines to carry *Othello* before him for trial upon the charge of magic. "Mine," says he,

> " Mine's not a middle cause; the duke himself
> Or any of my brothers of the State
> Cannot but feel the wrong, as 'twere their own:
> For if such actions may have passage free,
> Bond slaves and Pagans shall our statesmen be."

And Steevens, in his note on this passage, says, " He alludes to the common condition of all blacks who come from their own country, both *slaves* and *pagans;* and uses the word in contempt of *Othello* and his complexion. If this Moor is now suffered to escape with impunity, it will be such an encouragement to his black countrymen, that we may expect to see all the first offices of our state filled up by the Pagans and bond-slaves of Africa." *Othello* himself in his narrative says that he had been taken by the insolent foe and sold to slavery. He *had been* a slave.

Once more—When *Desdemona* pleads to the Duke and the Council for permission to go with *Othello* to Cyprus, she says,

> " That I did love the Moor, to live with him,
> My downright violence and storm of fortune
> May trumpet to the world; *my heart's subdued,*
> *Even to the very quality of my lord;*
> I saw Othello's visage in his mind;
> And to his honours and his valiant parts
> Did I my soul and fortunes consecrate."

In commenting upon this passage, Mr. Henley says, " That *quality* here signifies the Moorish *complexion* of Othello, and not his military profession (as Malone had supposed), is obvious from what immediately follows : ' I saw Othello's visage in his mind;' and also from what the Duke says to *Brabantio*—

> " If virtue no delighted beauty lack
> Your son-in-law is far more fair than black."

The characters of *Othello* and *Iago* in this play are evidently intended as contrasted pictures of human nature, each setting off the other. They are national portraits of man—the ITALIAN and the MOOR. The Italian is *white, crafty,* and *cruel;* a consummate villain; yet, as often happens in the realities of that description whom we occasionally meet in the intercourse of life, so vain of his own artifices that he betrays himself by boasting of them and their success. Accordingly, in the very first scene he reveals to *Roderigo* the treachery of his own character:

> " For when my outward action doth demonstrate
> The native act and figure of my heart
> In compliment extern, 'tis not long after
> But I will wear my heart upon my sleeve
> For daws to peck at : I am not what I am."

There is a seeming inconsistency in the fact that a double-dealer should disclose his own secret, which must necessarily put others upon their guard against him ; but the inconsistency is in human nature, and not in the poet.

The double-dealing Italian is a very intelligent man, a keen and penetrating observer, and full of ingenuity to devise and contrive base expedients. His language is coarse, rude, and obscene : his humor is caustic and bitter. Conscious of no honest principle in himself, he believes not in the existence of honesty in others. He is jealous and suspicious ; quick to note every trifle light as air, and to draw from it inferences of evil as confirmed circumstances. In his dealings with the Moor, while he is even harping upon his honesty, he offers to commit any murder from extreme attachment to his person and interests. In all that *Iago* says of others, and especially of *Desdemona,* there is a mixture of truth and falsehood, blended together, in which the truth itself serves to accredit the lie ; and such is the ordinary character of malicious slanders. Doctor Johnson speaks of " the soft simplicity," the " innocence," the " artlessness " of *Desdemona. Iago* speaks of her as a *supersubtle* Venetian ; and. when kindling the sparks of jealousy in the soul of *Othello*, he says,

> "She did deceive her father, marrying you :
> And when she seemed to shake and fear your looks,
> She loved them most."

"And so she did," answers *Othello*. This charge, then, was true ; and *Iago* replies :

> "Why, go to, then ;
> She that so young could give out such a seeming
> To seal her father's eyes up, close as oak.—
> He thought 'twas witchcraft."

It was not witchcraft ; but surely as little was it simplicity, innocence, artlessness. The effect of this suggestion upon *Othello* is terrible only because he knows it is true. *Brabantio*, on parting from him, had just given him the same warning, to which he had not then paid the slightest heed. But soon his suspicions are roused—he tries to repel them ; they are fermenting in his brain : he appears vehemently moved and yet unwilling to acknowledge it. *Iago*, with fiend-like sagacity, seizes upon the paroxysm of emotion, and then comes the following dialogue :—

> "*Iago*. My lord, I see you are mov'd.
> *Othello*.   No, not much mov'd :—
> I do not think but *Desdemona's* honest.
> *Iago*. Long live she so ! and long live you to think so !
> *Othello*. And yet, how nature erring from itself,—

> *Iago.* Ay, there's the point:—As,—to be bold with you,—
> Not to affect many proposed matches,
> Of her own clime, complexion, or degree;
> Whereto, we see, in all things nature tends:
> Foh! one may smell, in such, a will most rank
> Foul disproportion, thoughts unnatural."—

The deadly venom of these imputations, working up to frenzy the suspicions of the Moor, consist not in their falsehood but in their truth.

I have said the character of *Desdemona* was deficient in delicacy. Besides the instances to which I referred in proof of this charge, observe what she says in pleading for the restoration of *Cassio* to his office, from which he had been cashiered by *Othello* for beastly drunkenness and a consequent night-brawl, in which he had stabbed *Montano*—the predecessor of *Othello* as Governor of Cyprus—and nearly killed him; yet in urging *Othello* to restore *Cassio* to his office and to favor, *Desdemona* says—

> "—in faith, he's penitent;
> And yet his trespass, in our common reason,
> (Save that, they say, the wars must make examples
> Out of their best,) *is not almost a fault*
> To incur a private check."

Now, to palliate the two crimes of *Cassio*—his drunken fit and his stabbing of *Montano*—the reader knows that he has been inveigled to the commission of them by the accursed artifices of *Iago*; but *Desdemona* knows nothing of this; she has no excuse for *Cassio*—nothing to plead for him but his penitence. And is this the character for a woman of delicate sentiment to give of such a complicated and heinous offence as that of which *Cassio* had been guilty, even when pleading for his pardon? No! it is not for female delicacy to extenuate the crimes of drunkenness and bloodshed, even when performing the appropriate office of raising the soul-subduing voice for mercy.

Afterwards, in the same speech, she says—

> "What! *Michael Cassio*,
> That came a-wooing with you; and many a time,
> When I have spoke of you dispraisingly,
> Hath ta'en your part; to have so much to do
> To bring *him* in!"

I will not inquire how far this avowal that she had been in the frequent habit of speaking dispraisingly of *Othello* at the very time when she was so deeply enamored with his honors and his valiant parts, was consistent with sincerity. Young ladies must be allowed a little concealment and a little disguise, even for passions of which they have no need to be ashamed. It is the rosy pudency—the irresistible charm of the sex; but the exercise of it in satirical censure upon the very object of their most ardent affections is certainly no indication of innocence, simplicity, or artlessness.

I still retain, then, the opinion—

First. That the passion of *Desdemona* for *Othello*

is *unnatural*, solely and exclusively because of his color.

Second. That her elopement *to* him, and secret marriage *with* him, indicate a personal character not only very deficient in delicacy, but totally regardless of filial duty, of female modesty, and of ingenuous shame.

Third. That her deficiency in delicacy is discernible in her conduct and discourse throughout the play.

I perceive and acknowledge, indeed, the admirable address with which the part has been contrived to inspire and to warm the breast of the spectator with a deep interest in her fate; and I am well aware that my own comparative insensibility to it is not in unison with the general impression which it produces upon the stage. I shrink from the thought of slandering even a creature of the imagination. When the spectator or reader follows, on the stage or in the closet, the infernal thread of duplicity and of execrable devices with which *Iago* entangles his victims, it is the purpose of the dramatist to merge all the faults and vices of the sufferers in the overwhelming flood of their calamities, and in the unmingled detestation of the inhuman devil, their betrayer and destroyer. And in all this, I see not only the skill of the artist, but the power of the moral operator, the purifier of the spectator's heart by the agency of *terror* and *pity*.

The characters of *Othello* and *Desdemona*, like all

the characters of men and women in real life, are of
" mingled yarn," with qualities of good and bad—
of virtues and vices in proportion differently composed. *Iago*, with a high order of intellect, is, in
moral principle, the very spirit of evil. I have said
the moral of the tragedy is, that the intermarriage
of black and white blood is a violation of the law of
nature. *That* is the lesson to be learned from the
play. To exhibit all the natural consequences of
their act, the poet is compelled to make the marriage
secret. It must commence by an elopement, and
by an outrage upon the decorum of social intercourse. He must therefore assume, for the performance of this act, persons of moral character sufficiently frail and imperfect to be capable of performing it, but in other respects endowed with pleasing
and estimable qualities. Thus, the Moor is represented as of a free, and open, and generous nature;
as a Christian; as a distinguished military commander in the service of the republic of Venice;—
as having rendered important service to the State,
and as being in the enjoyment of a splendid reputation as a warrior. The other party to the marriage
is a maiden, fair, gentle, and accomplished; born
and educated in the proudest rank of Venetian
nobility.

Othello, setting aside his color, has every quality
to fascinate and charm the female heart. *Desdemona*, apart from the grossness of her fault
in being accessible to such a passion for such an

object, is amiable and lovely; among the most attractive of her sex and condition. The faults of their characters are never brought into action excepting as they illustrate the moral principle of the whole story. *Othello* is not jealous by nature. On the contrary, with a strong natural understanding, and all the vigilance essential to an experienced commander, he is of a disposition so unsuspicious and confiding, that he believes in the *exceeding honesty* of *Iago* long after he has ample cause to suspect and distrust him. *Desdemona, supersubtle* as she is in the management of her amour with *Othello;* deeply as she dissembles to deceive her father; and forward as she is in inviting the courtship of the Moor; discovers neither artifice nor duplicity from the moment that she is *Othello's* wife. Her innocence, in all her relations with him, is pure and spotless; her kindness for *Cassio* is mere untainted benevolence; and, though unguarded in her personal deportment towards him, it is far from the slightest soil of culpable impropriety. Guiltless of all conscious reproach in this part of her conduct, she never uses any of the artifices to which she had resorted to accomplish her marriage with *Othello.* Always feeling that she has given him no cause of suspicion, her endurance of his cruel treatment and brutal abuse of her through all its stages of violence, till he murders her in bed, is always marked with the most affecting sweetness of temper, the most perfect artlessness, and the most endearing resigna-

tion. The defects of her character have here no
room for development, and the poet carefully keeps
them out of sight. Hence it is that the general
reader and spectator, with Dr. Johnson, give her
unqualified credit for soft simplicity, artlessness, and
innocence—forgetful of the qualities of a different
and opposite character, stamped upon the transac-
tions by which she effected her marriage with the
Moor. The marriage, however, is the source of all
her calamities; it is the primitive cause of all the
tragic incidents of the play, and of its terrible catastrophe. That the moral lesson to be learned from it
is of no practical utility in England, where there are
no valiant Moors to steal the affections of fair and
high-born dames, may be true; the lesson, however,
is not the less, couched under the form of an admirable drama; nor needs it any laborious effort of the
imagination to extend the moral precept resulting
from the story to a salutary admonition against all
ill-assorted, clandestine, and unnatural marriages.

J. Q. A.

From Mr. Washington Irving.

NEW YORK, April 17, 1848.

MY DEAR SIR:—I have detained your manuscript
notes an unconscionable time, but I could not help
it. I wished to read them attentively, for they are
remarkably suggestive, and not to be read in a

11*

hurry; but for the last two or three months spent among my friends and relatives in my native city after an absence of several years, I have been kept in such a round of engagements, and such constant excitement, that I have only now and then been able to command a little leisure and quiet for reading and reflection. At such moments I have perused your manuscripts by piecemeal, and now return you my many thanks for the great pleasure they have afforded me. I will not pretend to enter at present into any discussion of the topics they embrace, for I have not sufficient faith in my critical acumen to commit my thoughts to paper, but when I have the pleasure of meeting with you personally, we will talk over these matters as largely as you please. I have seen all the leading characters of Shakespeare played by the best actors in America and England during the present century; some of them too, admirably performed in Germany: I have heard some of them chanted in the Italian Opera, and I have seen the Ballet of *Hamlet* gravely danced at Vienna. Yet with all this experience, I feel that I am an amateur rather than a connoisseur; prone to receive great pleasure without nicely analysing the source, and sometimes apt to clap my hands when grave critics shake their heads.

Excuse this scrawl, written in a hurried moment, and believe me, with great respect and regard,

Your obliged friend and servant,
WASHINGTON IRVING.

James H. Hackett, Esq.

43 St. James's Place, London,
December 26, 1851.

My Lord :—In compliance with your complimentary request, and in the hope of furnishing a little discursive and desultory entertainment, I submit herewith to your lordship's convenient perusal copies of my correspondence respecting *Hamlet* and other Shakespearean subjects, together with comments thereupon by certain literati.

The "*manuscript volume*" of mine referred to in the letter of Mr. Washington Irving, and also in the later of the two letters of the late Hon. John Quincy Adams, I would hesitate—had I it with me—to obtrude upon your time and notice ; as—though copiously mingled with explanations of points mootable by a professed Shakespearean student and critic—much of the matter involved having special reference to the different styles of rendering the text by certain *actors* whom I have seen (and noted) within the last thirty years represent *Hamlet* and *King Lear*, it might prove too didactic to be interesting to the general and unprofessional reader.

The latest intelligence from Washington respecting our venerated friend, *Mr. Clay*, announces a fearfully rapid and visible decline of health in that personally beloved and nationally respected statesman.

Your lordship's obliged and obedient servant,
(Signed)
Jas. H. Hackett.

R. H. the Earl of Carlisle.

Lord Carlisle's Reply.

GROSVENOR PLACE, February 9, 1852.

MY DEAR MR. HACKETT :—I am afraid I have kept your volume longer than I ought to have done, as I had not leisure for some time to render justice to its contents, but I have now perused them with great pleasure and interest.

The meanings and characters of Shakespeare supply matter for reflexion that can never be exhausted. I must be allowed to think that upon the points in controversy between you and Mr. Adams on the character of *Hamlet* I am disposed to side entirely with you. I know the great respect and deference which are due to a person so really eminent as Mr. Adams. I think him probably quite in the right about *Juliet*, but you must excuse me for observing, with respect to his views upon *Othello*, that I feel assured there is not a single man in Europe who would coincide in his views of what the chief moral is, that is to be deduced from that surpassing tragedy. I see none of your criticisms are addressed to the play of *Macbeth*, in my mind the very highest in order of all the few which seem to me indisputably higher than all the rest—*Macbeth, Hamlet, Othello, Lear.* When I say this, however, I never could quarrel with a person who puts *Hamlet* even above *Macbeth.*

Again thanking you for the perusal of this very
interesting volume,

Believe me, dear sir,
Your very faithful servant,
CARLISLE.

---

44 St. James Place, July 7, 1845.

*To John Payne Collier, Esq.**

My Dear Sir—As you expressed a desire not
only to read my Note-Book, but to see a specimen
of our American edition of Shakespeare, I send
you herewith "No. 4," an odd part, but the only
one which I happened to have with me in your
country. It contains some scenes of *Hamlet* with
original and selected notes by our American editor,
Mr. Verplanck, to which have been added by myself some very cursory and detached marginal scrib-
blings of my own ideas, as I glanced over the work.

---

* *Mr. Collier* had been often met by me at the Garrick Club, of
which he was an original, and I whenever visiting England elected an
honorary member. He was distinguished at that time as an anti-
quarian of great research, and has since published an edition of Shakespeare, and subsequently a volume of "*Notes and Emendations to the
Text of Shakespeare's Plays.*"—*J. H. H.*, 1854.

> "In the dead *wast* and middle of the night."—*Folio* 1623.
> "   "   *waist*   "   "—*Malone's edit.*
> "   '   *waste*   "   "—*Verplanck's* "

I think, "The *dead* waist of the night," is simply what we term "the dead of night," viz. midnight; that *part* of the night which the poet refers to in another place—

> "Thus twice before and jump at this *dead* hour,"

because, then—

> "O'er the one half world
> Nature seems dead,"

the word "dead," prefixed to the word "waist" in the above quotation, therefore, means, the *exact* waist and middle of the night; the use of the word "*waist*" is figurative; Night, in various places, by poetic license, being invested with human shape, for examples—

> "Beshrew the *witch!* with venomous wights she stays."
> [*Troil. and Cressida.*
> "Blackbrow'd Night."—*Mids. Night's Dream.*
> "Night, whose black contagious breath."—*King John.*
> "——whose pitchy mantle over-veiled the earth."
> [1 *K. Henry VI.*

Respecting the ancient orthography of the word which we now write "*waist*," Shakespeare, in the

Folio 1623, spells it " *wast* " and " *waste,*" promiscuously; but his context admits of no question as to his meaning; for examples—

> "His neck will come to your *wast;* a cord, Sir."
> [*Meas. for Meas.*

> "Then you live about her *waste* or in the middle of her favours."—*Ham.*

In another play he puns upon *wast* and *waste,* thus—

> "Indeed, I am in the *waste* two yards about, but now I am about *no waste,* I am about thrift."—*Merry Wives of Windsor.*

That Shakespeare confounded, in his spelling, " *vast,*" with what he means where he writes " *wast* " or " *waste,*" I cannot admit; wherever I have found them in the *Folio,* these words are used in distinct senses, and never seem intended as synonymous. It is true, as Mr. Verplanck remarks, that " *vast* " is " taken in its primitive Latin sense, for desolate, void," which might pass for a synonyme of the modern word, " *waste,*" but certainly not for *waist;* for examples—

> ———" urchins
> Shall, for that *vast* of night that they may work,
> All exercise on thee."—*Tempest, Act* 1, *Sc.* 1.

which sentence, I take it, means that these tormentors (the urchins) shall, for that open or vacant *space* during the *night* time wherein they are, by witchcraft, privileged to be mischievous, practise *altogether* upon Caliban.

Again—

"Though absent, shook hands as over a *vast*, and embraced,
&c."—*Winter's Tale, Act 1, Sc. 1.*

Again—

"I can call spirits from the *vasty* deep."—*Henry IV.*

the adjective "vasty" partaking of the same quality
as *Vastum*, its Latin radix—"In gurgite *Vasto*"—
Virgil.

It seems to me, therefore, that *vast*, and *wast* or
waste, could not reasonably have been written by
Shakespeare to express one and the same idea;
besides, to call any part of the night time, between
the hours of twelve and one, a "dead waste," or
useless superfluity, or barren desert, as Mr. Verplanck seems to understand it, is a far-fetched figure
in *poetry* whilst it is an absurdity in *fact;* because,
in the economy of Nature, the *darkest* hour of the
night is no more a *barren waste* than the *lightest* one
of the *day;* inasmuch as Time proceeds at the same
pace in each alternation, and, whether night or day,
one is the sequence of the other, and both together
consummate the *natural* day.

"I boarded the king's ship: now on the beak,
　Now in the *waste*, the deck, in every cabin."—*Tempest.*

Yet notwithstanding this and the numerous other
instances of the signification obviously attached to

Shakespeare, when he spelled the word "*waste*,"
Mr. Verplanck says—

"To suppose that the poet meant *waist*, for middle, as several editors have maintained, and many printed the text, seems
ludicrously absurd."—*See Verplanck's Hamlet.*

whereas, I must contend for its *strict* propriety in
this particular line, whether considered in its simple
and ordinary, or its lateral and figurative sense; if
it be argued against *waist*, that the addition ("and
middle") makes palpable tautology, let it be observed that these pleonasms, or *double* expressions
of a *single* idea, are not uncommon to Shakespeare's
style, and more deeply impress and powerfully
enforce a sentiment; for examples—

"Or given my heart a working, *mute* and *dumb*."—*Hamlet.*
"Many a time and oft."—*Merchant of Venice.*
"Time and the hour run through the roughest day."—*Macb.*
"Then you live about the *waist* or in the *middle* of her fa-
vours."—*Hamlet.*

The same gain of strength in expression, may be
imputed, however ungrammatical to modern taste, to
Shakespeare's *double comparatives*, as—

"Your wisdom would shew itself *more richer*."—*Hamlet.*
"O, throw away the *worser* part of it."—*Hamlet.*
"The unkindest beast *more kinder* than mankind."
                                        [*Timon of Athens.*

"*Polonius.* Do you know me, my lord?
Hamlet. Excellent well! you are a fishmonger."

"You are sent to fish out this secret. That is Hamlet's meaning."—*Coleridge.*

With due reference to Coleridge, and to Mr. Verplanck's taste in adopting his idea, I beg leave to differ; because, if such *had* been *Hamlet's* meaning, Shakespeare would have selected the word, *fisher*, or *fisherman;* the former he uses in his *Comedy of Errors*, and in *Romeo and Juliet;* and the latter in *King Lear;* a *fishmonger* is a *dealer* in fish; one who buys to sell again, and *Hamlet* calls *Polonius* "a fishmonger," not because he thinks he is "sent to fish out this secret," but because of his habitual importunity to procure a stock of news and then to hasten to the king, his ready customer, and deal it out to him before the commodity, *fish-like*, can become *stale* on his hands; the same pregnancy of reply is discernible afterwards when *Hamlet* compares Rozencrantz to *a sponge,*

> "that soaks up the king's countenance,
> His rewards, his authorities."

> "I know a hawk from a handsaw."

See my comment on this passage, in Notice of *Macready's Hamlet.*

> "The croaking raven doth bellow for revenge."

Mr. Verplanck says—

> "It resembles the poet's own strong figure elsewhere."

Of course, the figure referred to elsewhere, can be no other than—

> "——the raven himself is hoarse
> That croaks the fatal entrance of Duncan
> Under my battlements."

There may be some analogy in the sentiment, but not the least in the *occasion ;* the figure in *Macbeth* has special reference to the *messenger*—

> " Who, almost dead for breath, had scarcely more
> Than would make up his message,"

and who is therefore compared by Lady Macbeth to a *raven*, because he could only *croak* out his news.

> " Now could I drink hot blood,
> And do such *bitter business* as the day
> Would quake to look on."

I fully concur with Mr. Verplanck in his preference to this reading, which is that of the *Folio*, because, the meaning of " bitter " is obvious, when applied to " business," which it qualifies in concordance with—

> "——the bloody book of law
> You shall yourself read in the *bitter* letter."—*Othello.*

again—

> " My spirit and my place have in them power
> To make this *bitter* to thee."—*Ibidem.*

Reply from J. Payne Collier, F.S.A.

VICTORIA ROAD, KENSINGTON, 10 July, 1845.

MY DEAR SIR—I return your Notes with my best thanks. Of course you do not expect any man to go all lengths with you, but I have been much gratified by the novelty, ingenuity, and acuteness, of some of your views, even when I did not agree in them.

I return you also the number of the American Shakespeare with your MS. notes thereupon. I perceive that you do not always accord with Mr. Verplanck, and I am of your mind in several instances.

I remain, my dear sir,

Yours very sincerely and much obliged,

J. PAYNE COLLIER.

James H. Hackett, Esq.

SHAKESPEREAN VERBAL NICETIES.

SOME of my fellow-members of the Union Club, having had a very nice discussion, and been unable to agree, sought the favor of my written opinion on the subject.

The point to be settled was: *which* of two words —differing widely in their sense, though slightly in their orthography—was *intended* by Shakespeare, in that line of *Macbeth*, which, in the *first* edition of his plays, is printed,

"Sleep—that knits up the ravell'd *sleeve* of care,"

but by modern editors has had the word "*sleave*" substituted for that of "*sleeve*" in the original.

I replied to the foregoing inquiry, thus :

"When things appear unnatural and hard,
Consult your author with *himself* compar'd."
Roscommon.

In order to satisfy one's self of Shakespeare's meaning in the line,

"Sleep—that knits up the ravell'd *sleeve* of care,"

it is expedient to examine minutely every context, in his range of plays, wherein either of the following words are used by him—viz. *sleeve, sleep, knit up, ravel,* and *care ;* because, connected with one or other of these words, some concordance may be detected which would render clear the poet's intention.

Mrs. Cowden Clarke's complete Verbal Index to Shakespeare, furnishes a very ready medium for reference to every context of each of the above words. She gives the word "sleave" but once as a noun, throughout Shakespeare's works, and *that* in the passage quoted above—being so spelled in Knight's (modern) "Pictorial Edition," to which her compilation expressly refers; she finds however the word "sleeve" in some twenty-five *other* places and where its *special* reference to "a covering for the human arm" is palpable and indisputable. Now, though many of the modern editions have printed in this text, "sleave," the *First Folio*, commonly called "The Players' edition," has no such orthography of the word as "sleave"—being in this passage, as in *all others*, "sleeve;" however, that, *per se*, is not conclusive evidence that a distinct meaning may not have been designed; forasmuch as, in that same old edition, published in 1623, *wast, waste*, and *waist*, are printed indiscriminately for the human waist; but, as it is unusual for any author to use the same word to express two such very distinct and dissimilar things as "a knitted covering for the arm," and a "skein of unwrought silk," and, as Shakespeare in no *other* place out of twenty-five examples, uses "sleeve" or "sleave," where it can possibly be intended to mean *skein*, it seems singular that if he so intended he should not have *written* "skein" instead; being a word used by him elsewhere in his writings. The metre of the line too would have stood the same, and the sense of the reader, and especially the *audience*—for which he specially wrote —would not then have been so naturally confounded. The only approximation throughout Shakespeare to any form of the word "sleave," ("a skein or knot of silk,") may be seen in a line of "Troilus and Cressida," which (in the folio of 1623) reads thus,

"——thou immaterial *skein* of *sleyed* silk ;

and again in " Pericles,"

"—— weaved the *sleided* silk."

These references to unwrought silk, are so clear and distinct, that it seems very incongruous that the noun "sleave" should have been made a solitary use of, in the whole course of his works, to indicate " skein or knot of silk," though it is proved satisfactorily by lexicography that such a word as " sleave," and in such sense, was used by other writers of Shakespeare's time—see *Todd's Johnson's Dictionary*, 3 *vols.* 4*to.*, *London*, 1827, for definition of, and authorities for " sleeve" and " sleave ;" also, the " Notes" of various commentators upon this passage, in Malone's edition of Shakespeare, 21 vols. 8vo., London, 1821.*

---

* Extracts from Commentators' notes upon *Macbeth*. Malone's edition, 21 vols. 8vo.. London, 1821.

"—— the ravell'd sleave of care."

Sleave signifies the " ravelled knotty part of the silk, which gives great trouble and embarrassment to the knitter or weaver."—*Heath.*

Dayton, a Poet of Shakespeare's age, has likewise alluded to "sleaved" or "ravelled" silk, in his Quest of Cynthia:

> " At length I on a fountain light,
>   Whose brim with pinks was platted,
>   The banks with daffodillies dight
>   With grass, like *sleave* was matted."—*Langton.*

Sleave is properly *silk* which has not been twisted. It is mentioned

After a patient search throughout Shakespeare for, and a deliberate consideration of, every word elsewhere, which relates to either in the line—

"Sleep that knits up the ravell'd sleeve of care,"

I am inclined to the opinion that the metaphor it contains specially refers to some ancient, and now perhaps by-gone use, or possibly manufacture, of the covering for the human arm, called a "sleeve," of which history may not have conserved to us any precise description : consequently, the figure may seem somewhat obscure when first presented to the mind ; and hence, the proposed emendation of "sleeve" into "sleave," but too readily commends

in Hollinshed's History of England, p. 835 : "Eight wild men all apparelled in green moss made with *sleved* silk."

Again, in Muse's Elizine by Drayton,

> "—— thrumb'd with grass
> As soft as *sleave* or sarcenet ever was."

Again *Ibid.*

> "That in the handling feels as soft as any *sleave*."—*Steevens.*

Sleave appears to have signified *coarse*, *soft*, unwrought silk, *Sela grassolona*, *Ital.* See also Florio's Italian Dictionary, 1598 : "*Sfilazza*, any kind of ravelled stuffe, or *sleave silk.*" "*Capilone*, a kind of coarse silk, called *sleave silk.*" Cotgrave, in his Dictionary, 1612, renders *soye flosche* "*sleave silk.*" See also, *Ibid:* "*Cadarce*, pour faire *capilon.* The tow or coarsest part of silke, whereof *sleave* is made." In Troilus and Cressida we have—

> "Thou idle immaterial skein of *sleave*[1] silk."—*Malone.*
> [1] *Slev'd* silk. *Folio.*

itself to our adoption, and involves the idea that—
Sleep knits up the skein of care, the fibres of which had been ravelled in the weaving; a solution very plausible, if not satisfactory.

It seems, however, from various references to the fact in Shakespeare, that it was customary, when any object was near any one's heart, to " pin it upon his sleeve," where it would be sure to be constantly under his eye ; as—

> " The gallant *pins* the wenches *on his sleeve.*"
> *Love's Labour's Lost.*

Also, to hang out or expose his secret motives, *Iago* says,

> " I'll wear my heart upon my sleeve."—*Othello.*

Further, among Shakespeare's poetic figures of care are these—

> " Golden care
> That keep'st the ports of slumber open wide."
> *Henry the Fourth, Part Second.*

> " *Care* keeps his watch in every old man's eye,
> And where *care* lodges, *sleep* will never lie."
> *Romeo and Juliet.*

In connection, too, with the thoughtfulness of *care*, the following quotation is not irrelevant :

> "Then your hose should be ungarter'd, your bonnet unbanded, your *sleeve unbuttoned*, your shoe untied, and everything about you demonstrating a *careless* desolation."
> *As You Like It, Act* 3.

Now, if Care's "sleeve" was a "skein of silk," he was unworthy of his *name* to *let* it become "ravell'd" at all. In conclusion, I would submit whether the following is a far-fetched or an incongruous comprehension of the line in question:

"Care," who is called "busy," and whose sleeve from habitual use has been "ravell'd," finds it restored by sleep: the ravelled meshes of his "sleeve" having been "knit up" whilst busy Care's senses were steeped in forgetfulness, and afforded the requisite opportunity.   J. H. H.

Ravelled means *entangled.* So, in the *Two Gentlemen of Verona, Thurio* says to *Proteus,* speaking of *Sylvia,*

> "Therefore as you unwived her love from him,
> Lest it should *ravel,* and be good to none,
> You must provide to bottom it on me."—*M. Mason.*

Among other significations confirmed by quotations from standard authors in Todd's edition of Johnson's Dictionary, 3 vols. 4to. London, 1827, are found the following, under the word

"Sleeve,—In some provinces signifies a knot, or skein of silk, which is by some very probably supposed to be its meaning in the following passage,

> "Sleep that knits up the ravell'd *sleeve* of care."—*Macbeth.*

Under the caption of SLEAVE, Dr. Johnson says : "Of this word I know not well the meaning: *sleave-silk* is explained by Gouldman *floccus sericus,* —a lock of silk ; and the women still say, 'sleave the silk' for untwist it.   Ainsworth calls a weaver's shuttle or reed, a *slaie,* or *sley.*   To *sley* is to part a twist into single fibres."

Various other authorities are also quoted.   See *Todd's Johnson.*

A FUGITIVE NOTE.

"Nor the *gail* of Christian, Pagan, *or Norman.*"
Folio, 1623.   *Hamlet.*

Modern editors have altered " or Norman " to " nor man," by striking out the conjunction and dividing the word.

Imprimis.—As *Christians* and *Pagans,* too, were *men,* the change is pointless and nonsensical :—and I would submit whether Shakespeare did *not* write " *or Norman ?* "   When one takes the pains to search, and discover, and reflect upon the following reference to " *a Norman :*"—

" *King.*   Two months since,
    Here was a gentleman from *Normandy,*—
    I have seen myself, and serv'd against the French,
    And they *ran* well on horseback : but this gallant
    Had witchcraft in't ;* he grew into his seat;

* *Mr. Steevens* says :—"This is from Sidney's *Arcadia, book* 2.   As if, Centaur-like, the rider had been one piece with his horse."

> And to such wondrous doing brought his *horse,*
> As he had been incorps'd and *demi-natured*
> With the brave beast:* so far he passed my thought,
> That I, in forgery of shapes and tricks,
> Come short of what he did.
> *Laertes.*   A Norman, was't?
> *King.* A Norman."   *Hamlet, Act 4, Sc. 7.*

I furnished the Editor of the *New York Evening Post* certain matter respecting *Harvey and Shakespeare's knowledge of the circulation of the blood,* and what follows appeared in the columns of that public journal, Wednesday, Oct. 19, 1861.

HARVEY AND SHAKESPEARE.

HAD SHAKESPEARE A KNOWLEDGE OF THE CIRCULATION OF THE BLOOD?

Two papers on the "Medical Knowledge of Shakespeare," from the pen of Mr. James H. Hackett, the actor, have been handed us for publication. In the first of these papers, which is given below, Mr.

---

* *Witchcraft in't:* that is, in his movement *on "horseback."* Is it not reasonable that Shakespeare, in characterizing an unnatural *gait,* could find neither among Christianized nor pagan man, nor even in the *half-horse Norman,* such a *gait* as certain players had when "they strutted and bellowed," and that it caused him to conclude that, "Nature's *journeymen* had made such men;" because they imitated humanity so abominably?—See Amer. edit. (Redfield, N. Y.), 1853, p. 152.

Hackett takes issue with the biographers of Dr. Harvey, who claim for him the honor of the discovery of the circulation of the blood, and makes numerous citations from Shakespeare's plays in order to prove that the bard knew the secret before the physician. Mr. Hackett's speculations are certainly curious. Our readers will judge for themselves whether he has established his case.

SHAKESPEARE'S KNOWLEDGE OF THE CIRCULATION OF THE BLOOD.

BELLEVUE MOUND, CARLISLE, Illinois, Sept., 1859.

During the last summer I noticed in the London newspapers a paragraph referring to "a recent exhumation of the corporal remains of William Harvey, *the immortal discoverer of the circulation of the blood.*" My recollections of Shakespeare's writings suggested doubts whether Harvey could be truly and *exclusively* entitled to the distinction, for the reason that I had been early in life deeply impressed with the idea that at least a knowledge of the circulation of the blood had been conceded to Shakespeare by his readers, and that most if not all his plays had been written either prior to Harvey's birth, or to the period when he might have grown into contemporary manhood, or become professionally—like Shakespeare—known to fame.

By reference to chronology I ascertain that Shakespeare was born (1564) fourteen years prior to Harvey ; and that when he began to write his plays (1589) Harvey, who was born in 1578, could have been only about eleven years of age, and that the majority of them were completed during Harvey's adolescence, and the residue while he was still a young man. Shakespeare died in 1616, and had retired some years from dramatic composition and all connection with a theatre, and had resided at New Place, Stratford-upon-Avon. His plays, however, or most of them, had been printed and published, singly and severally, soon after they were respectively written and performed upon the stage, and may have been seen by Harvey, and have suggested a motive for his professional study and demonstration of such theory.

Four years after Shakespeare's death, viz. in 1620, Harvey (then about forty-two years of age), "from his chair as Professor of Anatomy and Surgery in London, announced to the College his conviction of the fact of the circulation of the blood ; and, as is also recorded, then began to investigate the subject minutely"—and (as I have been informed), " discovered and commenced his work to demonstrate the valves which prevented the return of the blood to the heart through the same channel whence it had issued and been propelled into the arteries." Harvey finished and published his book in 1628. Hence, it is obvious that if Shakespeare had any idea of the circulation of the blood he could not reasonably have obtained it from Harvey.

Without intending to detract in the slightest degree from the merit and scientific value of any of
Harvey's investigations and elucidation of a subject
so important to the practice of surgery and medicine, I must contend for the *internal* evidence furnished in Shakespeare's writings of his having, prior
to Harvey's imputed discovery and laborious investigations, a clear conception of the propulsory
action of the heart in forcing its

——" courses through
The natural gates and alleys of the body."

It should be premised and ever remembered, in
one's search into Shakespeare's writings for any
intrinsic evidence of his theory upon any scientific
subject, that it was not his *profession* to teach that
of anatomy or surgery, but to dramatize humanity;
and that only in so far as the moral action of man's
heart, or its influence upon his passions, became
necessary to his purpose of blending, truly and consistently with nature, his philosophic ideas with
dramatic poetry, did he refer to that conservative
fountain of life.

Among the great variety of references to the
blood—named within more than five hundred of
Shakespeare's sentences—I have selected the following, as indicating to me most clearly his understanding of the fact that the blood circulated. His
choice, too, of the word " *gate* " (" gates and alleys
of the body ") would seem to involve his idea of the

valves and their use in stopping the blood; else, why use such word?—a gate being a mechanical contrivance for opening or closing to any thing inclined to pass, according to occasion.

> " The leperous distilment, whose effect
> Holds such an enmity with blood of man
> That, swift as quicksilver, it *courses through*
> *The natural gates and alleys of the body.*"
>
> [*Hamlet*, Act 1.

" This does make some obstruction in the blood—this cross-gartering."—*Twelfth Night*, *Act 3, Scene 4.*

> " As dear to me as are the ruddy drops
> That *visit* my sad heart."—*Julius Cæsar*, Act 2.

> " Lord Angelo scarce confesses
> That his *blood flows*—a man whose *blood*
> Is very snow-broth; one who never feels
> The wanton stings and *motions* of the sense."
>
> [*Measure for Measure*, Act 1.

> " The resolute acting of your *blood*."
> " Why does my blood thus *muster* to my heart?"
>
> [*Ibid, Act* 2.

> " *Runs* not this speech like iron through your blood?"
>
> [*Much Ado About Nothing*, Act 5.

> " All the *conduits* of my blood froze up."
>
> [*Comedy of Errors*, (1592.)

> " ——————— make thick my blood,
> Stop up the *access and passage* to remorse."—*Macbeth.*

> " The spring, the head, the fountain of your *blood*
> Is stopp'd—the very source of it is stopp'd."—*Ibid.*

"———————— if that surly spirit, melancholy,
Had baked my *blood* and made it heavy, thick,
(Which else *runs tickling up and down the veins*.")
[King John, Act 2.

"The tide of blood in me
Hath proudly flowed in vanity, till now—
Now doth it turn and ebb back to the sea."
[2d Part Henry IV., Act 5.

"Where I have garner'd up my heart;
The fountain from the which my current *runs*,
Or else dries up."—*Othello*, Act 4.

"A good sherris-sack hath a two-fold operation in it," &c. "The second property of your excellent sherry is—the warming of the blood, which before cold and settled, left the liver white and pale," &c.; "but the sherris warms it, and makes it *course* from the inwards to the parts extreme," &c., &c.: "and then the vital commoners and inland petty spirits *muster* me all to their captain, the heart," &c.—2d *Part Henry IV.*, Act 4, *Scene* 4.

Further quotations seem to me needless to convince him who reflects that Shakespeare must at least have theoretically *conceived, if he had not been informed or learned*, that the blood circulated; but let him who doubts inspect his entire works, wherein may be found in various connections, the word heart, mentioned more than a thousand times ; and in many passages combining concordant confirmation of such a conclusion. Whether the word *circulation* (which is compounded of the Latin preposition *circum* and [Fero, Ferre, Tuli] *latum*, and signifies *carried*

12*

around,) was not in Shakespeare's time yet adopted in the vernacular, or not considered suitable for his rhythm or to express his prose sentiments, I am not philologist enough to decide; but as I can find neither of the words *circulate*, *circulated*, or *circulation* anywhere in his language, I infer that they had not *then* been included in his already copious vocabulary; else he would probably have chosen, if deemed more expressive, *circulation* (for " *the course*,") and *circulates* (instead of " *courses* ") in some one or other of the numerous references to the movements of the blood.

His text, however, seems to me quite sufficient for conveying the *idea* of the *circulation*.

James H. Hackett.

P.S.—An intelligent friend in New York, to whom I applied for chronological records of Harvey (not among my limited biblical collection here) has furnished some which tend to confirm my opinion that William Harvey could not have imparted to Shakespeare what the latter knew concerning the action or movements of the venous and arterial blood, and referred to in his plays.

" William Harvey did not return from Italy (where he studied) to England until 1602." (He was then aged twenty-four, and Shakespeare had already written twenty of his thirty-four dramas.) Nor " was he appointed Professor in the Royal College of Physicians until 1615," (several years after the retirement of Shakespeare, and only one prior to the poet's death.) Also, "about or between the years 1616 and 1619 Harvey first publicly announced his discovery, which met with universal ridicule— nor did he print his work until 1628," (twelve years after Shakespeare's death.) It was entitled "*Exercitatio Anatomia de motu cordis et sanguinis circulatione.*"

Hence, as Harvey could not have taught him, may not Shakespeare have received his impressions intuitively, perhaps when reading Hunter's theory respecting the blood, which, I think, without reference to chronology, had appeared prior to Shakespeare's commencement as a dramatist? My intelligent New York friend writes: "From the few passages in Shakespeare's plays which I can now recall, and which bear upon this subject [the circulation of the blood,] I incline to think that if they had been written by Shakespeare as prose observations, and not as poetic illustrations, we should resolve that he had, without anatomical knowledge, reached a conclusion which Harvey afterwards so carefully and triumphantly demonstrated."

The fact that Hume and Hallam, the historians, as well as all modern medical writers, with very few exceptions, yield Harvey the credit of the *discovery* claimed for him, weighs little in the scale of my opinions. Historiographers referring to events which have transpired long before their own time, are not apt to question or to hesitate to record the then undisputed authorities of a former age, and more especially upon subjects not within their own province to investigate and compare ; and with regard to modern medical writers, they would hardly consider their time profitably occupied in sifting and analyzing the poetry of a dramatist of the Elizabethan age, to find what elements of the healing art may have been amalgamated even by the genius of a Shakespeare.

J. H. H.

————

A Reply to Mr. Hackett.

October 30, 1861.

To the Editors of The Evening Post :

I was somewhat surprised by reading in your issue of the 19th instant a paper written by Mr. Hackett, endeavoring to render to Shakespeare the honor which for two centuries has been conceded to the immortal Harvey, viz. the discovery of the circulation of the blood. Had Mr. Hackett been as well acquainted with the literature of the profession to which Harvey belonged as with the numbers of the bard, he would have probably hesitated ere he endeavored to pluck from the great physician's brow a single leaf of his undying crown.

It is very natural in one treating a subject which is "not within his own province to investigate and compare," whose inquiries must be necessarily crude and superficial, and who probably has never read Harvey's elaborate treatise, entitled "*De Motu San-*

guinis," and devoted as little attention to similar works written before and since that author's time— it is very natural that such an investigator should be led into errors which even those more conversant with the subject might scarcely have avoided. "A little knowledge is a dangerous thing," appears to be well exemplified in the article to which I am replying. With all due deference to Mr. Hackett's superior attainments in other respects, and particularly in regard to Shakesperean lore, in whose interpretation he is certainly entitled to the highest consideration, allow me to suggest that his arguments in favor of Shakespeare as a medical discoverer are far from being proved by the passages which he quotes, or, in fact, by any others of a similar significance occurring in that poet's productions.

Shakespeare undoubtedly did possess, more than any other man who has bequeathed to us his own record of intellectual capacity, a most intimate acquaintance with all the motives of human action. As a student of human nature, his province was the anatomy of the mind and the soul—and with a most careful and delicate hand did he dissect apart the elementary tissues of those complex existences. As regards, however, his study and knowledge of the more material constituents of the human organism, we may be pardoned in entertaining great doubt, his works affording us but little enlightenment on the subject. In fact, where he displays a strange familiarity with many of the other sciences, it seems curious that there should be wanting, almost completely, any, except mere figurative commonplace allusions, to that of anatomy and physiology. It is related in his biography that he served for a short period of his youth in the office of a country attorney, and, as a consequence, we find introduced into his writings many technical phrases then employed only by those of the legal profession, many of whom figure quite conspicuously in his plays.

With the medical profession, however, he meddles but little; a doctor is occasionally introduced, but is either as vulgar and devoid of dignity as Dr. Caius, or so obscure, even when occupying the position of physician to the king, as to attract no special attention. Might we not suppose that had the poet been at all conversant with medical science he would have employed his knowledge to greater advantage? And certainly, had even superficial inquiries into the art led him to so important a discovery as the circulation (allowing it to have been unknown before), was he a person to have concealed his familiarity with such a fact, or merely to have thrown out obscure hints here and there?

But, letting rest the arguments for or against Shakespeare's acquaintance with anatomy or physiology, it is certain that we need impute to him no extraordinary knowledge in that respect, whereby to explain the meaning of the passages quoted by Mr. Hackett. They only prove that he was cognizant of a few simple facts which had been recognised and commented upon ages before, and an ignorance of which would have been impossible in a person of so comprehensive a mind. They suggest—1st: That the blood exists in conduits or vessels of some sort. 2d: That it moves through these vessels from one part of the body to another, though without undertaking to explain how or why. 3d: That it starts at the heart; and 4th (though the application seems to me very far fetched): That there are valves through which it passes, and which prevent its reflux.

Now all of these suggestions undoubtedly originated in a few facts which had been first promulgated many centuries before by the great Galen, who was the first to form any correct idea of the circulating system. His writings faithfully describe the blood as pursuing its course from the heart into the arteries, and as being prevented from returning by a system of valves, to which he contents himself with a mere allusion. Although his ideas upon the subject were indefinite, still his observations contain enough of plausibility to have produced a deep impression upon a reflective and philosophic mind, such as Harvey's, and to have led him to those investigations which were so prolific in great results. Indeed, Harvey even acknowledges these hints in referring to the statements of Galen, which he quotes as those of "*viri divini patris medicorum.*" From the period of Galen down to that of Harvey, the subject remained to a certain degree dormant; though it is said, I know not how truly, that the Italian physiologists had demonstrated, many years previous to Harvey's time, what is termed "the lesser circulation," *i. e.* from the heart through the lungs, and back again to the heart. Such theories and facts, therefore, as had previously been enunciated, we may admit that Shakespeare knew and hinted at, without any necessity of our considering him the discoverer of the circulation.

But now it may be asked: How can Harvey, then, be so regarded exclusively, if such and such things had been known ages before his birth? The answer is, that if we comprehend by the word " circulation" merely the movement of the blood through the heart and vessels, he is not entitled to the honor which posterity has bestowed upon him. But let us remember that he took up the subject in the primitive condition in which Galen had left it (whose suggestions, though given to the world so many centuries before, had yet been, curiously enough, the foundation of few inquiries); that he pursued it for years, by means of the most laborious dissections and experiments; that he unravelled the complex construction of the great propelling organ, the heart; that he traced the arteries from their very root in the great aorta onward through their gradually decreasing ramifications, until he arrived at their most minute divisions; that he thence watched the course of the blood through various and complicated tissues, through an intricate network of capillaries, until, re-collected into the veins, it returned to its original starting-place. And not only this, but he analyzed the mysterious causes of this circuit, the powers which start the fluid upon its round, and serve to propel it and assist it in its continual course. And what was the consequence of his herculean labors? A result, constructed step by step upon determined facts and logical conclusions, grand and comprehensive, the very foundation of modern medical science, and remaining almost a type of perfection even at the present period, when such tremendous strides are being taken in all scientific research.

Harvey, therefore, seems to me to bear the same relation to Galen that Morse did to Franklin. At all events, *he was the first to demonstrate the entire circulation ;* and, therefore, is he not entitled to be considered its discoverer?   C. P. R.

ORCHARD PLACE, YONKERS, Nov. 29, 1861.

To the Editors of the Evening Post :

Having just returned after some six weeks' business upon my landed estate in Illinois, I have been shown in your issue of October 30 an article capped "Harvey and Shakespeare—A Reply to Mr. Hackett;" wherein the author, signing C. P. R., in reference to my own article "No. 1" upon that subject, published in your issue of October 19, charges me with "endeavoring to render to Shakespeare the honor which for two centuries has been conceded to the immortal Harvey, viz. *the discovery of the circulation of the blood.*"

C. P. R. is wrong in his premises. I did not claim for Shakespeare the *discovery*, but only that by analogy he understood the theory, and could not have been ignorant of the fact before Harvey began to write. The words in my article were: "I must contend for the internal evidence furnished in Shakespeare's writings of his having, prior to Harvey's imputed discovery and laborious investigations, a clear *conception* of the propulsory action of the heart in forcing its

> ——' courses through
> The natural gates and alleys of the body.'"

My article referred to—No. 1—was written in 1859, and was intended rather as prefatory to my observations—"No. 2"—made a year after upon a book published in London, in 1860, entitled "Shakespeare's Medical Knowledge, by John Charles Bucknill, M.D.;" but only so far as its contents related to *Shakespeare's knowledge of the circulation of the blood.* Whenever it may suit the convenience of your press to publish said "No. 2," and that of your correspondent to peruse it, I would *prefer* to be spared further animadversion, and to learn his objections to the orthodoxy of my arguments, and to refer him to the profound and elaborate medical researches in that work of the erudite Dr. Bucknill,

who, alluding to the late Lord Chancellor Camp-
bell's interesting work on Shakespeare's legal attainments, observes that it "convinced him that the
knowledge of the great dramatist was, in each department, so extensive and exact that it required
the skilled observation of a professional mind fully
and fairly to appreciate and set it forth."

Doctor Bucknill, in his preface, continues:
" Although the author desires explicitly to disavow
the intention to put forward in behalf of his own
profession any rival claims for the honor of having
occupied the *unaccounted-for period* of Shakespeare's early manhood, he must confess that it
would be gratifying to professional self-esteem if he
were able to show that the immortal dramatist, who
bears, as Hallam says, 'the greatest name in all
literature,' paid an amount of attention to subjects
of *medical* interest scarcely if at all inferior to that
which has served as the basis of the learned and
ingenious argument, that this intellectual king of
men had devoted seven good years of his life to the
practice of *law*. For the honor of *medicine* it would
be difficult to point to any great author, not himself
a physician, in whose works the healing art is referred to more frequently and more respectfully
than in those of Shakespeare. The motive, however, for writing, and the excuse for publishing the
following pages, is not to exalt the medical profession, by citing in its glorification the favorable
opinion and special knowledge of the great bard,

but to contribute to the elucidation of his universal genius, and to prove that, among others, 'the myriad mind' had paid close attention to this most important and personally interesting subject of study."

I would reiterate my conviction that William Harvey, though he investigated and practically demonstrated, was not the original "discoverer of the circulation of the blood."

JAMES H. HACKETT.

Mr. Hackett's No. 2 we shall publish as soon as we can find room for it.—[EDS. EVENING POST.

Mr. Hackett's Second Letter.

[The following is Mr. Hackett's second letter on Shakespeare and Harvey.—EDS.]

December 12, 1861.

To the Editors of the Evening Post :

As I expected that Dr. John Charles Bucknill's work, entitled "*Medical Knowledge of Shakespeare,*" published in London, would necessarily involve, in a general disquisition of its subject, certain points deducible from some of the passages which I had quoted in order to prove that Shakespeare could not have been ignorant of the fact of the circulation of the blood, the discovery of which, after Shakespeare's death, had been claimed for Harvey, I eagerly sought and obtained a copy of Dr. Bucknill's book, and was much entertained and often instructed through the scope of its contents. However, as I, from ignorance of the science of surgery or anatomy, and its origin and progressive advancement, am not qualified for its general review, I will confine my extracts and comments to such portions as may seem to bear upon the specialty of Harvey's originality in discovering the circulation of the blood.

Page 10.—" The world saw nothing of the circulation of the blood in Servetus, Columbus, Cæsalpinus, or Shakespeare, until after William Harvey had taught and written."

Hallam's *Literary History of Europe*, though not questioning Harvey's discovery of the dual circulation, and conceding that the lesser circulation was known to the ancients, observes : " It may, indeed, be thought wonderful that Servetus, Columbus, and Cæsalpinus should not have more distinctly apprehended the consequences of what they maintained, since it seems difficult to conceive the lesser circulation without the greater ; but the defectiveness of their views is not to be alleged as a counterbalance to the more steady sagacity of Harvey ; " and as Dr. Bucknill has chosen to add Shakespeare to Hallam's catalogue, I will proceed with quotations from the poet, and leave my readers to judge whether he did not comprehend this duality and inter-dependence of the circulation ; but, previously, let me anticipate, for my readers' advantage, what Dr.

Bucknill has reserved in his arrangement of matter until page 201.

> " The flow of blood to the heart was a fact well known and recognised in Shakespeare's time. It was the flow of blood from the heart, that is, the circulation of the blood, which was not known to Shakespeare, or to any other person, before Harvey's immortal discovery."

> " I send it through the rivers of your blood,
> Even to the court, the heart—to the seat o' the brain ;
> And through the cranks and offices of man."
>
> —*Coriolanus, Act* 1, *Sc.* 1.

Dr. Bucknill, after first referring to the body's nutriment being sent " through rivers of blood to the court, the heart,"—" a fact well known in Shakespeare's time,"—continues : " The flow of the blood ' through the cranks and offices of man ' is a singular expression. ' Offices ' appear to mean functions, put for their organs, and ' cranks ' mean bendings or turnings, and, no doubt, refer to the elbows or turns in the blood-vessels." I regard the preposition " through " as very significant, but, firstly, I would suggest whether Shakespeare's choice of the word " visit " (by *Brutus* in his *Julius Cæsar*), and which signifies " to go and come," does not imply in that connection the flux and reflux of the blood ?

> " As dear to me as are the ruddy drops
> That *visit* my sad heart."—*Act* 2.

—and also, how the propulsory action of the heart

can be denied, after reading and digesting the following direct expression of it, independent of many lateral ones :

—————"My heart,
Where either I must live or bear no life;
The fountain FROM *the which my current runs,*
Or else dries up," &c.—*Othello, Act* 4, *Sc.* 2.

Page 12. "—instances appear, and amount not merely to evidence, but to proof, that Shakespeare had read widely in medical literature."

Pages 35, 36. " Shakespeare's eldest daughter, Susanna, married Dr. John Hall, a physician of great provincial eminence, practising at Stratford upon Avon. The registration of his marriage stands thus:

" '1607, June 5. John Hall, gentleman, and Susanna Shakespeare.' It will be an interesting subject of inquiry whether such of the dramas as were written after their author entered into terms of intimate relationship with a physician well educated in the professional knowledge of his time, bear any impression of the mental conduct; since it is scarcely possible but that some influence should have been exercised upon the impressible mind of the poet by the husband of his favorite daughter—living with him in the same house."

It seems reasonable, certainly, between " the instances in proof that Shakespeare had read widely in medical literature," and the circumstances of an eminent physician, his son-in-law, residing, after 1607, in the same house, and with whom he may have been intimate long previous to the marriage, that Shakespeare should have made himself acquainted clearly with every important fact or theory relating to such a subject, which had transpired; and, indeed, out of his own intuitive and comprehensive genius might have originated others, or new ones, which neither his leisure nor his avocations allowed him to explore, prove, or demonstrate, even for his own satisfaction.

Page 74

"' Why does my blood thus muster to my heart,
Making both it unable for itself,
And dispossessing all my other parts
Of necessary fitness?'

Measure for Measure, Act 2, *Sc.* 4.

" This mustering of the blood to the heart is referred to by Warwick, in describing the death of John of Gaunt; it is perfectly in accordance with modern physiological science, and when it is remembered that in Shakespeare's time the circulation of the blood, and even the relation of the heart to the blood, was yet undiscovered, the passage is in every way remarkable."

If Dr. Bucknill's premises are true, the passage is indeed not only "in every way remarkable," but unaccountable, not to say miraculous.

Page 82. "Shakespeare may, with the intuition of genius, have guessed very near the truth respecting the circulation of the blood, &c., &c. See also Falstaff's reflections on Prince John, part 2; King Henry IV., act iv., scene 3."

Page 123. "The absence of blood in the liver was the supposed property of a coward. 'The liver white and pale' is Falstaff's pathological badge of pusillanimity and cowardice. Fear is called 'pale-hearted' in Macbeth. Also, Lucio, in Measure for Measure (act 4, scene 3), says: 'I am pale at mine heart,' &c.: and was not that too (the absence of blood there) the supposed property of a coward, according to the old theory of the circulation of the blood which (Dr. Bucknill writes) gave rise to this opinion?"

Page 133. "The expression in King John, act 3, scene 3, that 'the blood runs trickling* up and down the veins,' seems to point to the thought that there is a flux and reflux of the current."

Pages 157–158. "Shakespeare follows Hippocrates, &c., &c., and has reference to another theory of Hippocrates, namely, that the veins, which were thought the only blood-vessels, had their origin in the liver. The Father of Medicine maintained that they come from the liver, the arteries from the heart. It appears, however, that in different parts of his works he expressed different opinions on the relation existing between the veins and the heart," &c.

Dr. Bucknill follows up by extracting a lengthy passage from the Sydenham Society's edition of *The Works of Harvey*, and also quotes "Rabelais, who was both a practising physician and a medical author," and his translation of the works of both Hippocrates and Galen; and adds, "Rabelais expresses the doctrine of the function of the liver which is implied in Falstaff's disquisition," namely, "that the liver conveys blood through the veins for the good of the whole body." Indeed, Dr. Bucknill continues through several pages afterward to refer to "the old opinions," and compares, in an apparently

---

* Trickling is Shakespeare's word, alluding to an occasional sense of the motion of the blood in the veins. "To trickle" signifies to "drop gently." Shakespeare has only used trickling once, and then as a synonyme of tricky, "trickling tears are vain."—*Henry IV., Part* 1.

learned manner, the theories which existed among the medical professors prior to Harvey, respecting the functions of the liver and of the heart.

> —— "and let my *liver* rather heat with wine
> Than my *heart* cool with mortifying groans."
>
> [*Merchant of Venice*.

Shakespeare, who was neither a medical author nor a practising physician, was not bound to ascertain, and may have confounded the respective functions of the heart and the liver, and the causes; but at the same time have distinctly understood the fact of the circulation of the blood, which is simply that for which I have thus far contended and been trying to convince my readers.

Page 213:
> " You are my true and honorable wife,
>   As dear to me as are the ruddy drops
>   That visit my sad heart."—*Julius Cæsar*.

" 'On these three lines,' (writes Dr. Bucknill) 'a short essay, the only one bearing upon Shakespeare's physiological opinions I have anywhere been able to find, has been written by Mr. Thomas Nimmo, and has been published in a second volume of the Shakespeare Society Papers. Mr. Nimmo considers that this passage (quoted)—'containing what I cannot view otherwise than a distinct reference to the *circulation of the blood*, which was not announced to the world, as is generally supposed, until some years after the death of Shakespeare.'"

Dr. Bucknill remarks: "Assuming the truth of this, Mr. Nimmo argues either that the play was not written so early as 1603—the date fixed by Mr. Collier—or that 'Shakespeare had been made acquainted by Harvey himself with his first notions on the subject.' Mr. Nimmo afterwards speculates thus: 'Is it, then, impossible that Harvey, a young medical practitioner, may have become acquainted with Shakespeare—may have become intimate with him, and may have acquainted him with those great ideas by which also he hoped to become famous?'"

Dr. Bucknill resumes: "In some comments on the article Mr. T. J. Pettigrew satisfactorily disposes of Mr. Nimmo's suggestion, observing: 'There is no evidence that Shakespeare knew Harvey; and as Shakespeare died in 1616, when the first ideas of Harvey upon the subject were promulgated at the college, he could not, through that medium, have been acquainted with it; but if the date of 1603, as given by Mr. Collier as the period at which the play of "Julius Cæsar" was written, be the correct one, it is quite clear that Shakespeare could not have then known Harvey, because he (Harvey) must at that time have been abroad (in Italy), and, whatever may have been his reflections upon the discovery of the existence of valves in the veins, there are no traces in any of his writings to show that he had then entertained any particular views upon the nature of the circulation.'"

With regard to my own sentiments concerning the probability whether Shakespeare was indebted to Harvey or Harvey to Shakespeare for their respective and original ideas of "the circulation," I must ask my reader, if he cares to consider them, to refer to their expression, in the course of my postscript to letter dated 15th September, 1859.

Dr. Bucknill goes on:

"Shakespeare might indeed have known Harvey, as he no doubt was intimate with many of the leading minds of the age; but, in addition to the fact that Harvey's first notice of his discovery was made in the year of Shakespeare's decease,

Mr. Nimmo's suggestion is easily refuted from the other writings of the poet, with which it seems probable that Mr. Nimmo had not made himself acquainted. There are several passages in the plays in which the presence of blood in the heart is quite as distinctly referred to as in this speech of Brutus; but the passages quoted in these pages from 'Love's Labor Lost,' and from the 'Second Part of Henry IV.,' distinctly prove that Shakespeare entertained the Galenical doctrine universally prevalent before Harvey's discovery; that, although the right side of the heart was visited by the blood, the function of the heart and its proper vessels, the arteries, was the distribution of the vital spirits, or, as Byron calls them, 'the nimble spirits in the arteries.' Shakespeare believed, indeed, in the flow of the blood, 'the rivers of your blood' which went even to the court, the heart;' but he considered that it was the liver, and not the heart, which was the cause of the flow. There is not, in my opinion, in Shakespeare, a trace of any knowledge of the circulation of the blood. Surely the temple of his fame needs not to be enriched by the spoils of any other reputation."

Certainly not, good Dr. Bucknill; nor, as I hope, does the temple of Harvey's fame which the medical profession have constructed need any support to be obtained by denying Shakespeare his obvious intelligence prior to "Harvey's discovery." May not an effect, like the circulation of the blood, be obvious, whilst its cause may be hidden and obscured, or confounded by one's imputing to the liver the distinct propulsory action of the heart?

Finally, recommending my readers to ascertain precisely Dr. Bucknill's definition of the word circulation, and to remember that it is not to be found

in Shakespeare, and to satisfy himself whether or
not the word "course," as used by Shakespeare
when referring to the blood, is synonymous with
circulation, I take my leave of the subject; and
though I differ with him in many of his interpreta-
tions of Shakespeare's text, I have derived much
pleasure from his book, and would commend it to
the attentive perusal of every one who may be
gratified by perceiving that the immortal dramatist,
who bears, as Hallam says, "the greatest name in
all literature," paid an amount of attention to subjects of medical interest scarcely if at all inferior
to that which has served as the basis of the learned
and ingenious argument, that the intellectual king
of men had devoted seven good years of his life to
the practice of the law.

Jas. H. Hackett.

P. S.—After a deliberate reconsideration of the
mooted question, whether William Harvey can be
justly entitled to the fame and honor of having
been "the immortal discoverer of the circulation
of the blood," it seems to me that the point of the
argument after all resolves itself into what may be
the direct, or lateral, or longitudinal signification of
the word discover, which literally means—to find
out, to expose to view, to make known that which
was unknown before. Restricted to this sense,
Columbus was unquestionably the first discoverer
of this Western Continent. Its very existence was
conceived by his genius, and ascertained only

through his practical faith, energy, and enterprise, having been previously unknown, at least to civilized Europe; yet, Americus Vespucius, by reason of his secondary efforts, and progressive discernment in the premises, was enabled to build and to perpetuate his own name, and to eclipse, if not almost supersede, the fame of Columbus, its original discoverer.

Sir Isaac Newton, born in 1642, is generally regarded by his enthusiastic eulogists at this day as the discoverer of the attraction of gravitation; whereas, absolutely, he only investigated and explained the laws which regulate the solar system. The solar system of the ancients was that of Ptolemy, and is poetically referred to by Shakespeare in his play of "Troilus and Cressida," (written some fifty years before Sir Isaac was born), thus:

" *Ulysses.* The heavens themselves, the planets, and this centre,
    Observe degree, priority and place,
    Insisture, course, proportion, season, form,
    Office and custom, in a line of order.
    And therefore is the glorious planet, Sol,
    In noble eminence enthron'd and spher'd
    Amidst the other."—*Act* 1, *Scene* 3.

But, on special reference to the attraction of gravitation—the discovery of which has been imputed to Newton—can any reader of common understanding doubt Shakespeare's knowledge of that fact when perusing the following sentence put into the mouth of his heroine?—

" *Cressida.*   *   *   *   *   Time, force and death,
    Do to this body what extremes you can;
    But the strong base and building of my love
    Is as the very centre of the Earth
    Drawing all things to it!"—Act 4, Scene 2.

J. H. H.

IAGO.

In the year 1828, soon after I had adopted the stage as a profession, I studied and attempted to act Shakespeare's *Iago*, but although I was received encouragingly at the Park Theatre, New York, a few times, and favorably reported by the Press, I found it not attractive; and though the result confirmed me in the correctness of the conception I had formed after an elaborate study, I was by no means satisfied with my own personation, and for that reason, and also because the New York public had seemed to identify my stage-abilities only with Yankee and other American Originals, and some dialect and eccentric characters, and with imitations of popular actors, and also inasmuch as I had then never attempted any other serious performance with the exception of *Richard the Third*, and that in direct and avowed imitation of *Edmund Kean*, I regarded my *Iago* but as an experiment, and at once resolved that it was inexpedient for me in my novitiate to persist in trying to represent such a very difficult character, and hence abandoned further attempts accordingly.

Mr. John Inman, then noted for his literary and critical discernment and who afterwards became associate editor of the Commercial Advertiser, witnessed my first effort to personate *Iago*, and reported it for the New York Evening Post. For the reason that Mr. Inman gave a rather minute and careful description of what seemed to him to be my *understanding* of certain points which I had not yet acquired art enough to strike out *effectively* in my *acting*, I will reprint his report herewith as a record of my peculiar notions of this character.

MR. HACKETT'S IAGO.

PARK, Thursday, April 10, 1828.

The character of *Iago* has, in our opinion, been almost universally mistaken, both by players and critics. Actors in general have been struck only with the wickedness of the character, and have represented him as a monster, a fiend, revelling in malevolence and mischief—devoting his time, his talents, and his life to the perpetration of gratuitous villanies, and actuated by no other motive than the mere love of wickedness. This is an unnatural conception; and Shakespeare, who was quite as good a philosopher as he was a poet, never intended to exhibit such a picture. The same error has been fallen into even by the first critics in England—Hazlitt says, " The general groundwork of the character of *Iago*, as it appears to us, is not absolute malignity but a want of moral principle, or an indif-

ference to the real consequences of the actions, which
the *perversity* of his disposition and *love of immediate excitement* lead him to commit. He is an amateur of tragedy in real life. The character is a complete abstraction of the intellectual from the moral
being; or in other words, consists in an absorption
of every common feeling in the virulence of his
understanding, the deliberate wilfulness of his purposes, and in his *restless, untameable love of mischievous contrivances.*" Now it appears to us that
the *motives* of *Iago's* conduct are so plainly described
even in the very first scene, as to render it almost
impossible to mistake them. They are, jealousy and
disappointed ambition. When *Roderigo* adverts to
the hatred which *Iago* had expressed towards the
Moor, what is his reply?

> " Despise me if I do not—Three great ones of the city
>   In personal suit to make me his lieutenant,
>   Oft capped to him; and by the faith of man,
>   I know my price—I'm worth no less a place;
>   But he, as loving his own pride and purposes,
>   Evades them, with a bombast circumstance, &c."

And immediately after, having spoken disparag-
ingly of the abilities of *Cassio*, he goes on—

> " *He*, sir, had the election,
> And I, (of whom his eye had seen the proof
> At Rhodes, at Cyprus, and on other grounds,
> Christian and Heathen) must be be-leed and calmed
> By debtor and by creditor; this counter-caster,

13*

He, in good time, must his lieutenant be,
And I, (Heaven bless the mark) his Moorship's ancient—"*

This is the origin of *Iago's* hatred, and for this insult, he determines to be revenged. In the third scene, we find that there is another barbed arrow rankling in his heart. He says—

" I hate the Moor;
And it is thought *abroad*, that 'twixt my sheets
He has done my office."

To which, referring again, in the first scene of the second act, he displays an intensity of feeling, which we consider as the strongest confirmation of our idea of his character.

" For that I do suspect the lusty Moor
Hath leaped into my seat; the thought whereof
Doth, *like a poisonous mineral, gnaw my inwards;*
And nothing can, or shall content my soul
Till I am even with him—"

But his jealousy is not confined to *Othello*—He

"fears *Cassio* with his night-cap too;"

and it is for this, that he selects *him*, to be the instrument wherewith to work his vengeance upon

---

* Mr. Hackett has (very wisely) restored this passage, beginning " But he, sir, had the election," which has been heretofore most injudiciously omitted: it has such a direct and palpable bearing upon the character, that we cannot but wonder why it should ever have been left out.

Othello. These passages, if rightly considered, we cannot help looking upon as affording redeeming points in the character of *Iago*—as tending completely to do away the imputation of gratuitous villany, which has been so generally affixed to it.

It is from Mr. Hackett's performance, that we have chiefly derived this idea of *Iago.* This we are confident is his conception, and for it, we consider Mr. Hackett entitled to all praise, although his execution was by no means perfect. We have once before said, that "with time and practice, Mr. Hackett would become a good tragedian," and in that opinion we are confirmed rather than shaken by his performance of *Iago.* He has faults, but they are such as practice will remove. He wants acquaintance with "stage trick" as it is called; that is, with the crossings, the pauses, the minutiæ of stage business which are so necessary to give the greatest effect to an actor's readings—his utterance and his action are altogether too quick : and he has a habit of keeping his head and his limbs in continual motion, which he *must* avoid. The *intention* of his *Iago* was evident and excellent, and gave proof of the close attention and deep study which, we are confident, he has bestowed upon the character. He makes *Iago* assume three distinct characters ; to *Othello,* that of a frank, blunt, honest-hearted friend, but withal a close observer, betrayed involuntarily by his attachment to his general, into the revelation of what leads to *his* destruction—*Othello* often calls him "honest." "This *honest* creature" —" this fellow's of *exceeding honesty ;*" and here we cannot help noticing the strange error into which Hazlitt's view of *Iago's* character has betrayed him ; he says, "He (*Iago*) is repeatedly called 'honest *Iago*,' which looks as if there were something suspicious in his appearance, which admitted a different construction." Now we imagine that *Othello* calls him honest, because he thinks he actually is so. If *Iago* were the open undisguised villain, Hazlitt thinks him, *Othello* must have been a fool, an egregious blockhead, to be so duped by him.

To *Roderigo* Mr. Hackett makes *Iago* assume the bearing of a light-hearted philosopher (capable, however, like all Venetians, of strong feelings), who has been deeply injured by *Othello*, and good-natured enough to take upon him the furtherance of his comrade's wishes, while he is working his own purpose upon his enemy ; to *Cassio* he appears merely an honest, faithful soldier, and his friend. Mr. Hackett's well known versatility is of the most essential service to him in the assumption of these different characteristics, and still more in the soliloquies, where his feelings and the workings of his active mind are exhibited without disguise. Throughout the whole five acts his scenes with *Othello* were given with very great tact and effect ; but there was one which we do not hesitate to pronounce masterly. The first of the third act, from the moment in which *Iago* first begins to work upon the

susceptible nature of the *Moor* with his artful insi-
nuations, to the fine hypocritical burst of indignation
with which he breaks out,

"Oh grace! Oh Heaven defend me!
  Are you a man? Have you a soul or sense?
  Heaven be with you—take mine office—Oh wretched fool,
  That liv'st to make thine honesty a vice," etc.

And the half sullen air of honest friendship with
which he says,

  "I should be wise, for honesty's a fool
    And loses that it works for—"

The whole scene was sustained throughout with
admirable force and spirit. But our purpose in
writing this article is not merely to praise Mr.
Hackett, but rather to point out those particulars
wherein he has succeeded in presenting something
original in his performance of a character which
has been so often and so variously played that
novelty would almost seem to be impossible. We
noticed, then, a point which we have not seen made
before—in the second scene, where *Iago's* merry
conversation with *Cassio* is interrupted by the sudden entrance of *Othello:*

  "*Iago.* Faith, he to-night hath boarded a land-carack;
    If it prove lawful prize, he's made for ever.
  Cassio. I do not understand.
  Iago. He's married.
  Cassio. To whom?
  Iago. Marry to—"

Here he stops abruptly in his jesting, and seeing *Othello*, suddenly exclaims, "Come, captain, will you go?" and, in an instant, changes his sneering tone and manner to an appearance of the utmost cordiality and devotion. This is happily conceived, for it is by such touches as these that the Machiavelism of *Iago* is most strikingly exemplified. Another good idea is the significant look to *Roderigo* with which Mr. Hackett singles him out as his opponent in the subsequent scuffle—intimating that they two understand each other. Mr. H. makes another fine point in the second act, when, after making malicious remarks upon the grace of *Cassio's* manner in saluting *Desdemona*, he suddenly bursts out, on hearing the trumpet of the *Moor*, with an assumption of exultation at his safe arrival. We observed a new reading, also, in the first scene of this act—

> "I'll have our Michael Cassio on the hip;
>   Abuse him to the Moor in the *right* garb,"

which we have always before heard read "*rank garb*." Mr. H. probably has some authority for his correction, and it certainly appears just: the "right garb" would signify that very way, which, while it *seems* a palliation, shall, in reality, be an aggravation—*rank* garb we do not understand at all. We think Mr. Hackett correct, also, in making

* The Folio of 1623 reads "*right* garb;" all the later editions substitute the word "*rank*" for "right." When *Iago* says—

Iago pretend to be somewhat affected by the liquor he has drunk in the next scene, where he beguiles *Cassio* with intoxication. Unless he does this, his design upon *Cassio* is too evident; and *Iago* is too crafty to risk the failure of his contrivance by the detection of so clumsy an artifice. The finest point, however, that we noticed (and it is new to us), was the air of earnest and interested attention with which he leaned forward to catch the words of *Othello*, in the second scene, and the involuntary and suddenly suppressed start of joy which he gives when he hears him pronounce the sentence—"Cassio, I love thee, but never more be officer of mine." In the first scene of the third act Mr. H. introduces a reading, which is certainly new, but which we do not approve.

"I'll abuse him to the Moor in the right garb,"

he means—"I will assume the right kind of covering to hide any nakedness of my sinister purpose. I'll seem at first reluctant when ask'd to give *Othello* my evidence—

"*Othello.* Honest Iago, that look'st dead with grieving,
    Speak, who began this? On thy love I charge thee,

"and then I'll so color my narrative of the brawl, and seem so exceedingly anxious to excuse *Cassio's* behavior, as to have forgotten myself and become too hasty and voluble in expressions, and by interjecting apparently conscientious stops and reflective breaks in my specious story, (as, 'Yet *surely Cassio—I believe*—received,' &c.). I shall the more thoroughly *criminate Cassio*, in proportion to my seeming earnestness of effort to *excuse* him to the understanding of *Othello*." That such was the "*right* garb" or cloak to cover his design is proved by the succeeding remarks of *Othello*—

"*Othello.* I know, Iago,
    Thy honesty and love doth mince this matter,
    Making it light to Cassio."

J. H. H.

> "*Othello.* I do not think but Desdemona's honest.
> *Iago.* Long live she so—and long live you to think so.
> *Othello.* But yet, how nature, erring from itself—
> *Iago.* Ay, there's the point, as (to be bold with you)
>   Not to affect," etc.

Mr. Hackett gives quite a different signification to the words in the parenthesis and reads them thus, " as, to be bold, with *you* "—as if he were referring in his own mind to a former observation of her father, who says of her, " a maiden never bold," and now applied the epithet to her conduct, heightening its force by making it refer particularly to *Othello.* To be bold, with *him*, of all men, whose difference of age and complexion should naturally have made him an object of dislike or fear to her. This reading may be correct enough, but the other is quite as good, and has the sanction of long established custom to justify it.

But it is time to put an end to this notice, which, when we began it, we had no thought of extending to such an unreasonable length. We will therefore only mention one more touch in Mr. Hackett's performance, with which we were much pleased, and then conclude with a few words of advice to him— which he will adopt or disregard at his pleasure. The point that we like is the manner of his exit when *Cassio* declares that he had found the handkerchief in his chamber, where it had been dropped by *Iago.* *He* meets the inquiring eyes of *Othello* (naturally directed to him for confirmation), with a significant look and action, expressive of his contempt for the credulity and weakness of his dupe; then gazes fixedly and with a look of exultation upon *Othello* and the fatal bed, and seems to be absorbed in self-gratulating meditation upon the successful issue of his villany, from which he is roused by a touch upon the shoulder from one of the guards, turns, and goes out rapidly and cheerfully, as if content to endure whatever might be in store for him.

The advice we have to give Mr. Hackett is, to play *Iago* again as soon as possible, and to turn his attention, as much as may be, exclusively to tragedy.   Q.

These notices were written by Mr. John Inman for the *N. Y. Evening Post*, where they may be found in its files for April, 1828. I did not take his advice—" to turn my attention as much as may be to tragedy "—because it did not *draw*, as did my *comedy;* besides, it demanded continued study and constant practice, and brought me, who was a *novice*, in continual comparison with old stagers of stereotyped conventionalities, and before audiences containing scarcely one educated critic among them, or capable of discerning and indicating by applauding or condemning my innovations of conception and nice subtleties in collating the text, however *crude* my *acting* might be.

                                                    J. H. H.

Iago has been classified by its players as "a very uphill part;" the reason is obvious. *Iago's* vices and villany are so flagrant that when discovered his very presence becomes hideous and repulsive. *Othello*, on the contrary, displays many ennobling traits of character which enlist and carry along with him the sympathies of an audience, and his *actor's* pretensions to public favor are promoted accordingly; whereas, the *player* of *Iago* has not only no aid towards winning their partiality by its *goodness*, but is in some measure bound to partake of the *demoralizing* effect of their indignation at his character's *baseness*.

An instance of such effect is said to have occurred when *King George the Third* witnessed the performance of *Iago* by the famous George Frederick Cooke; that simple-minded sovereign remarked, "Cooke must be a very bad man *at heart*, because if he were not, he could not so well perform such a *heartless* villain."

When Junius Brutus Booth, who had been brought from the Provinces to the British Metropolis by the Covent Garden Manager, for the special purpose of disputing Edmund Kean's superiority as *Richard the Third* at Drury Lane, had afforded the London public sufficient opportunities for instituting comparisons of their respective pretensions in the part, and concerning the merits of which the great majority appeared in favor of Kean, though Booth had many ardent admirers in the same roll,

Elliston, the Drury Lane Manager, who was a wily politician in theatricals, tempted Booth to "come over from Covent Garden for a night and play *Iago* to Kean's *Othello*," his most favorite part, and pronounced by Lord Byron and all the critics "Kean's most intellectual and artistical performance." Booth was persuaded, and pitted against Kean, who had become thoroughly established in London as "the *Othello* of the age," whilst Booth was comparatively a stranger in London. The result was, that many, who had previously contended that their style and personal peculiarities were very similar and their genius equal, upon seeing the two act together, agreed there was "*no comparison;*" that "Booth could not stand by the side of Kean," and the critics reported that "Kean had floored Booth and walked over him completely." Mr. Booth never recovered any position afterward in London, and in reference to that event, in conversation with me at New York some years afterward, Booth said—"Kean's *Othello* smothered *Desdemona* and my *Iago* too." Edmund Kean returned from his second visit to America to Drury Lane, where he appeared in January, 1827. After performing his established parts repeatedly there was great desire expressed to see him play *Iago*, which he had not acted for a number of years, his *Othello* having become his favorite and established as such with the public. In order to gratify the curious, Mr. James Wallack, then the leading tragedian of that theatre, was cast *Othello*, and Mr.

Kean reappeared on the occasion as *Iago*. Mr. Wallack's *Othello*, though accepted by the great majority of the audience, especially under the exigency, was not satisfactory to a few who expressed disapprobation at his delivery of certain of Kean's points, ungenerously comparing him with Kean's standard, when Mr. Wallack had had no ambition, and indeed had *unwillingly* consented to play *Othello* with him; nevertheless Mr. Kean made no feature then of his *Iago*, and I believe never performed it again.

During the winter of 1832–33 Captain Polhill, the lessee, through Alfred Bunn, his acting-manager, engaged Macready to play *Iago* to Kean's *Othello*, with the understanding that Kean, after a few performances of *Othello*, would appear as *Iago* alternately to Macready's *Othello*. Macready's *Iago* was generally commended by critics, and seemed to me a very creditable performance of his own conception, but it was not generally admired as much as Charles Young's. Macready, however, could not obtain an opportunity to perform *Othello* with Kean, who, though urged again and again by the manager, positively and repeatedly refused.

The fact is, the conventional idea was then and generally still obtains among the theatrical public that *Iago* should be acted in a black wig and with heavy black eyebrows, and betray in his countenance throughout, and in all his outward semblance, the characteristics of a barefaced ruffian, whereas

Nature furnishes black-hearted villains of all complexions, and the records of crime have shown more of light than of a dark complexion; besides, if *Iago's* villany is made so apparent to *all* around him, and not confined as it should be to his *soliloquies*, and where only by his self-communion the audience are let into his secrets as he *exposes* his subtlety, *Othello* could not have been so deceived by him as to remark, "this fellow's of exceeding honesty and knows all qualities with a learned spirit of human dealings" and repeatedly calling him "*honest, honest Iago*." Though Shakespeare intended *Iago* to *dupe* that silly young gallant *Roderigo*, he surely never designed that he should make *easily* and *readily* a *fool* of *Othello;* though he apostrophizes to himself as such after the denouement, "Oh! fool, fool, fool!"

The character of *Iago* is composed of such peculiar traits, some of his very words in soliloquy have such particular significance, and require such marked emphasis to make them the more intelligible to his audience, his subtlety and hypocrisy, his direct and his sinister motives and purposes are so skilfully blended, and carefully or more or less artfully concealed according to his respective objects and the different penetration or circumstances of each one with whom he has any intercourse, that the part requires to be diligently and patiently studied in *all* its bearings before even the most comprehensive genius can clearly perceive the immortal dramatist's design; and then, none but some actor of great talent in portraying dissimulation, and of sound judgment and long experience, may reasonably hope to produce *such* effects upon an ordinary audience as will prove satisfactory to them *generally* and to himself as an *artist* particularly.

Iago may indeed be regarded by professional actors as one of the most uncertain " and least profitable of *great* parts which can be attempted within the whole range of Shakespeare's dramas," and if an actor would become *popular* in that character, he must, for the sake of effect upon the uninstructed and impracticable majority of play-goers, submit to their false but settled notions respecting *Iago*, and sacrifice as a condition his own *true judgment* and an orthodox *consistency* with the poet's words and his obvious meaning.

FALSTAFF.

PART VI.

FALSTAFF.

FALSTAFF,

IN THE FIRST PART OF KING HENRY IV.

LATE in the month of May, 1831, whilst Charles Kean and myself were starring upon alternate nights at the Arch Street Theatre, Philadelphia, and were fellow-guests in Head's Mansion House—then the most favorite hotel of that city—we strolled about the town together.

In the course of our promenade, Charles Kean asked me if I had "ever thought of acting *Falstaff?*" I replied that "with such object I had partially studied the character." He observed, " I have a strong desire to play *Hotspur*, and if you will undertake to be ready within a week to make a first appearance in *Falstaff*, I will essay *Hotspur* on the occasion for the first time also." We performed accordingly, and both were favorably received, *May* 31, 1832. The weather that evening was very warm, and the costume I wore covering a

14

heavy padding or stuffing of curled hair—to give the requisite rotundity to *Fat Jack's* large proportions—together with my anxiety and nervousness about the result, caused me to perspire very profusely.   Towards the conclusion of the play, the manager, Mr. Duffy, came behind the scenes, and repeated some complimentary remarks which he said certain critics among the audience had made to him, and inquired, " How do you feel now ?"   I replied, " Severely punished by the heat of the weather, intensified as it is by confined space, the gaslights, and the breath of the audience."   " Psha!" rejoined Mr. Duffy, " you don't suffer at all when compared with *Cooper*" (*Thomas A.*), " just such a night as this about a year ago.   After *Falstaff's* running away and roaring for 'Mercy,' when surprised and chased from Gad's Hill by the Prince and Poins, Cooper insisted upon having the large double-doors at the back of the stage—constructed in order to admit elephants, horses and cars, on occasion—thrown wide open ; and, regardless of the rear being upon a public alley, ordered his servant to bring a chair, which he placed in that opening and sat himself there, to pant and try to cool himself.   Every time thereafter, as he came off the stage, he threw himself into the chair, and commenced by crying aloud to his servant—'Where's that brandy and water?'   'Here, sir!'   Having swigged it down, Cooper next ordered him, ' Bring here a looking-glass!'   After reconnoitring his features in the mirror—'There's that bloody-red nose of mine, and more characteristic than Bardolph's; get some chalk and whiten it!' His servant had hardly time to effect it, when Cooper was called to the stage. Upon returning, as before, he called first for 'brandy and water!' then for the looking-glass, and, again surveying his face, he rebuked his servant—'Didn't I tell you, sirrah, to chalk my nose?' His man replied, 'I did, sir, but you sweat so much the chalk won't *stay* on it!' 'Well, then, take a towel and wipe my nose *dry*, first, and then rub *more chalk* over it.' He was interrupted by the *call-boy*—'Mr. Cooper, the stage is waiting for you!' 'Is it? I'll pray to be d——d if ever I undertake to act this infernal old vagabond again!'"

With respect to my own and peculiar conception and rendition upon the stage of the character of *Falstaff*, and concerning which I may be expected to write something, I would premise, that, as it is seldom given to us to see ourselves as others see us, perhaps I cannot convey to such as never have and never may see my performance of the part an idea of it better than by transcribing some of the most graphic reports of various critics for the press in Great Britain and America, beginning in 1840.

FALSTAFF:

A SHAKESPEREAN TRACT.

As a curious native American, my attention has been occasionally arrested by the labored attempts of certain London theatrical critics at what is termed "fine writing;" and as my own *debût* in *Falstaff*, at Drury Lane theatre, elicited a critique of this species "in the leading journal of Europe," I will merely take up and review the writer's *premises*, which relate solely to the *character* itself, in order that, as its *actor*, I may escape any imputation of an unbecoming captiousness towards a professional censor about what follows and treats specially of my stage readings.

A critic of the "Times" Newspaper of 2d November inst., in reporting the representation of the "*First Part of Henry the Fourth*," advances the following characteristics, as constituting his "ideal" of *Falstaff*, which, by sentences, I will here recapitulate in *italics*, and then attempt, link by link, to unravel his *conceptions*, coiled with such seeming subtlety. After capping his notice with the title of the play, and some general remarks, he commences thus :—

  " *What an accurate balancing, a nice adjustment of qualities, is necessary to portray Falstaff, that he may be the proper mixture of debau-*

*chée, coward, bully, wit, and courtier, without
being one to the exclusion of the rest, or an
unfortunate, disjointed succession of all!"*

Such a problem, I should imagine, would be
unavoidably solved if the actor justly and accu-
rately delivers Shakespeare's own ingredients,
accompanied by such action as may be natural
to one of his bulk and breeding, in his relative
situations.

*" What richness in every word that is to be ut-
tered!"*

Vocal "richness" depends upon each listener's
own ideas of what is the quality of voice peculiar
to *obesity;* my own observation of human nature
has determined me that fat men generally have
either *thin* voices, or such as are constantly alternat-
ing between a bass and a falsetto, as if escaping a
throat partially clogged with a surplus of flesh.

*" What unctuosity of tongue as well as person;
what an assumption of maudlin uneasiness
that ever pinches Falstaff into a sort of repentance!"*

I cannot imagine any, inasmuch as he never exhibits the slightest proof of a sincere disposition to
repent of anything. Once, indeed, being " troubled
by him with vanity," he affectedly threatens the
Prince with his own amendment, by " giving over
this life;" and in almost the same breath, being
tempted, yields, and relapses "from praying to
purse-taking." At another time, when apostrophiz-

ing his loss of flesh—his fear of becoming "out of
heart shortly"—his forgetfulness of "what the inside
of a church is made of," and the spoliatory effects
of "villanous company," Bardolph insinuates he is
"so fretful, he cannot live long;" whereupon,
instead of any sign of *repentance*, he calls for "a
bawdy song, to make him merry."

> "*What rapidity in the discharge of the apt epi-
> thets which beget one another with such astound-
> ing fertility,*"——

Doubtless as much rapidity in articulation as is
consistent with his physical short-windedness, and a
zealous desire to return promptly the personalities
heaped upon him, at one time, by the Prince with
such exemplary volubility, mutually unrestrained
(as they are) by any well-bred consideration of the
presence of their low companions.

> "——*what courtesy to the heir apparent are
> necessary, before even the most careless peruser
> of Shakespeare can see the Falstaff of his
> imagination.*"

What *courtesy?* Indeed, very little of any sort
can reasonably be expected from "an impudent,
embossed rascal," who, whenever annoyed, is hardly
restrained by intimidation from pursuing his scur-
rility towards a prince, not only habituated to *his*
familiarities, called "rascalliest," and told to "hang
himself in his own heir-apparent garters," but *such*
an one as, to indulge his "inordinate and low
desires, barren pleasures—rude society," invites

general disrespect, by descending (as himself describes) to "sound the very base-string of humility, and to become sworn brother to a leash of drawers, calling them Tom, Dick, and Francis," and proficient enough to drink "with any tinker, in his own language, the rest of his life."

Such *bold* shew of "*courtesy*" as is compatible with his venturing a familiar, if not impertinent, joke on Worcester's defection in the presence of Majesty itself; for example when the King animadverts thereon, he interjects—"Rebellion lay in his way, and he found it!"

Such *respectful* "*courtesy*," under the most trying circumstances, as may merit the rebuke of the Prince in the heat of the battle, when refused his sword, and misled by the offer of his "pistol," he draws *Falstaff's sack-bottle*, and rushes away angrily, exclaiming—"Is it a time to jest and dally now?"

> "*With all the bold outline and full-facedness of a coarsely painted Dutch clock, he has all the delicate organization of a Geneva watch; and hard is it for the actor to avoid marring some part of the fine machinery.*"

This clock-and-watch figure may be *striking* to *others*, but to discover the most remote analogy between such mechanism and *Falstaff's* bodily exterior, with its soul's motive shining clearly through every action, puzzles *me* as much as I think it would have done the Prince to compare the minutes of that "long hour by Shrewsbury clock," wherein the dead *Percy* and the prostrate and death-counterfeiting *Falstaff*, "both rose at the same instant and fought" so valiantly.

Indulgent British reader! Accustomed as we *Americans* have been to reverence the chastening rod of *London* criticism,—once the fiat of each new Shakespearean actor's fate, and hallowed, as in by-gone days, for its stimulating and restraining influence upon many, whose genius then illumined, and whose memories still reflect a glimmering glory on the British stage, how unavoidably must our esteem decline at such specimens of degeneracy!—and when, also, such a journal as the "Morning Chronicle," (in reference to the same occasion,) after premising that "Mr. Hackett is indisputably a good comedian,"—his "*Falstaff* about as good as any now on the stage," &c., sagely remarks, "there was a good deal of jollity about him, but withal, coarse: THOUGH FALSTAFF IS A HUMORIST, HE IS A GENTLEMAN."[*]

Falstaff a GENTLEMAN!!! I should like to learn in what *one* respect beyond the ideal quality associated with a *knighthood*. The Prince sketches to him the following picture of himself,—viz. "a *devil* in the likeness of a fat old man—a tun of man—a trunk of humors—*a bolting hutch of beastliness*—a swoln parcel of dropsies—a huge bombard of sack—a reverend vice—grey iniquity, father-ruffian, vanity in years—neat and cleanly only in carving a capon

* *Mad Tom*, in *King Lear*, says "The Prince of darkness is a gentleman."—J. H. H.

and eating it—villanous in all things, and worthy in nothing." Are any of *these* innate characteristics of a gentleman? Even what prepossessing *personal appearance* does *Falstaff's* own vanity claim? "A good portly man—of a cheerful look, a pleasing eye, and a most noble carriage!" and admits withal that he is "old and merry." What is his *conduct?* Is he not mean, cowardly, and selfish?—addicted to "incomprehensible lying?"—lawfully due to the gallows for highway robbery?—guilty of "abusing the king's press damnably," by a fraudulent exchange of soldiery, and of cruelty in leading his "ragamuffins where they are so well peppered that not three out of a hundred and fifty are left alive?" Is he not overbearing to his humble dependents? Is not the poor hostess, who has trusted him a long score for "his diet and by-drinkings, and bought him a dozen shirts to his back, and lent him twenty pounds besides," slandered most wantonly and grossly by him, whom she may well call "a foul-mouthed man?" If so, the sentiments and feelings of a *gentleman* cannot be predicated of his *words* or his *actions;* nor can any actor who delivers certain of his language, and that the least objectionable to modern ears polite, as, "*you lie, hostess,*" &c., avoid being identified with vulgarity and *coarseness.* As for *Falstaff's* disposition to cultivate a dignified and court *manner,* his ambition in that particular may be inferred from his own words, that "to become a rare *hangman,* jumps with his humor as well as

waiting in the court;" in fact, except for a few
moments when meeting Westmoreland, there is no
situation in the acting-play where *Falstaff* would
not consider an assumed *refinement of manner*, useless affectation.

In conclusion, Shakespeare has invested that philosophic compound of vice and sensuality, with no
amiable or tolerable quality to gloss or cover his
moral deformity, except a surpassingly-brilliant and
charming wit, and a spontaneous and irresistible flow
of humor. That the character was designed for
stage effect is evident from his many practically-
dramatic situations, and the idea that it is beyond
the reach of histrionic art to represent him properly
can only originate in a hypercritical and fantastic
imagination ; one of that sickly cast, which, like
unto a peevish child, would not rest satisfied even if
humored with its own fancies ; therefore, the ends
of *criticism* would be far more beneficially gained
by the public and the performer, if censors for the
press would occasionally analyze, where they differ
about prominent traits of character, and particular-
ize any new candidate's defects, whether of judgment, art, or physical qualifications ; then could
every reader judge for himself, instead of being, as
now, obliged to yield his premises to the *ipse dixit*
of some Sir Oracle, who may confound the faculties
of his cursory observer, by a sweeping *ad-captan-
dum-vulgus* display of pseudo-intelligence, and
impose also upon the player, who, having made a

study of character the business of his life, may possibly have *forgotten* more than such a mere occasional peruser ever knew of the subject-matter.

JAMES H. HACKETT.

22 CHARLOTTE STREET, BEDFORD }
SQUARE, LONDON, Nov. 5, 1839. }

Extract from the London Times, Feb. 7, 1845.

" *Mr. Hackett*, the American comedian, has re-appeared at Covent Garden as *Falstaff* in the First Part of Henry IV., a character on which, we have heard, he has bestowed great study ; and his performance bears the mark of study. There is probably not a gesture, look, or motion, on the part of Mr. Hackett, which has not in his mind its meaning and significance. This is in itself a commendation. It is something now-a-days to find an actor desiring earnestly to give a view of a character, when it is so ordinary a plan to learn by rote a few conventionalities, and conceive nothing. As for the view itself, that is another matter. We should say that Mr. Hackett looks upon *Falstaff* as a slower and more deliberate person than he is usually considered—less rejoicing in the play of his own fancy, more premeditative with his jokes, more seriously irascible. The exterior of the character, as he gives it, is touchy, fretful, even serious ; it is only on occasions that the mirth breaks out, and then, by the intensity of the laugh, he marks a strong contrast with the usual deportment. * * If we rightly interpret Mr. Hackett's meaning, as displayed in his acting, it is this: that *Falstaff* is a man of cynical temperament, with the infirmity of age already weighing upon him—that he has a kind of mental as well as bodily obesity, and that though the internal humor of the man is unquestionable, it does not readily rise to the top. To this view of the character Mr. Hackett seems to have worked up most conscientiously. Two isolated speeches we heard with unmingled satisfaction. *Falstaff's* description of his ragged regiment was given with a real sense of enjoyment at the ridiculous. The " fun" was allowed free play—the laugh at the exit was capital. The other speech was that on the futility of honor— good for a different reason. The deliberate qualities of the actor were well placed in this soliloquy, which, though comic, is deeply reflective, and in- volves the destruction of the whole life of the mid- dle ages."

Remarks upon the Foregoing.

LONDON, Feb. 7, 1845.

After many years of stage-practice in the *Falstaff* of both parts of *King Henry IV.*, and also in that of *The Merry Wives of Windsor*, I think there was not a phase of the character—either as exhibited in his own words, or as relatively indicated by their context—which has escaped my minute observation and very careful consideration before I resorted to histrionic art to embody and represent it to an audience; still, as I claim no infallibility of judgment, I hold my senses ever open to conviction, and am pleased rather than offended whenever a critic will take any *reasonable* exception to my own *understanding*, or will *specify* his objections to my *personation* of *Falstaff*. By a critic, I mean one who at least remembers each of the plays wherein Shakespeare has introduced *Falstaff*. I have made the character a practical study the greater portion of my professional life, and feel ready to maintain my conception with the poet's text and its most obvious interpretation.

Every *trait* of my representation, described by "The Times," I contend for, and I am gratified in discovering that I succeeded in depicting each so clearly. The specific character of *Falstaff*'s humor changes with the *circumstances*. When *Poins* has hidden *Falstaff*'s horse behind the hedge, and by such practical joke has compelled old *Fat Jack* to clamber Gadshill on *foot*, *Falstaff* is said to "*fret like a gummed velvet;*" he also fumes out a long soliloquy of splenetic invective, ending with—"I hate it!"

The "Times" critic charges that I look upon *Falstaff* as "more seriously irascible than he is usually considered." I would submit whether *Falstaff* would *not* be in *earnest* when *Poins* confesses the trick he had put upon him, and shelters himself behind the *Prince* to escape punishment, in saying—

"*Now*, can not I *strike* him if I were to be hanged;" and also, whether it was not *Poins's* agility or the *Prince's* personal interference, or the urgency of their predatory expedition, which *prevented Falstaff* from "*striking him.*"

In *Falstaff's* abuse of the hostess, and when back-biting the *Prince*, he interjects—

"The Prince! He is a Jack! a sneak-cup! and if he were here and were to say so, *I'd cudgel him like a dog!*"

In fact, the *Second* Part of Henry IV., and the Merry Wives of Windsor, too, furnish many instances of *Falstaff's* habitual recourse to his "cudgel," and of the indulgence of his "*irascible*" humors. Is not *Falstaff* "*touchy?*" Mark! When *Bardolph*, encouraged to become familiar with him, ventures a jest confirming *Falstaff's* own report of his condition—"Now, I live out of all *order*, and out of all compass," and remarks, "Why, Sir John, you are so *fat* you must needs be out of all compass!" *Falstaff proves* himself "*touchy;*" because *Bardolph* finds cause to *qualify* his observation immediately by adding, "out of all *reasonable* compass;" yet, it does not restrain an immediate display of *Falstaff's* "*cynical temperament,*" for which *Bardolph's* face and appearance furnish a subject.

I contend that there *should* be "marked, a strong contrast between" the *heartiness* of *Falstaff's* mirth according to *circumstances;* for example, when he is cornered into his wit's end, to escape detection in the lies which he has just told the *Prince* and *Poins*, and swears—

> "I *knew* ye, as well as he that made ye!"

the *exigency* of the occasion (to "hide himself from the open and apparent shame") and a *forced* mirth *ought* to be discernible in the *acting*—in order to characterize it distinctly from the *unctuous* kind, and wherever it is the spontaneous and the irresistible ebullition of his own exuberant fancy; as, for example, when he is surveying in soliloquy and luxuriating upon the features of his own ragged regiment.

That *Falstaff* feels "the infirmity of age already weighing upon him," may be proved from various expressions of his at different times; says he— "There live *not* three *good* men unhanged in England, and one of *them* is fat and grows old!" thus insinuating that there exist but *two ;* one of course being his *king,* and the other *himself,* that king's loyal subject.

Respecting *Falstaff's* "mental as well as bodily obesity," which the "Times" critic also discovers in my rendering on the stage, the *Prince* tells him, when *Falstaff* inquires the "*time of the day,* "Thou art so fat-*witted* with drinking of old sack," &c., &c.

Extract from The Times, London, June 27, 1851.

"*Mr. Hackett,* the American comedian, who

favors us with visits at very long intervals, comes
back to us with precisely the same qualities which
he displayed years ago. There is probably not a
more conscientious actor on the stage. He has
evidently studied the speeches of the fat knight,
whether uttered in *Henry IV.* or *The Merry Wives
of Windsor*, with a carefulness worthy of a com-
mentator on Sophocles. He has a definite manner
of giving every phrase, and of introducing every
jest. The finest mosaic work could not be more
carefully laid down. And there is not only care,
but considerable intelligence evinced in the rendering. The mind of an acute artist has evidently
been devoted to a character, with the view of digging everything out of its hidden recesses, and
making of it the completest thing in the world.
And yet there is one deficiency, which prevents the
Falstaff from producing its full effect on the audience. This is, the want of the *ars celare artem;*
you approve of the result at which the artist has
arrived, but you always see the pains he takes to
reach it."

Remark.

If this critic, in the subtlety of his penetration,
could find but "*one* deficiency" in my making my
Falstaff "*the completest thing in the world*," and
that deficiency, too, such a one as none but the
most unsophisticated of spectators could fail to

detect to be, after all, no more than *acting*, or stage-art, and *intended*, by "an acute artist," to only represent *naturally* an *imaginary* character, under the particular circumstances of his varying scenes, I can't ask nor expect more from "The Times" newspaper—ever notorious for its parsimony of praise and its liberality of censure : the rule of *that* press being never to compliment any body or action without a "*but*," or some *qualifying* reservation. The dignity of its policy on every subject and in every department forbids that its *editor* can be fallible in judgment, or ever surprised or instructed on any occasion.

JAMES H. HACKETT.

SKETCH OF JAMES H. HACKETT.

BY CHARLES J. FOSTER.

Chief Justice. What's he that goes there ?
Attendant. Falstaff, an't please your lordship.

IT has often been said that though the triumphs of the actor are immediate, they are not lasting. The fruition of his efforts is quickly gathered ; he hears the thunder of applauding multitudes while he is yet upon the stage, but it is as brief as it is boisterous and intoxicating. It confers no enduring fame like that which, ripening slowly, rewards the author, the painter, the sculptor, and the statesman, and lives for ever. Shakespeare himself may have been of this opinion, for he likens life to the "poor player, that struts and frets his hour upon the stage, and then is heard no more." With all due deference to the great authorities who have propounded this idea, it may well be questioned. The fame of the really great actor is not as evanescent as has been supposed. His profession is one of the polite arts; and he who elevates and adorns it does not merely revel in exquisite applause while upon the stage, to sink into oblivion when the curtain falls upon this mortal scene. He is the companion of those whose pencils write their names upon the pedestal of fame, and whose chisels carve out immortality in indestructible marble. He is the friend of the poet and biographer, whose pens illustrate and embalm the men and manners of their time for all succeeding ages. His fame is but little more evanescent than their own, than that of most of those who win glory in command of armies, or shape the fate of nations in the deliberations of senates. Roscius is not forgotten. We know as much of Betterton as of Bradshaw, the regicide. Garrick's fame will survive the memory of the monarch who fed mutton upon his own turnips at Kew, and philosophising over the baked dumpling, asked, how got the apple in? Kean and Kemble will have a name among polished nations after the vagaries of "the finest gentleman in Europe" are no more remembered; and Talma will go down to later ages in company with the " Man of Destiny " and Talleyrand. It is very true that the actor leaves nothing of his own behind him, by which after generations can revise the verdict of his contemporaries, nor is it necessary to his fame. His finest efforts instantly are " melted into air—into thin air! " but this is nearly so with those of the great orator as well. From the necessities of the case, we accept the judgment of those who saw and heard them, as the unquestionable guarantee of that genius which commands the admiration of every generation of men. The fame of poets, painters, and sculptors does not rest upon the judgments of the mass of mankind upon their works. How many men in this age have seen a fragment from the hand of Phidias? How many of those who hold Raphael to have been the greatest of painters have looked at one of his pictures? How many of those who believe in Homer have read him, except through the ground and polished spectacles of Alexander Pope? I grant that the notoriety which some actors mistake for fame is as short-lived as, to any man of genius and sensibility, it would be unendurable ; but this is also true of daubers who think they are artists, of scribblers who believe themselves authors, and of charlatans who pretend to be statesmen. It scarcely needs the investigations of future ages to detect the imposture. The foolish of Dryden's time thought Settle a poet—the wise knew him to be a dunce. Pensioners and parasites, in all ages, proclaim the minister who pays them "a heaven-born statesman;" but the bold and honest leave it upon record that he is a wretched jobber. Everybody knows the brazen-faced and brazen-throated mountebanks who purchase venal praise with little cash and many bibulous gratuities; everybody knows the versatile sons of genius, for whom no tragedy is too high, no farce too low; everybody knows the admirable men who are equally excellent in presenting the almost divine creations of Shakespeare, and the delirious conceptions of any fustian rascal who will murder the English language, and massacre his characters expressly and solely for their use and behoof. For a brief space, and among the green ones (but not in the green-room), the fame of such persons seems almost to equal, and sometimes to surpass, that of the really great actor. While his greatest excellence is rarely seen in more than two or three characters, these fellows are declared by their puffers to be fine in all. The real difference in kind, however, is fully as great as the apparent difference in degree. It is a cat's-eye diamond to a ton of coal. Both have carbon for a base, but one is constituted brilliant, to endure for ever; the other will be dust and ashes long before its lucky owner is. In every polished age vast numbers of people, and those not the least informed, have taken much interest in the reminiscences and memoirs of truly great actors. They enter into the spirit of their early struggles, sympathise with their disappointments, dwell upon their triumphs, and devour the gossip of the stage and its antechambers with avidity. Something of one of these great actors I am about briefly to sketch. It is a labor of love, for I believe that could Shakespeare see his plays, as they are performed in our day, he would esteem Hackett as the best exponent of one of the most delightful and difficult of his characters that has trod the stage since his bones were laid by Avon side. Nor will this actor's fame be evanescent, in my opinion. From the very nature and degree of it, he is without a rival living, he will never be without admirers dead. When he, and you, and I, and sixty years have gone, old gentlemen will say to the play-goer of the day, "I saw Hackett in *Falstaff*, sir. He was the finest '*Sir John*' that ever enacted the character!" And when sixty times sixty years have elapsed, I have little doubt but the dramatic critic and antiquary will declare, "the real *Falstaff* died with Hackett; and one of Shakespeare's masterpieces is, as yet, no more!"

James H. Hackett was born in New York, in the year 1800. He came of good stock, and is now the oldest male lineal descendant of *Haket*, a Norman knight, who crossed the Channel with the Conqueror, and whose descendants were, no doubt, men of mark among the Hackems and Slashems who followed Strongbow to Ireland, and Richard to the Holy Land. The actor is heir to the title long held by the

* *Haket*, of Hackett's-town, County Carlow, and Shelton Abbey,

Barons Hackett, of Hackett's Court in Ireland.
Some of our cotemporary journals have put forth a
good deal of nonsense about his reasons for not
asserting his right to the peerage. The story goes,
that he does not claim the title because being a
recognized gentleman, the equal of any, in America,
a British Barony, the third degree in the peerage,
would degrade him, and make his rank relatively
below what it is at present. Then follows the old
formula about "good breeding," "worth makes the
man," "honor and shame from no condition rise,"
&c. Stuff like this could scarcely have emanated
from Mr. Hackett; and it is quite certain that Sir
John Falstaff would have treated it with sovereign
contempt. Those who tell the story are not even
consistent in their nonsense. They begin by prais-
ing Mr. Hackett for not claiming certain rank, and
then assert that he does not claim it because it will
lower the rank and consideration he already enjoys.
But the absurdity does not stop here. No man of
sense really believes that the descendant of a long

County Wicklow, derived from *Dominus Paganus de Hackett*, who
himself descended from one of the great Norman Barons under the
Conqueror at Hastings, whose name appears on the Roll of Battle
Abbey.   Paganus, in more than a century afterwards, accompanied
Henry II. into *Ireland*, and acquired broad lands and Seignories there;
and his descendants, generation after generation, were subsequently
parliamentary barons and potent magnates in Ireland."—*Burke's
Armorie of England, Scotland, and Ireland.   London, 4to. 1844.*

line of valiant and honorable men would be degraded below other gentlemen, anywhere, by reason of his succession to the title they bore for centuries. Is it any worse for a gentleman to be a baron than to be an actor? Grant that the descendants of Nell Gwynne, and the Duchess of Portsmouth, will have precedence of him at Court on certain State occasions—they have *now*, if he goes there. They have it over the American Minister, but who declines the embassy on that account? Again, if dukes, marquises and earls, rank above the Barons Hackett in Dod's Peerage and the book of the Court Chamberlain, they do not in the estimation of the English people. The baron of ancient degree does not owe his patent to the compliances of wantons, or the services of chamberers. The names of his kin are in Doomesday Book, and on the roll of Battle Abbey! His ancestors were among those "barons" who wrested the Great Charter from John, at Runnymede, after having spilt their martial blood under his valiant brother, beneath the walls of Ascalon.

> "The knights are dust—
> Their swords are rust,
> Their souls with the saints I trust;
> And honor their names we must."

The man of fine genius and rare intelligence, never talked as this idle tale supposes. It smacks of the demagogue, who, believing the people to be as foolish as he really is himself, endeavors to impose upon them by clap-trap as wretched as that shouted to clowns in country theatres by buffoons barely fit to grin through a horse's collar. Hackett declined to claim the title he might have had, because he had achieved fame by his own efforts, and because he is of a nation which has wisely discarded titles in its economy of place and honor. This was sensible, a proper respect for principle, which everybody can understand; whereas, nobody can understand how the taking of the title could have been degrading in any sense of the word.*

* The basis of this newspaper-story was constructed out of an after-dinner and incidental conversation in England in the autumn of 1839; and Mr. Hackett was reported, by an American correspondent who happened to be a guest also, to have replied—when asked, "Why, possessing an attested pedigree,* he had not claimed the *title* of a *Baron?*"—"Because, it is now only an *honorary* one. It was derived originally from a descendant of *Haket* (whose name is still visible upon the Pillar at Battle Abbey near Hastings, as one of the Norman nobles and Generals of *William the First*, that shared richly with him in his *Conquest of England*) who attended *Henry the Second* into *Ireland*, and obtained large landed estates there, but has become *extinct*, and is now only recognised as having, through many centuries, lastly and properly belonged to the Peerage of a by-gone and since disintegrated Irish Parliament. Hence the *title* is now only the shadow of a departed dignity, and such as could offer no temptation to a native and an unostentatious *American* to parade anywhere as an appendage to his family-name."   J.

* Issued in 1834, by the *Ulster King at Arms*, to the late Edmond—the last of the Barons—*Hackett*, who died when visiting New Orleans in 1839.

In 1815, after the turbulent star of Talma's friend, Napoleon, had set in a sea of fire and blood, young Hackett was entered at Columbia College. His poor health, however, prevented a close and long devotion to classical studies. A severe attack of sickness compelled him to leave the college, and after his recovery he began the study of the law. But even thus early, the works of our great dramatists had for him an irresistible charm, and much time that might have been devoted to Coke upon Lyttleton, and the Commentaries of Mr. Justice Blackstone, was given to Shakespeare's plays. He began to lay the foundation of that large and accurate knowledge of these works, which has since guided him to truthful conceptions in the closet, and borne such splendid fruit upon the stage. He did not pursue the study of legal principles and practice long, but I dare say he mastered enough of them to appreciate the almost marvellous wisdom which built up the structure of the Common Law, and then devised the maxims and rules of equity to assuage the sometime harshness of its strict application. In 1819 Mr. Hackett was married to Miss Catharine Lee Sugg, a young actress of much ability, fine vocal talent, and many charms of mind as well as person. The young couple settled at Utica, in this State, where he embarked in mercantile pursuits. In Utica they remained six years, at the end of which time, desiring to extend his business operations, Mr.

Hackett removed to New York. The change was unfortunate for the merchant, but happy for the man. He failed in business, and his wife returned to the stage, where she received the welcome eminently due to her talents and virtues. On the first of March, 1826, at the Park Theatre, Mr. Hackett made his *début* in public, as Justice Woodcock, in Love in a Village, his wife playing Rosetta. He was not successful, for his efforts were frustrated by extreme nervousness. Perhaps his supposed failure on this occasion was not an unfavorable omen as to his future career. There is an order of mind in which high powers are joined to a self-possession not to be shaken, but it is very rare. There are also two or three other things which may enable a man to stand such an ordeal without emotion. One is stolid insensibility, but he who is preserved from nervousness on his first night by that, had better quit the stage at once and go to rail-splitting. In that case he may, in time, come to be President, whereas he can never, under any circumstances, become a good actor. Another is a flippant self-conceit which keeps its possessor in blissful ignorance of the fact that he is making a fool of himself. The first effort of such a man is apt to be as good as his last, and that is not saying much for either of them.

Nine days after Mr. Hackett's first appearance, he availed himself of the opportunity afforded by his wife's benefit to go before the audience of the Park Theatre again. He played *Sylvester Daggerwood*, with imitations of Matthews, Kean, Hilson, and Barnes. His efforts on this occasion were so highly applauded, that his resolution to adopt the profession of an actor was confirmed. He soon made another " hit," as the bills have it, as *Dromio*, in the *Comedy of Errors*, Barnes playing the other brother. Hackett gave such a capital imitation of the voice, manner, and peculiarities of Mr. Barnes, that the audience were confused as to their identity, and convulsed with laughter all through the play. In the spring of the following year Mr. Hackett visited England. I can imagine the bounding spirit and emotion with which such a man treads for the first time the boards of Covent Garden and Old Drury, and becomes familiar with the haunts of Shakespeare and rare Ben Jonson. He first appeared in London, at Covent Garden, in *Sylvester Daggerwood*, with imitations of Kean and Macready, and stories of American life and manners. The latter, no doubt, of the old Knickerbocker folk, and of Western characters, such as those in the Arkansaw Traveller, were vastly amusing; the imitations of Kean were so good, that Jones induced Mr. Hackett to play a whole scene from *Richard* in the style of the great tragedian. Hackett, however, soon returned to this country, where his excellent performances of *Dromio, Solomon Swap, Nimrod Wildfire, Rip Van Winkle, Monsieur Mallet, &c.*, procured him many friends and hosts of admirers. At this time he was interested in the management of the old Chatham and Bowery Theatres, but did not find the treasury of either establishment a Californian placer. In the fall of 1832 he again went to England. During this sojourn in London he played at Covent Garden, Drury Lane, and the Haymarket, concluding his engagements by playing *Falstaff*, in which part he had appeared once before in America. In this great and subtle creation of Shakespeare, the fame of Hackett was mainly won. He may have played other characters very well, but they had not for him the scope and significance of this. We do not see the stars when the sun is shining. Nobody cares about *Dromio* or *Solomon Swap* when sweet *Sir John*, portly, rollicking, full-to-the-brim-and-running-over *Falstaff*, with his flashing, many-sided, diamond-cutting wit, is in question. This is quite natural. Washington may have been an excellent surveyor, Jenner may have had a capital salve for a cut finger, James Watt may have improved cooking stoves or candlesticks, but, inasmuch as the first wrought the deliverance of America, the second discovered vaccination, and the third invented the condensing engine, nobody thinks of their minor achievements. Hackett's name has become identified with the personality of *Sir John Falstaff* wherever our language is spoken. To play the part as he plays it is to do what no other man, certainly no other of this age, has ever done. *Falstaff*, one of the most glorious creations of our great dramatist, was lost to the stage for want of a competent interpreter, and with him sank the lesser lights who revolve around him in three plays. Why was this? Fat men were plenty enough, as models, and roguery and wine-bibbing have always been extant. Thinking that these are the essentials of the part, every low comedy man is persuaded that he could play it. The manager, however, who, according to said comedian, was once hissed in it himself, refuses, out of sheer envy, to let the favorite of the gallery appear as *Sir John*. The judicious are very glad of it, for in ninety-nine cases out of a hundred we should have all the grossness of *Jack Paunch* and none of the wit of *Sir John Falstaff*. The subtle, mercurial essence which informs the character would escape to no purpose in hands like these. Corporeally, *Sir John* is heavy; intellectually, he is lightsome and nimble as the "tricksy spirit" who ministered to *Prospero*, when he

> "———————— be-dimmed
> The noontide sun, call'd forth the mutinous winds,
> And 'twixt the green sea and the azure vault
> Set roaring war."

Hackett is as near perfection as can well be conceived in this character. It is one of the most difficult of those we owe to the immortal author, whose genius created it; and it must have been a favorite with him. The marvellous readiness, the rich fancy, the exuberant wit, the imperturbable self-possession in circumstances which would confound a hundred others, the manners of the gentleman never departed from in the most ludicrous situations, the real good-nature which underlies the disposition of the great, roguish roysterer, and, above all, the luscious, unctuous humor with which *Falstaff* really "lards the lean earth as he walks along," are all admirably preserved by Hackett. *Sir John*, mark you, drinks much sack, but he is never reeling ripe, like *Sir Toby* and *Sir Andrew*, in Twelfth Night. "If sack and sugar be a fault, God help the wicked!" He goes out to commit highway robbery, but he is no thief. He offers *Bardolph* as security to *Master Dumbleton*, for a new doublet and slops, but he is no swindler. He borrows a thousand pounds of *Justice Shallow*, but says to him, when he hears that the young King has come to the throne, "Choose what office thou wilt in the land, 'tis thine!" He runs away at Gadshill, but he is not a poltroon. "Not John of Gaunt, your grandfather, but yet no coward, Hal." The real highwayman ran away too. Each took his fellow for an officer. It is true that the "instinct" and epicurean philosophy of the knight, induce him to keep his person out of harm's way as much as possible, but he had more of it to care for than other men. The common notion is, that the knight is without courage; but this is a mistake. I will go to the death for it that *Sir John* was no coward. Let us look at the circumstances of the time, and what was happening. England was streaked through and through with the turbulent passions which marked the era of "the roses red and white." The fourth prince of the house of Tudor had mounted the throne by violence, and the second Richard had been murdered in his prison, in Pontefract Castle, after having stretched four or five of his assassins dead at his feet with a pole-axe, wrested from one of their number. The Percys, Nevilles, and Douglases, with other of the barons who enabled Henry to seize upon the crown, are now in arms against him. The dynasty of the Tudors is menaced. *Hotspur* rages in the north, and marches south to Shrewsbury. The commotion about the court of the old king penetrates the haunt of the *Prince* and *Falstaff* in Eastcheap, and young *Henry*, taking arms himself, procures a charge of foot for *Sir John*. He must have known whether he was fit for it or not. At that time, battles were decided at sword point and lance's thrust, and everything depended upon the conduct and example of the leaders. Later than that, *Richard of Gloucester* and the *Earl of Warwick* won great victories by their personal daring and courage. The Tudors, father and son, had everything at stake. The *Prince*, afterwards a great captain, procured a command for *Falstaff*. It is incredible that Shakespeare would have permitted young *Henry* to do this, if *Sir John* had been a poltroon. The latter would have disgraced him in the field. *Falstaff* was a captain of his making—the chief of those boon companions with whom he " daffed the world aside to let it pass!" It is true the *Prince* calls him a coward; but *Sir John* calls him a coward, and *Poins* another. " An' the Prince and Poins be not two arrant cowards, there's no equity stirring! there's no more valor in that Poins than in a wild duck." Yet *Falstaff* knew better. All the epithets they applied to each other were but parts of the great joke their lives then were. But here is irrefragable testimony, under Shakespeare's own hand, that *Jack Falstaff* was, in real action, a brave and doughty soldier. What does he make him say upon the field, where there was " no scoring but upon the pate?" " I have led my ragamuffins where they are peppered. There's but three of my hundred and fifty left alive; and they are for the town's end, to beg during life!" He has led them into the very heat of the fray—the current of the heady fight; and now, " hot as molten lead, and as heavy, too," he breathes awhile, and jests upon the dangers and incidents of the fight. Is this the conduct of a coward? would such a one have led the ragamuffins where they got peppered? Would he not have been pale and silent, instead of hot and cracking jokes upon the stricken field? Again, see how *Falstaff* draws upon *Pistol* and drives him out, when the latter vapors and flourishes his sword at the Boar's Head in Eastcheap, where the *Knight* is carousing with *Doll* and *Quickly.* And then again, in the Merry Wives of Windsor, he puts *Pistol* and *Nym* down by that authority of courage which they know he has, and they have not:

> " Rogues, hence avaunt! vanish like hailstones—go
> Trudge, plod away o' the hoof; seek shelter, pack!
> Falstaff will learn the humor of this age,
> French thrift, you rogues; myself and skirted page."

Friends! I beseech you, for the credit of Shakespeare and the hero of Agincourt, as well as for that of the knight himself, never think of sweet *Jack Falstaff* as a coward again.

At his end, we see that the great poet loved him. In his last moments he "played with flowers," and when "his nose was as sharp as a pen, 'a babbled of green fields!" Memento mori! His dependants, too, scamps as they were, loved the man, as appears in King Henry the Fifth.

Pistol. ————for *Falstaff* he is dead.
    And we must yearn therefore.
Bardolph. Would I were with him, wheresome'er he is, either in heaven, or in hell!

*   *   *   *   *   *   *

Nym. They say, he cried out of sack.
Quickly. Ay, that 'a did.
Bardolph. And of women.
Quickly. Nay, that 'a did not.
Boy. Yes, that 'a did, and said they were devils incarnate.
Quickly. 'A could never abide carnation; 'twas a color he never liked.
Boy. 'A said once the devil would have him about women.

None of these " base companions " had an end like that the poet gave *Falstaff*, unless it were the *Boy*. *Bardolph* is hanged for pix of little price. *Quickly* is " dead i' th' 'spital of malady of France." *Pistol*, soundly cudgelled, goes home to follow a wretched and infamous calling. These contrasts are thrown in to mark the superior nature of *Sir John*. The rebuke administered to him in such harsh terms by the young King, would have better become the lips of Chief Justice Gascoigne. *Harry* had shared his dissolute way of life, and I regard this sermon to *Sir John*, as a sort of vicarious atonement, very convenient, but not very creditable to the King. Some think Shakespeare inserted it as a homage to virtue. I think it was a homage to that resolute and imperious woman, Elizabeth Tudor. For her he made Richard Plantagenet a hump-backed fiend ; for her he made Harry Tudor a saint on his coronation day. The *Merry Wives*, in which *Sir John* is made a dupe and butt, was written at her request. Even in this play, *Falstaff* rises superior to what would overwhelm another man. Besides, look at the charms of the females, Ford and Page, employed to compass his undoing. Seductiveness and treachery have been the downfall of many a man since Jack gravitated to the bottom of the Thames, like a whale sounding in the shallows of the Antarctic Seas.

Mr. Hackett, in 1839, had a very interesting correspondence with John Quincy Adams, respecting the character of *Hamlet*, and his letters establish his critical acumen. In 1840, he visited England again, and repeatedly performed *Falstaff* at Drury Lane, with great success. On his return to this country, he played *King Lear*, at the Park Theatre, and also at Philadelphia and Boston. Two years afterwards he appeared as *Hamlet* at the Park Theatre. His success in these characters led him to undertake Richard. In 1845, Mr. Hackett lost his wife, and his engagements on the stage became fitful and irregular after the sad bereavement. In the winter of that year we find him again in London, playing *Falstaff* and *Rip Van Winkle*, at Covent Garden. He also appeared at the Haymarket, and there, by desire of the Queen, enacted *Monsieur Mallet*, to the great amusement of her Majesty and Prince Albert. His experience as a manager, like his walk as an actor, has been large. The Howard Athenæum, at Boston, was built for him; and he was lessee of the Astor Place Opera House in 1849, when the Macready riots occurred. The circumstances of that affair, and those which grew out of it, disgusted him so much that he threw up his lease. In 1851, he made another visit to England, more for pleasure than with a view to acting. He played *Sir John*, however, in *Merry Wives of Windsor*, at the Haymarket, and the comedy had a great run.

Even the brief sketch that has here been given will suffice to show how varied, as well as great, are the powers of Hackett. *Sir John Falstaff* is all his own. Another actor of reputation would be insane to afford the opportunity for comparison by attempting it. *Falstaff's* belt has become like Shakespeare's magic—" within that circle none durst walk but he!" Hackett is one of the most natural actors that ever trod the stage. He affects no rant. He " mouths no sentence, as dogs mouth a bone." Too many of our players imagine that swiftness of utterance is vehemence, and that volume of sound is power. In no character did Hackett ever make these mistakes. He is not as rapid as a mock auctioneer, nor as loud as the town bell-man, and yet he moves his audiences as those who rave prodigiously can never do. His engagement at Niblo's has shown the hold he has upon the taste and affections of the public. May it not be his last! Mr. Hackett resides in the vicinity of New York. With a generous competency, the reward of his own exertions, appreciated and cherished for his knowledge and learning, and having but just crowned and passed the heights which decline gently into the vale of years on the farther side, his life must needs be happy and dignified ; and when his steps pass down, near the clods in the valley, where the long shadows, betokening that the sun is about to set, still point towards its place of rising for a longer and more glorious day, " all that should accompany old age, as honor, love, obedience, troops of friends," this man may look to have.— *Wilkes's Spirit of the Times, Feb.* 1862.

REMARKS.

As may be perceived by reference to my "*Shakesperean Tract*," page 316, my opinion of Falstaff's *moral* claims to our respect is in direct antagonism to that of Mr. Foster, the author of the foregoing *sketch*.

In the latter part of the last century *Maurice Morgann, Esq.*, the same who had filled the office of Under-Secretary of State to the Marquis of Lansdown during his first administration, and who became afterwards Secretary to the Embassy for ratifying the peace with the U. S. of America in 1783, wrote, as he professes in his Preface, "originally to *amuse* his friends, though he subsequently consented to its publication," "*An Essay upon the Dramatic Character of Sir John Falstaff*." Mr. Morgann seems to have been so charmed by *Falstaff* that he became blinded to the enormity of his *immoralities*, and undertook, like some professional advocate, to maintain, contrary to the general opinion, and apparently against his *own* conviction, "the worse to be the better reason," and that "the character was not intended to be shown as *a coward*." Though his arguments were palpably sophistical, and utterly failed to vindicate *Falstaff's* courage, I could not but admire the talent he displayed in the effort, and I remember his "*Essay*" as one of the most amusing and ingenious which I had ever perused. As an actor of the *character* I am far from thinking it necessary to dignify it or to hide or excuse its moral deformity in order to elevate any merit in its personation, or to furnish an audience an apology to themselves for being attracted and amused whilst instructed by such an old reprobate as *Sir John Falstaff*.

Shakespeare has been censured, and unjustly, for making the Prince, after he became *Henry V.*, dissolve his former intimacy with *Falstaff*, who had been the misleader of his youth, and banish him some miles distant from his person ; for had he continued him in favor and allowed him near his Court, *Falstaff* would have become a constant cause of annoyance, if not an absolute nuisance to him. Besides such personal reasons of the *King*, Shakespeare evidently had a *moral* to inculcate. To crown *Falstaff* with *Henry the Fifth's* favor would have been to reward vice and immorality instead of punishing them. According to the history of Shakespeare's time, when he wrote " *The First Part of King Henry IV.*," the character now known as *Falstaff* was first named *Oldcastle*, for which offence, as *Sir John Oldcastle* had been historically a valorous knight and an honorable gentleman, the great dramatist was censured, and he therefore coined for the *character* a new and an appropriate or *indicative* name. The staff upon which Fat Jack relied to support him through life was composed of his *wit and humor* and self-assurance, but it proved in the end a *false staff*; he died, after the "*King had killed his heart*," disgraced and neglected by Court friends, and in the tavern at Eastcheap, where he was surrounded only by his hostess, and his former lewd and licentious companions or his humble dependents. The idea entertained by some critics that Shakespeare had, in so changing the *name*, been again unfortunate in selecting that of *Sir John Fastolf*, who historically, like *Sir John Oldcastle*, had been also a *brave* man, is absurd; he intended, when he explained that "Oldcastle died a martyr, and this is not the man," to avoid the possibility of such another *personal* imputation, and, by the *new* name, to point the *moral* whilst the character should adorn his historical play; *such suggestive name*, too, requiring the omission of only two letters in its orthography, superfluous to its *sound* upon the ear, whilst its *significancy*, when *pronounced*, was fully preserved—*Fal(se)staff*.

Falstaff was one of such as had "put their trust in princes." The *staff*, upon which this huge and extraordinary mental and physical compound depended to procure him a secure and prominent position about the *Court*, and to sustain him during his latter days in Royal favor; and indeed, to render his own presence near his future king's person so indispensable, as a source of continuous pleasure to his new majesty, that, after hearing of the death of the father, he flattered himself "the young king would be *sick* until he should see him" at his coronation, consisted of certain ingredients; such *staff* had been formed by himself out of his natural gifts and his artful accomplishments; a rare wit and of an ever-amusing quality, whether proceeding from his good or his ill humors; the cultivation of a social and familiar intercourse, boon companionship with the *heir apparent*, a common fellowship among "barren pleasures and rude society;" a ready participation even in absolute highway robbery, which had been suggested by Poins, and consented to by the Prince as a frolicsome *jest*, and the basis of a practical joke against *Falstaff*, and involving some personal danger to him certainly; but all seemingly consistent with his selfish policy, and well calculated to establish his special favoritism with, and his influence over a wild young prince thereafter. Out of such materials was Fat Jack's *staff* constructed, with which he hoped and expected to continue to live licentiously, and to defy the good ordering of society, but at last he found it to be as *false* as a jack-o'-lantern.

The great and always moralizing dramatist, *Shakespeare*, whose immortal mind has made its stores of reflections as treasurable to us as they will be imperishable throughout all time, teaches, by the career of *Falstaff*, to *Youth* the danger of becoming corrupted by intimacy with old and vicious company, who may have a high order of intellect, yet pervert it to base uses; and also furnishes *Courtiers* a popular example and an instructive caution to beware of placing any reliance upon hopes founded upon ministering to the vices of great patrons, lest they too, like *Falstaff*, be left to die in despair.

JAMES HENRY HACKETT.

NEW YORK, April 23, 1862.

THE END.